THE BELATED WITNESS

Cultural Memory

in

the

Present

Mieke Bal and Hent de Vries, Editors

THE BELATED WITNESS

Literature, Testimony, and the
Question of Holocaust Survival

Michael G. Levine

STANFORD UNIVERSITY PRESS

STANFORD, CALIFORNIA

2006

Stanford University Press
Stanford, California

THE IMAGES by Art Spiegelman in Chapters 2 and 3 are reprinted from:

Comix, Essays, Graphics, and Scraps: From MAUS *to Now to* MAUS *to Now,* © 1998
by Art Spiegelman. Reprinted with the permission of the Wylie Agency.

MAUS *I: A Survivor's Tale. My Father Bleeds History,* copyright © 1973, 1980, 1981, 1982,
1984, 1985, 1986 by Art Spiegelman. Used by permission of Pantheon Books, a
division of Random House.

MAUS *II: A Survivor's Tale. And Here My Troubles Began,* copyright © 1986, 1989, 1990, 1991
by Art Spiegelman. Used by permission of Pantheon Books, a division of Random House.

THE POEMS AND EXCERPTS OF POEMS by Paul Celan are reproduced from:

Mohn und Gedächtnis, © 1952 and 1955 by Deutsche Verlags-Anstalt, München,
Verlagsgruppe Random House GmbH. Used by permission of the publisher.

Selected Poems and Prose of Paul Celan, translated by John Felstiner. Copyright © 2001
by John Felstiner. Used by permission of W. W. Norton & Company.

This book has been published with the assistance of Barnard College.

Printed in the United States of America on acid-free, archival-quality paper

Library of Congress Cataloging-in-Publication Data

Levine, Michael G.
  The belated witness : literature, testimony, and the question of Holocaust survival /
Michael G. Levine.
     p. cm.—(Cultural memory in the present)
  Includes bibliographical references and index.
  ISBN 0-8047-3080-6 (cloth : alk. paper)—ISBN 0-8047-5555-8 (pbk. : alk. paper)
  1. Holocaust, Jewish (1939-1945), in literature. 2. Holocaust survivors' writings—
History and criticism. 3. Literature, Modern—20th century—History and criticism.
4. Holocaust, Jewish (1939-1945)—Psychological aspects. I. Title. II. Series.

PN56.H55L49 2006
809'.93358—dc22   2006011302

Typeset by Classic Typography in 11/13.5 Adobe Garamond

For Juliann

Contents

Acknowledgments

This book has grown out of conversations with students and colleagues over the past decade. When I began teaching courses on Holocaust historiography, testimony, literature, and film in the mid-1990s, I was not prepared for the tremendous challenges my students and I would face. I have learned a great deal from the students at Yale University, Barnard College, Cornell University, and New York University who took part in these classes, and I am deeply grateful to them for their thoughtful questions and unsettling reflections. I owe a special debt of thanks to John Felstiner, who introduced me to the work of Paul Celan in the early 1990s. His sensitivity as a translator and generosity as an interlocutor are greatly appreciated. The manuscript is much improved thanks to the feedback and encouragement I received at critical moments from Ulrich Baer, Bella Brodzki, Cathy Caruth, Stanley Corngold, Shoshana Felman, Andrew Frisardi, Deborah Geis, Geoffrey Hartman, Marianne Hirsch, Janet Jacobsen, Richard Klein, Anna Kuhn, Dominick LaCapra, Dori Laub, David Levin, Anne-Marie Levine, Maya Maxym, John Michael, Daniel Purdy, Esther Rashkin, Peter Rudnytsky, Ilana Szobel, Georges Van Den Abbeele, Sheri Wolf, Sidra Ezrahi and her wonderful students at Hebrew University, and especially Jared Stark. This book could not have been written without the institutional and collegial support of Judith Shapiro, Elizabeth Boylan, and Richard Gustafson at Barnard. I would also like to thank Eric Trump, who prepared the index, and my research assistants, Meredith Doster and Melanie Flamm, for all their hard work. Generous support of the project was provided by a Yale University Faculty Fellowship and a Littauer Fund Grant for Research in Jewish Studies. I am grateful to Helen Tartar, who first encouraged me to bring the project to Stanford University Press, for her guidance, vision, and intellectual integrity. My sincere thanks as well to Norris Pope,

Mariana Raykov, Rob Ehle, and Angie Michaelis at Stanford for helping this book into the world. Finally, I would like to thank my wonderful wife, Juliann Garey, to whom I dedicate this book, and our children, Gabriel and Emmanuelle, for their patience, love, and unwavering support.

Abridged versions of Chapter 2 appeared in *American Imago*, Special Issue on Memory, Post-memory, and False Memory after the Holocaust, vol. 59, no. 3 (Fall 2002): 317–41, and in *Considering* Maus: *Approaches to Art Spiegelman's "Survivor's Tale" of the Holocaust*, Deborah Geis, ed. (University of Alabama Press, 2003), 63–104. An earlier draft of Chapter 4 was published in *Diacritics*, vol. 27, no. 2 (Summer 1997): 106–23. Portions of Chapter 5 appeared in *Teaching the Representation of the Holocaust*, Hirsch and Kacandes, eds. (The Modern Language Association of America, 2004), 396–411. Chapter 6 is a revised version of an article previously published in *New German Critique*, Special Issue on Paul Celan, no. 91 (Winter 2004): 151–70. I thank these publishers for permission to use this material.

THE BELATED WITNESS

1

Introduction

"We wanted to survive so as to live one day after Hitler, in order to be able to tell our story," Helen K. tells interviewers at the Fortunoff Video Archive for Holocaust Testimonies at Yale University.[1] This book attempts to listen to such stories and, in doing so, to explore the relationship between narration and survival, between a desire to survive in order to tell and the equally intense need to tell—and to be heard—in order to survive.[2] The book is also, more enigmatically, an effort to listen to stories carried by the survivor that exceed his or her capacity to access and relate.

It is this element of excess and the impact of these *untold stories* upon the lives of Holocaust survivors and their children that is at the heart of Art Spiegelman's MAUS: *A Survivor's Tale*, discussed at length in Chapters 2 and 3. The subtitle of the first volume of MAUS, *My Father Bleeds History*, conveys a sense not only of physical injury, but of psychical wounding and emotional anguish. It suggests that the literally unbearable pain of the first generation will have spilled over somehow into the next, that the still unassimilated historical experience of the father will have bled through the pages of the "survivor's tale" drafted by his son. Spiegelman's highly resonant and unsettling metaphor draws our attention, in other words, both to a certain hemorrhaging of his father's story and to the spaces between the frames of his own Holocaust "comix," to openings in the body of his work where something else appears to be going on—something that could not be contained as an object of narration, that could not be framed in pictures or in words, that could not be communicated as the discrete content of an eyewitness account, be it the account of the father or the son.

The following chapters seek to develop ways of attuning ourselves to this element of excess in Holocaust writing, to that "something," in the words of Jean-François Lyotard, that "remains to be phrased which is not, something which is not determined."[3] The book seeks in this way to reorient the study of Holocaust literature and survivor testimony, shifting the focus from the often sacralizing and awestruck language of the "unspeakable" toward an investigation of what transpires in the unstable borderland between speech and silence, body and text.[4] Such an approach, I argue, enables us to tune in to those between-spaces in Spiegelman's work—and in Holocaust writing more generally—associated with the fluid language and silent outpourings of the body as witness.

In what follows I examine the ways in which such bodies are transfused with and mutely driven by historical energies that have yet to be metabolized, how they are inhabited by memories painfully lodged in particular openings, organs, tissues, and cavities.[5] In the context of this examination we will have occasion to deal with what I would call the "uneven development" of the traumatized body, a psychosomatic economy that manifests itself in some instances as a reorganization of corporeal space—a redistribution of psychical investments in the body—around the open wounds it bears; in others it may appear as a withdrawal of such investments and be associated with the deadening of particular bodily spaces. In the latter case, the benumbed area seems out of synch and out of touch, as though its development had not kept pace with the rest. Seemingly frozen in time, such underdeveloped regions of the body appear to speak a language or idiolect different from the rest.

The Witness to the Witness

In order to begin to attend to these bodies in pain, to learn their languages, and to attune ourselves to the untold stories they bear—to stories which all too often have been unconsciously lived out and silently passed on by survivors—it is necessary to cultivate not only another, more analytically informed mode of listening but a different, more ethical way of responding, a way of assuming co-responsibility for the act of bearing witness.

To bear witness to the degrading and dehumanizing atrocities of the Holocaust is not simply to address one's story to others. It is more fundamentally—and more tentatively—to speak in search of "an addressable you." As the poet Paul Celan, whose parents were murdered by the SS, and who was himself condemned "to haul stones" in the Ukraine during the war, said of his own poetic testimony, "a poem, as a manifestation of language and thus essentially dialogue, can be a message in a bottle, sent out in the—not always greatly hopeful—belief that it may somewhere and sometime wash up on land, on heartland (*Herzland*) perhaps. Poems in this sense are always under way: they are making toward something. Toward what? Toward something standing open, occupiable, toward an addressable you perhaps, toward an addressable reality."[6]

I return at length in subsequent chapters to the metaphor of the poem—and of the testimonial act—as a message in a bottle, a figure Celan borrows from Osip Mandelstam, the Russian writer with whom he felt a keen sense of poetic and existential kinship. For the moment I want only to stress the place made for the other, for "an addressable you," in his poems—for another, indeterminable and unpredictable *place* which these errant poems are themselves said to be "making toward." As drifting messages in a bottle, Celan's poems leave themselves essentially open to chance, letting themselves open with an unprecedented sense of vulnerability, exposure, and woundedness in the direction of an unforeseeable encounter, in the direction of "something standing open" which perhaps, in its turn, might open in them the possibility of speaking otherwise while still speaking German. Celan's poetry bears witness to his lifelong struggle not only to orient himself in the German language after "that which happened," but also to open it—this language which "had to pass through the thousand darknesses of deathbringing speech"—to a different heading.[7]

For Celan, who continued to write in his mother tongue after emigrating in the late 1940s from the Eastern European province of Bukovina via Vienna to Paris, where he would commit suicide in 1970, it was never simply a question of the "working of language itself, language as such, but always of an 'I' who speaks from the particular angle of inclination which is his existence and who is concerned with outlines and orientation."[8] "Reality is not simply there," he stressed in his 1958 Bremen speech, "it must be searched for and won.["9"] It is this search for "an addressable you," for "an addressable reality," that not only destines the speaking "I" of his poetic testimony toward "something standing open" but defines its own essentially *dialogical* structure. In other words, there will have been no "I," no witness, without a witness to the witness, without an opening of that dialogically constituted "I" to and by the essential *possibility* of address. This is why Celan speaks of "an address*able* you, an address*able* reality" (emphasis added). Like this "reality," the "I" destined to search for it "is not simply there." It, too, must be "searched for and won." Only in its orientation toward the other, toward the *weak* possibility (Celan's "not greatly hopeful belief") of a *chance encounter* it cannot, by definition, be assured of in advance, does this "I" dialogically constitute itself first and foremost as an act of language, an act of witnessing, which must be performed each time anew.["10"] As a performative speech act, witnessing is structurally open to the possibility of failure, to the possibility of *not* reaching its destination, of *not* washing up on that shoreline of the heart (*Herzland*) of which Celan speaks.

"If someone else could have written my stories," writes Elie Wiesel, "I would not have written them. I have written them in order to testify. My role is the role of the witness . . . Not to tell, or to tell another story, is . . . to commit perjury."["11"] Whereas the notion of a witness is traditionally defined by his or her singular status, by his or her irreplaceability with regard to the truth of an experience which has been lived through or seen firsthand, the notion of bearing witness that is developed in the following chapters focuses more on the singularity of each act of witnessing itself, on an illocutionary speech act which must be performed each time, as though for the first time, on the contingency of an act that in each instance tests— and contests—the limits of narration. My focus is thus less on the stories *already* in the speaker or writer's possession, less on the constative dimension of his or her testimony, than on what *happens* in the very act of testifying, on what untold and unpossessed stories are *unwittingly accessed and unconsciously performed* in the very process of speaking toward another in the fluid space of transmission opened between the precariously fluctuating positions of the witness and the witness to the witness. The precariousness of these fluctuations is at once a sign of danger and an indication of the risks necessarily incurred in opening the act of witnessing to the chance of a dialogically transformative encounter.[12] What then are these risks and why must they be taken?

"The listener to the narrative of extreme human pain," writes the analyst and cofounder of the Fortunoff Video Archive for Holocaust Testimonies, Dori Laub, "faces a unique situation."

> While historical evidence to the event which constitutes the trauma may be abundant and documents in vast supply, the trauma—as a known event and not simply as an overwhelming shock—has not been truly witnessed yet, not been taken cognizance of. The emergence of the narrative which is being listened to—and heard—is, therefore, the process and the place wherein the cognizance, the "knowing" of the event is given birth to. The listener, therefore, is a party to the creation of knowledge *de novo*. The testimony to the trauma thus includes its hearer, who is, so to speak, the blank screen on which the event comes to be inscribed for the first time.
>
> By extension, the listener to trauma comes to be a participant and a co-owner of the traumatic event: through his very listening, he comes to partially experience trauma in himself. The relation of the victim to the event of the trauma, therefore, impacts on the relation of the listener to it, and the latter comes to feel the bewilderment, injury, confusion, dread and conflicts that the trauma victim feels. He has to address all these, if he is to carry out his function as a listener, and if trauma is to emerge, so that its henceforth [*sic*: possibly, *heretofore*?] impossible witnessing can indeed take place. The listener, therefore, by definition partakes of the struggle of the victim with the memories and residues of his or her traumatic past.[13]

While it is important not to conflate Celan's notion of "an addressable you" with the position of the analytic listener or testimonial interviewer assumed by Laub, it is useful to begin by noting how in both cases the focus has shifted from a traditional notion of the speaker qua witness to the other's necessary implication in the act and *transaction* of witnessing; from the witness viewed as a privileged locus of knowledge, as someone *independently* capable of translating his or her firsthand experience of a traumatic event into a "knowing" of it; from the witness as owner of a story *already* in his possession and at his disposal to the space of transmission as the place where such "knowing" first takes place, where cognizance of the event is *belatedly* "given birth to."[14]

The Hazards of Listening

While Spiegelman's description of his father as someone who "bleeds history" and Celan's metaphor of the poem as a drifting message in a bottle both implicitly draw attention to the fluidity of this space of transmission, Laub explicitly describes the hazards of listening to survivor testimony as "a threat of flooding." In all three cases what is implied is a relationship in which the boundary separating the speaker from the listener is always in danger of dissolving, a situation in which, as Laub says, "the fear of merger with the atrocities being recounted" may bring about a sense of total paralysis on the part of the audience. The listener, he adds, may experience a "flood of awe and fear." We tend, in other words, to endow the survivor with a kind of sanctity, both to pay our tribute to him and to keep him at a distance, to avoid the intimacy entailed in knowing.

Insistently privileging a language of inundation and overflow as though to emphasize an elemental fear which all the various modes of audience response analyzed by him may have in common, Laub also addresses the danger of hyperemotionality, a response, he says, "which superficially looks like compassion and caring." In such cases it is the testifier who is "flooded, drowned and lost in the listener's defensive affectivity" (72). Fears of engulfment may also prompt the listener to overidentify with the victims, to *drown out* in effect the intolerable otherness of their stories. "These are some of the ways," Laub concludes, "in which the listener feels the need to protect himself from the offshoots of the trauma and from the intensity of the flood of affect that, through the testimony, comes to be directed toward him" (73).

Fraught with numerous and incalculable hazards, the act of transmission threatens not only to overwhelm the listener to survivor testimony but also to retraumatize and re-silence the returning witness. "They speak . . . among themselves," Primo Levi says of his indifferent audience, "as if I was not there."[15] Such risks of deferred or repeated annihilation cannot be avoided, however, if the heretofore "impossible witnessing" of which Laub speaks is to be given a chance to "take place belatedly as though retroactively" (85).

Toward an Addressable You

"To bear witness," Shoshana Felman writes, "is to take responsibility for truth: to speak, implicitly from within the legal pledge and the juridical imperative of the witness's oath."

To testify—before a court of law or before the court of history and of the future; to testify likewise, before an audience of readers or spectators—is more than simply to report a fact or an event or to relate what has been lived, recorded and remembered. Memory is conjured here essentially to *address* another, to impress upon a listener, to *appeal* to a community. To testify is always, metaphorically, to take the witness stand, or to take the position of the witness insofar as the narrative account of the witness is at once engaged in an appeal and bound by an oath. To testify is thus not merely to narrate but to commit oneself, and to commit the narrative to others: to *take responsibility*—in speech—for history or for the truth of an occurrence, for something which, by definition, goes beyond the personal, in having general (nonpersonal) validity and consequences.

The present study seeks to develop the notion of responsibility discussed by Felman through an examination of the role played by the listener, interviewer, or reader in the testimonial act. Such a *supplementary* witness, I argue, implicitly commits himself to the task of assuming *co-responsibility* for an intolerable burden, for an overwhelming charge, for the crushing weight of a responsibility which the witness had heretofore felt he or she bore alone and therefore could not carry out.[16] Indeed, as the clinicians Bessel van der Kolk and Onno van der Hart have observed, it is the intensely isolating quality of traumatic memory that distinguishes it from narrative memory. Whereas the latter is a social act, the former is inflexible, invariable, and monologic. "Traumatic memory," they note, "has no social aspect; it is not addressed to anybody . . . it is a solitary activity."[17] In seeking to assume co-responsibility for the act of testifying, the witness to the witness helps to transform such traumatic memories into social acts, into narrative memories addressed to others—to others who are not simply located *outside* the self. Indeed, as Laub remarks, "The testimony is . . . the process by which the narrator (the survivor) reclaims his position as a witness; reconstitutes the *internal 'thou,'* and thus the possibility of a witness or a listener inside himself" (85).

Yet why the necessity of this internal "thou"? Why must the possibility of such a listener inside the witness be *reconstituted* in the first place? According to Laub,

one has to conceive of the world of the Holocaust as a world in which the very imagination of the *Other* was no longer possible. There was no longer an other to which one could say "Thou" in the hope of being heard, of being recognized as a subject, of being answered. The historical reality of the Holocaust became, thus, a reality which extinguished philosophically the very possibility of address, the possibility of appealing, or of turning to, another. But when one cannot turn to a "you" one cannot say "thou" even to oneself. The Holocaust created in this way a world in which one *could not bear witness to oneself*. The Nazi system turned out therefore to be foolproof, not only in the sense that there were in theory no outside witnesses but also in the sense that it convinced its victims, the potential witnesses from the inside, that what was affirmed about their "otherness" and their inhumanity was correct and that their experiences were no longer communicable even to themselves, and therefore perhaps never took place. This loss of the capacity to be a witness to oneself and thus to witness from the inside is perhaps the true meaning of annihilation, for when one's history is abolished one's identity ceases to exist.[18]

The "imagination of the *Other*," whose historical foreclosure is so poignantly sketched in this passage, is ultimately for Laub the imagination of the Other as *another Self*. It is a Self imagined as a speaking subject dialogically constituted through its relation to someone else, as an "I" that addresses itself to a "you," "in the hope . . . *of being recognized as a subject*" (emphasis added). For Laub, the "you" is itself but another "I." Indeed, it is the *mutual recognition* of speaker and listener, and the essential possibility of the one dialogically exchanging places with the other, that maintain within each "I" the space of an internal "you," that hold open the space of an inner dialogue in which one can "say 'thou' . . . to oneself." While I agree with Laub's contention that the "historical reality of the Holocaust became . . . a reality which extinguished philosophically the very possibility of address, the possibility of appealing, or of turning to, another," I argue that his conception of the Other as *another subject*, of the "you" as a kind of *alter ego*, prevents us from seeing some of the more radical ways in which the question of address is reposed and rethought in post-Holocaust writing—specifically in the work of Spiegelman, Wolf, Ozick, and Celan discussed in the following chapters.

In contrast to Laub, I argue that what is "reconstituted" in the testimonial alliance forged between the witness and the witness to the witness is not merely an "internal 'thou,'" but something which was never exactly "there" in the first place, something on the order of what Lacan refers to as "the discourse of the Other." In developing the notion of a testimonial contract, which is related to Laub's sense of "the encounter and the coming together between the survivor and the listener," while differing from it in important ways, the following chapters ask: How is it possible to assume co-responsibility for the emergence of such a discourse? How can one open oneself to the possibility of speaking—and of listening—otherwise? How can one begin to heed Celan's strange injunction voiced in his poem "The Trumpet's Place" to "listen in with your mouth"? How, in other words, might it be possible in listening at the very limit of the "you's" addressability, at what might be described as the mouth of the ear, to leave oneself open to the chance of being surprised by the foreignness of what happens in the fluid space of testimonial transmission?[19]

To begin to respond to these questions, it is necessary to return to the text "On the Interlocutor," from which Celan derives his figure of the poem as a message in a bottle. There Mandelstam writes:

When I speak to somebody, I do not know with whom I speak, and I do not wish to know him. There is no lyric without dialogue. Yet the only thing that pushes us into the arms of the interlocutor is the desire to be surprised by our own words, to be captivated by their novelty and unexpectedness. The logic is ineluctable. If I know to whom I speak, I know ahead of time how he will regard what I say, whatever I might say, and consequently I shall manage not to be astonished by his astonishment, to be overjoyed by his joy, or to love through his love.[20]

The dialogic relationship outlined here is developed by Celan in his "Meridian" speech. Regarding the poem's relation to the Other, he says, it "wants to move toward an Other, it needs this Other, it needs this interlocutor. It seeks it out, speaks toward it. For the poem making toward an Other, each thing, each human being is a figure [*eine Gestalt*] of this Other."[21] "A poem," he says later in the same speech,

becomes conversation—often desperate conversation. Only the space of this conversation can establish what is addressed, can gather it into a "you" around the naming and speaking I. But this "you," come about by dint of being named and addressed, *brings its otherness into the present*. Even in the here and now of the poem—and the poem has only this one, unique, momentary present—even in this immediacy and nearness, the otherness gives voice to what is most its own: its time.[22]

The complicated syntax of Celan's speech does not lend itself to easy paraphrase. Nevertheless, important differences between his notion of address and the notion proposed by Laub begin to emerge. Whereas for Laub the "you" is addressed by a speaking "I," "in the hope of being recognized as a subject," for Mandelstam and Celan the dialogic relation to the interlocutor is one that opens a space of *self-distance*, a gap through which an "encounter," as Celan calls it, might emerge. Whereas for Laub the "you" is ultimately another "I," another person, for Celan each human being is instead a figure, *eine Gestalt*, of the *impersonal* Other toward which the poem is making and speaking. For Celan it is less a question of the specular relation which may obtain between an "I" and a "you," less a matter of their respective identities being mutually recognized, than of according a place to the otherness which the "you" "brings with" it (*bringt mit*) and which it in a certain sense impersonates. It is a question, moreover, of listening to the other voices and the haunting silences which the poem itself—in its very self-estrangement—*lets speak through it* (*läßt es das ihm, dem Anderen, Eigenste mitsprechen*). In short, Celan's use of the prefix *mit-* in the pivotal verbs *mitbringen* and *mitsprechen* shifts the focus in this passage from the "I" and the "you" conceived of as intact identities engaged in a dialogic exchange to the *parasitic others* they bring along with them, to the way the host bodies of the "I" and the "you" leave themselves open to that which speaks with and through them as the uncanny otherness of their own voices.[23]

"There is no lyric without dialogue," Mandelstam asserts. Yet, as we have seen, it is no longer dialogue in the sense of a reciprocal exchange of words and of illocutionary positions, of taking turns speaking and listening, but rather in the sense of *mitsprechen*, in the sense, that is, of voices speaking with and through one another, *at the same time*. It is dialogue in which interruption is no longer the exception but the rule, in which one speaks in the hope not merely of being recognized as a subject but rather of being interrupted, provoked, and "surprised by one's own words." To bear witness to the witness in this context is thus to assume co-responsibility for that which *mitspricht* in the discourse of the witness, for that which remains adrift on its surface as a floating message in a bottle, as a letter in sufferance, as the flotsam and jetsam of unconnected and still unassimilated memory fragments.

The Compulsion to Repeat

The act of bearing witness to traumatic experience has often been conceived of as an act of procreation, as a process, in Laub's terms, of "creating knowledge *de novo*."[24] Yet, it is important to emphasize that both the knowledge given birth to and the process of its delivery are themselves traumatic. In what follows I explore the relationship between the act of bearing witness and the figure of birth trauma, a figure which is itself often associated in the texts under discussion with the witnessing of a traumatic death. Indeed, it is this uncanny configuration of birth and death—of birth *as* death trauma—that plays a crucial organizing role in all the texts examined in this study. In an effort to account for the peculiar frequency with which this configuration recurs, I suggest that the act of witnessing be viewed as a process of *Entbindung*—that is, as a way of giving birth that is also at the same time a struggle to *unbind* fixed psychical energies, to re-open closed, static, and fatally repetitive cycles of compulsive return.

As for the "knowledge" given birth to in such moments of unbinding, I argue that it is itself available only in the mode of repetition. The following chapters therefore pay particular attention to moments of repetitive stammering, labored breathing, and breathless panting in the texts under discussion. Like Spiegelman's father, Vladek, who is often shown pedaling a stationary bike while telling his story to his artist son, the testimonies in question seem themselves *to move in place*, to go in circles, to "proceed" in an apparently stagnating manner "from threshold to threshold" (Celan).[25] It is as though these testimonies were themselves trapped at the very frontier of speech and silence, as though the "knowledge" they seek to give birth to were caught in the act of transmission, remaining somehow stuck in the throat above or suspended in the cervical opening below.[26] Incommunicable and undeliverable as such, this traumatic knowledge is all too often left to resonate not only in the painfully congested narrows of the witnessing body, in a place Celan refers to as that of an *Engführung* or straitened passage, but also in the body of the witness *to* the witness, where

it is left to wander—like a summons one cannot simply heed or ignore—
in the labyrinthine passageways of the inner ear.[27]

It is therefore necessary to invent new ways of listening to this "knowledge," which is articulable and indeed only audible in the mode of repetition. To begin to attune ourselves to that which perseverates at the very
threshold of speech and silence, insisting like an unlaid ghost—or a specter
of what is yet to come—at the limit of life and death, we must also begin
to treat the question of repetition in a different way. The following chapters therefore seek to view repetition as a movement that is never one with
itself, as a *com*pulsion that is not only internally divided but doubly driven,
impelled by *competing impulses* at work within it. Indeed, what comes together and insists in the mode of repetition, I argue, are both a drive to return obsessively to the same place and a driving, desperate search for someplace different—for an uncanny difference that might emerge in the place
of the same.

It is this inherent otherness of the very movement of repetition, this
internal dislocation and reorientation of its trajectory, that is silently ac-
centuated by Dominick LaCapra in his book *Writing History, Writing
Trauma*, when he strategically hyphenates the term *re-petition*. Making a
place for the other impulses silently and unwittingly at work in the repetition compulsion, LaCapra invites us to view it not merely as a process
of "acting out" but also as a stammering movement of *petitioning again*,
which he associates with the process of "working through."[28] While my
own understanding of repetition is indebted to LaCapra's work on trauma,
I view "acting out" and "working through" not as different *stages* in a process of coming to terms with the past, as he often does, but rather as two
moments *simultaneously* inhabiting an internally divided and doubly
driven movement.[29] To claim, in other words, that re-petition *is* repetition
is to say that there is one impulse silently at work within another, one
which seeks to alter the very spacing of repetition, to open *in it* a space of
self-difference, a space marked by LaCapra's hyphenation of the term *repetition*. To better grasp what is to be found in such a space—or, to be
more precise, in the *spacing out* of re-petition—it is necessary to return for
a moment to Celan's "Meridian" address, where the competing impulses
inhabiting the compulsion to repeat may be said to go by the names of
"poetry" and "art."

And poetry? Poetry, which still has to take the path of art? . . . Perhaps—I'm just asking—perhaps poetry, in the company of the I which has forgotten itself, travels the same path as art, toward that which is mysterious and alien. And once again— but where? but in what place? but how? but as what?—it sets itself free. . . .

Can we now, perhaps, find the place where strangeness was present, the place where a person succeeded in setting himself free, as an—estranged—I? Can we find such a place, such a step? . . .

Is perhaps at this point, along with the I—with the estranged I, set free . . . —is perhaps at this point an Other set free?[30]

Celan's extremely tentative, stammering effort to locate such a place, to find where the "I" is unbound in its very self-estrangement and where, along with it, an Other is set free, is, I would suggest, itself the drive to open the movement of compulsive repetition to the otherness it bears, to the movement of re-petitioning silently at work and unconsciously insisting within it. Insofar as this movement is associated in Celan with that of "poetry" still obliged to travel the same path as "art," its re-petitioning should be viewed as the poem's "own" uncanny and erratic path, as its uncertain *way* of blindly searching out "something standing open," of stutteringly speaking toward the very wound around which the "you" will have gathered, toward an opening of that "you" to the petitioning address of an as yet "unbound" and still undeliverable Other.

Uncanny Configurations

In Spiegelman's MAUS the question of compulsive repetition is articulated with the language of birth-as-death trauma through the figure of a tightening umbilical cord, a figure that appears in the text at the very moment that Art's mother, Anja, is about to commit suicide. Chapters 2 and 3 trace this passage opened at the limit of life/death, a passage which is not only enacted at various points *within* the text—most notably in the story of Art and his brother's own births—but also in the publication history of the text itself, in the story of its own traumatic *Entbindung* as text.

My reading of Christa Wolf's *Patterns of Childhood* in Chapter 4 is similarly focused on a moment of birth alluded to at the end of its opening chapter, in which a child is said to begin to stir—or rather "to bestir herself [*sich . . . zu regen beginnt*] independent of certain promptings."

These stirrings are accompanied by a feeling of anxiety that suddenly seizes the narrator—"the feeling," she says, "that overcomes any living being when the earth starts moving underfoot." Losing her footing as the ground seems to open beneath her and as the lost child of her youth begins to emerge unsummoned from the depths of memory, the narrator associates this anxiously ungrounding moment with the birth of her own text—or, to be more specific, with the emergence of that in it which writes itself otherwise in the very lapses of authorial control. The chapter examines how "writing otherwise" in Wolf involves the negotiation of a certain passage at the very "limits of the expressible," a passage which silently connects the "sentences that stick in our throats" above to a more fragmentary, stammering mode of articulation associated with the stirring of a certain *infans* below.[31]

In Cynthia Ozick's two-part narrative *The Shawl*, discussed in Chapter 5, the struggle to bear witness to a traumatic past is once again associated with an act of procreation. Here the intertwining of birth and death trauma is particularly complex, in part because the small child the protagonist, Rosa Lublin, loses in an unnamed camp is herself apparently conceived as the result of a rape. Not only does Rosa's strangely silent child first belatedly come to life, "spilling a long viscous rope of clamour," obviously evocative of an umbilical cord, at the very moment of her impending death, but this birth-as-death itself repeats the mother's own sense of having died at the moment of her daughter's violent conception. Traces of these intimately related traumas wash up in bits and pieces at various points in the second part of *The Shawl*, set in Miami Beach. It is here, moreover, that the inverted doubling of birth and death and the temporal structure of belatedness associated with it in the first part return as a movement of deferred parturition, as the very structure of the survivor's struggle to bear witness to—and from—her own indefinite suspension at the limit of life/death.

Whereas, in Ozick's fiction, the question of what it may mean to bear witness to and from this moment of suspension is explored through the figure of a belated birth which is itself already the repetition of a premature and unacknowledged death, in the poetry and life of Paul Celan these questions and figures assume a tragic literality. Chapter 6 discusses two poems written by Celan in fall 1953, both of which are contained in the 1955 volume *Von Schwelle zu Schwelle* (From Threshold to Threshold). The first, entitled "Die Winzer" (The Vintagers), was written at a time when the poet's wife, Gisèle, was pregnant with their first child. The second, "Grab-schift für François" (Epitaph for François), written approximately a month later, was composed in commemoration of the loss of this infant, who died shortly after birth. The chapter examines the structure of belatedness through which these poems are linked and the traumatic break inscribed in their uncannily intertextual relationship.

To begin to tease out the implications of this configuration of birth-as-death trauma for a theory of belated witnessing, we turn now to Spiegel-man's MAUS: *A Survivor's Tale*.

2

Necessary Stains

THE BLEEDING OF HISTORY IN SPIEGELMAN'S MAUS I

> Every word is like an unnecessary stain on silence and nothingness.
> —Samuel Beckett

> In making MAUS, I found myself drawing every panel, every figure, over and over—obsessively—so as to pare it down to an essence, as if each panel was an attempt to invent a new word, rough-hewn but streamlined.
> —Art Spiegelman

The publication of Art Spiegelman's MAUS "comix," the first volume of which appeared in 1986, the second in 1991, has helped to mark and define an important turning point in the history of Holocaust testimony.[1] Forty years after the events of the Second World War, many survivors had reached a point in their lives where they knew that it was getting late, that if ever there was a time to talk, to pass on their experience as a "legacy," it was now.[2] It was also a time when the children of survivors began to participate in increasing numbers in the process of bearing witness. For this second generation it was a question not only of helping to elicit their parents' stories, persuading them to write, speak, or agree to be interviewed, but also of coming to terms with their own implication in their parents' experiences. Indeed, many of these children had reached a point in their own lives where they were discovering that the first generation's stories had in a sense *already* been passed on to them, that they had themselves become the unwitting bearers of a legacy of pain, of a trauma which had in Spiegelman's words inadvertently "spilled over" from one generation to the next.

Various terms have been proposed recently to describe the situation of this second generation of survivors in general, and Spiegelman's own predicament with regard to his parents' memories in particular. Referring specifically to the photographs contained in MAUS, Marianne Hirsch has noted that they "connect the two levels of Spiegelman's text, the past and the present, the story of the father and the story of the son, because these family photographs are documents both of memory (the survivor's) and of what I would like to call postmemory (that of the child of the survivor whose life is dominated by memories of what preceded his/her birth)." For Hirsch, postmemory is not simply "beyond memory" nor it is "purely in history." It is distinguished from the former "by generational distance" and from the latter "by deep personal connection." "Post-memory," she argues, "should reflect back on memory, revealing it as equally constructed, equally mediated by the processes of narration and imagination."[3]

Although the "postmemories" of this second generation thus may be said to be more distanced and mediated than those of the first, in coming after they also have the retroactive effect of revealing things about the parents' memories which might not have been sufficiently appreciated the first time around—not just that they are "equally constructed, equally mediated by the processes of narration and imagination," but also that the overwhelmingly *immediate* impact of the Holocaust on the first generation was such that it was not fully assimilated as it occurred. It is ultimately this legacy of unassimilated memories unwittingly passed on from one traumatized generation to the next that Hirsch seeks to call attention to in coining the term *postmemory* and in reading MAUS as representative of an "aesthetic of the trauma fragment, the aesthetic of the testimonial chain." "The power of the photographs Spiegelman includes in MAUS," she argues, "lies not in their evocation of memory, in the connection they can establish between present and past, but in their status as fragments of a history we cannot take in."[4]

While Hirsch traces the insistence of these unassimilated historical fragments in MAUS and thereby helps us to appreciate some of the ways in which the first generation's "legacy" is passed on not just in words but in silence, she also suggests that this silent mode of transmission is itself strangely double-edged—at once a way of silently and unconsciously acting out that which "we cannot take in" and a way of repeating from one generation to the next the very *act of silencing*. Thus, in addition to Spiegelman's father, who effectively silences the mother's voice when he burns the diaries she had written after the war, and who compounds the violence of this act by refusing until much later to tell Art he had done so (a moment depicted on the last page of the first volume), the son is also guilty, in Hirsch's eyes, "of banishing female voices from his narrative."[5]

The "survivor's tale" Art draws in collaboration with his father, Vladek, is seen by her as a process of masculine, Orphic creation, as an Orphic song "about the internal workings of a Hades which few have survived, and fewer still have been able to speak about." This Orphic creation, she continues (drawing heavily on Klaus Theweleit's *Buch der Könige*),[6] results not only from such a descent into Hades but also from a reemergence. It is

a masculine process facilitated by the encounter with the beautiful dead woman who cannot herself come out and sing her own song. Orphic creation is thus an artificial "birth" produced by men—by male couples able to bypass the generativity of women, male couples whose bonding depends on the tragic absence of women. In this process, women play the role of "media" in Theweleit's sense, of intermediaries, not of primary creators or witnesses. In *Maus*, father and son together attempt to reconstruct the missing story of the mother, and by extension, the story of women in Auschwitz. . . . Art and Vladek perform the collaboration of the creative male couple: the difficulties that structure their relationship only serve to strengthen the ties which bind them to each other and to the labor they have undertaken.[7]

Hirsch is right to apply critical pressure to the question of creativity in MAUS, suggesting that there is something odd and perhaps even "artificial" about its "birth." Nevertheless, her attempt to describe this "birth" in terms of a process of masculine, Orphic creation based on female absence, and to link this explanation in turn to Art's "process of banishing female voices from his narrative," itself seems to domesticate a much more unwieldy connection forged in the text between birth and death trauma—to which I will return at length below. Let it suffice, for the time being, to note with Hirsch the strange appearance of an umbilical cord, a figure so obviously associated with the moment of parturition, in the very scene in MAUS in which Art describes his mother's death. Not only does this cord come to figure the complex ties through which Art remains bound to the traumatic moment of his mother's suicide, but, as the figure of a certain interweaving of life-and-death lines (itself woven through others in and around MAUS), it makes us see the "birth" of the text very differently from the view outlined above.

Whereas Hirsch seeks to explain the silencing of women in this male-centered text in terms provided by Theweleit, I would argue that, rather than endeavoring to *interpret* the one through the other, we view the roles of women and of the "media" as two related *questions*, so bound up with each other that in broaching one it is impossible not to address the other. These questions surface again in James Young's essay "The Holocaust as Vicarious Past: Art Spiegelman's *Maus* and the Afterimages of History." While Young does not speak of women as "media" in Theweleit's sense, he agrees with Hirsch that Spiegelman is "an accomplice to the usurpation of his dead mother's voice."[8] In Young's account, Art is no longer paired off with his father in a male couple "whose bonding depends on the tragic absence of women," but is described instead as "the midwife to and eventual representer of his father's story."[9] The choice of terms here is no doubt significant; for in depicting Art as a midwife to his father's story, Young suggests not only that the men have once again taken the place of a woman, usurping both Anja's voice and her role in the "creative process," but, moreover, that they have done so *as women*—as a father who gives birth and as a son feminized as a "midwife" who assists in the delivery. This strange crossing of gender and generational lines would hardly be worth mentioning were it not for the fact that the question of the woman's role—of the mother as a generative source—comes up again at another point in Young's essay, where the birth of the father's story seems once again to overlap with that of the son's. According to Young, "Art is on a mission, a self-quest that is also historical. '*I* still want to draw that book about you,' Artie says to his father, who answers, 'No one wants anyway to hear such stories,' to which Artie answers, 'I want to hear it.' And then he asks his father to begin, in effect, with his own implied origin: 'Start with Mom . . . ,' he says. 'Tell me how you met.' He did not ask him to start with the war, deportation, or internment, but with his mother and their union—that is, his *own* origins."[10]

Although there are other ways of reading this passage (and I will propose such a reading below), at this point it is important first to underscore the recourse to birth imagery in Hirsch's and Young's essays, to remark the way such imagery is repeatedly linked to the usurpation both of the mother's voice and of her procreative role, the way father and son, in bypassing the generativity of the mother, seek not only to engender their own stories but to do so in such a way that the son is made to assist in the birth of a paternal tale which is also in effect his own.

Both Hirsch and Young are concerned with the ways in which the first generation's traumatic tales—tales that in some fundamental sense will never have been entirely their own—have become their children's life stories as well. Yet, while Hirsch's notion of postmemory tends to stress the ways in which "a history we cannot take in" has been unconsciously passed on, Young coins the term *received history* to describe the highly self-conscious narratives produced by Spiegelman's "media-savvy generation, born after—but indelibly shaped by—the Holocaust." "This postwar generation," Young contends,

cannot remember the Holocaust as it actually occurred. All they remember, all they know of the Holocaust, is what the victims have passed down to them in their diaries, what the survivors have remembered to them in their memoirs. They remember not actual events but the countless histories, novels, and poems of the Holocaust they have read, the photographs, movies, and video testimonies they have seen over the years. They remember long days and nights in the company of survivors, listening to their harrowing tales, until their lives, loves, and losses seemed grafted indelibly onto their own life stories.[11]

Whereas Hirsch describes the women in MAUS as "media," as "intermediaries" who are never permitted to play the role of "primary creators or witnesses"—parts reserved in the text exclusively for the men—in Young this gender distinction becomes a generational one. Working with a surprisingly linear notion of generational descent (surprising, at least, in a context where the belated structure of traumatic experience significantly complicates such notions), Young repeatedly contrasts the first generation's "immediate" knowledge of the Holocaust with the second generation's "hypermediated experience of the memory of events." While such an approach clearly makes sense on one level, on another it fails to account for—or even to address—those moments in MAUS where it is a question not only of the initial trauma returning in disjointed fragments in the memory of the survivor, but of time itself being "out of joint."[12]

In contrast, then, to Young's notion of "received history" that ultimately frames the ways the events of the Holocaust are passed down to us in very traditional terms as a movement from "painful immediacy" to "somewhat less painful mediacy" or from "trying to remember events" to recalling one's "relationship to the memory" of them, I would urge that one view Spiegelman's "survivor's tale" instead as an act of *belated witnessing*, as a text in which Art may be said to function as a second-degree witness who is not just one step removed from the experiences of the first generation but otherwise implicated in them. In MAUS it is this implication of the second-generation survivor in the traumas of the first that not only tangles the lines of descent but makes Art a witness to the *delayed impact* of the Holocaust. In becoming a witness to the witness, Art elicits and records his father's testimony. Yet, in doing so he also opens a space in which the impact of that testimony is given a chance to register as if for the first time.

Translation and Survival

As critics have often noted, the act of transmission in MAUS involves various processes of translation.[13] Perhaps nowhere in Spiegelman's work are questions of translation so clearly raised as in the very title of his "survivor's tale." *Maus* is, after all, a German word, a cognate of the English term, *mouse. Maus* means "mouse."[14] Yet, it is precisely the seeming transparency of this translation that the text calls into question. For only in a particular historical and ideological context, one shaped by the visual media of posters, caricatures, and Nazi propaganda films such as *Der ewige Jude* (The Eternal Jew), does *Maus* begin to mean not just "mouse," but "Jew," and not just "Jewish mouse," but "plague-infested vermin." As such, a Jew is not a human being who is murdered, but a disease-ridden rodent that is "exterminated," and exterminated not just with poisonous gas but with the pesticide Zyklon B. In addition to raising questions about the translation of terms *between* languages—about the pseudotransparency of words which seem to *need no translation*—MAUS also draws attention to the deceptive sense of immediacy, the pseudofamiliarity with which one relates to one's own so-called "mother tongue"—and MAUS, as we have already begun to suspect, is very much a text about (the silence of) the mother. Whereas the dogs in MAUS speak English, the cats German, the pigs Polish, and the frogs French, the mice speak a variety of idioms, none of which could be said to be their own "natural language." It is certainly not by chance, in this regard, that the cat word for mouse is used in the title. Compared to the other animals of the text, the mice seem to have a less "natural"—that is, less transparent, unmediated—relation to a particular national language. Moreover, if Spiegelman makes a point of using the German word *Maus* in the title, he perhaps does so in order to allow it to resonate with the German verb *Mauscheln*, thereby intimating a particular

German-Jewish, cat-mouse, *linguistic* relation. As the Czech-Jewish writer of German animal stories Franz Kafka once observed in a famous letter to Max Brod, *Mauscheln* involves "a bumptious, tacit, or painfully self-critical appropriation of another's property. . . . It is an organic compound of bookish German and pantomime."[15]

Spiegelman has openly acknowledged his debt to Kafka on a number of occasions. Of particular relevance in this regard is his response to a question posed by Jonathan Rosen concerning the genesis of the text.

The real origin of *Maus* was being invited, 20 years ago, to do a three-page comic strip for an underground comic book called *Funny Animals*, the only requirement being that I use anthropomorphic characters. Fishing around for something led me toward my center. A number of things helped. One of them was sitting in on Ken Jacobs' film classes at SUNY Binghamton where he was showing racist cartoons and at the same time cat-and-mouse chase cartoons. They conflated for me and originally steered me toward possibly doing something about racism against blacks in America. Shortly thereafter, Josephine the Singer began humming to me and told me that there was something closer to deal with and I began pursuing the logic and possibilities that that metaphoric device opened up.[16]

In what language, one wonders, did Spiegelman hear Kafka's mouse humming to him? To respond to this question one might recall the words of one Kafka critic: "Although etymologically related to the names Mauschel, Moishele, and Moses, the verb *Mauscheln*—to speak German 'like a Jew'—recalls the German word for mouse. . . . In this sense the language spoken by the mice in 'Josephine'—what one might term their *Mäusedeutsch*—can be interpreted as Kafka's fictional version of *Mauscheldeutsch* and, perhaps, as a figure for his own Jewish-German language."[17] One might say in turn that Spiegelman uses the German word for mouse in the title of his book in order to allude to the ways his own text seeks to displace the dominant discourse from within,[18] to dislocate it by speaking not only "cat" but other established languages and protocols of verbal and visual representation "like a mouse."[19]

While MAUS may thus be said to be a text on translation, a text that invites one to begin translating precisely in those places where translation seems unnecessary, it is also one that deals with the question of Holocaust survival, the question not only of who survives as a witness to the Holocaust, but of the Holocaust's own lack of closure, its way of outliving its own apparent end. Claude Lanzmann's remarks about his film *Shoah* are particularly relevant in this context.

You know, this was a real question, the question of the end. I did not have the moral right to give a happy ending to this story. When does the Holocaust really end? Did it end the last days of the war? Did it end with the creation of the State of Israel? No. It still goes on. These events are of such magnitude, of such scope that they have never stopped developing their consequences. . . . When I really had to conclude I decided that I did not have the right to do it. . . . And I decided that the last image of the film would be a train, an endlessly rolling . . . train.[20]

Like Lanzmann, Spiegelman has spoken of the Shoah as an event without end, as a "cataclysmic world event the ripples of which keep seeping through the pages of *The New York Times* on a daily basis." Like Lanzmann's film, Spiegelman's MAUS comix struggle with the enigma of this survival, with the overlapping questions of who survives as a witness to the trauma of the Shoah, of who bears witness to *its survival*. In an interview Spiegelman has said that growing up his father *was* Auschwitz for him as much as he was its victim. When asked in a subsequent interview to comment on this statement he responded that "for a child, a father can be a very threatening figure, and the fact that he carried so much pain with him, well, that spilled over."[21] One begins to get a sense here of some of the ways in which the "cataclysmic world event" of the Shoah will have overflowed its apparent end—namely, as a dissolution of boundaries, as ripple effects seeping through the pages of the daily press, as the spilling over of unbearable suffering, and as ongoing cycles of victimization. It is no doubt telling in this connection that the first volume of MAUS bears the subtitle *My Father Bleeds History*.

In MAUS such bleeding is most obviously linked to the hemorrhaging of Vladek's left eye, which, the text suggests, cannot come to terms with what it has seen; it is physically wounded by what it is forced to see repeatedly in flashbacks and recurrent nightmares, so wounded in fact that eventually it must be removed by a surgeon and replaced by a glass facsimile.[22] What is perhaps less obvious, however, is the connection between this spectral presence of an unassimilated past, this bleeding of the past into the present through the very medium of vision, and the hemorrhaging of *visual images* in the text, which literally burst out of their pictorial frames on numerous occasions (fig. 1).[23] Although such moments may be said to stage a certain hemorrhaging of history in a particularly concentrated, painful, and graphic way, they also suggest more generally that one should pay close attention to the body of the text itself, a body composed of multiple narrative layers that repeatedly bleed into and through one other. The question raised

FIGURE I

by the text's enigmatic subtitle is thus: how is one to read this *internal* bleeding of history, this palimpsest of interpenetrating narrative layers?

Cartoon Narrative as (Slow-)Motion Picture

In order to pursue the question of narrative stratification in MAUS, it is necessary to examine what exactly it means for Spiegelman to tell a story in a medium that "mixes together words and pictures." In his introduction to *Breakdowns: from MAUS to Now* the author's 1977 "Anthology of Strips," Spiegelman notes that his "dictionary defines COMIC STRIP as 'a narrative series of cartoons.' A NARRATIVE is defined as 'a story.' Most definitions of STORY leave me cold. Except the one that says: 'A complete horizontal division of a building . . . From Medieval Latin HISTORIA . . . a row of windows with pictures on them'" (fig. 2).[24]

FIGURE 2

These definitions are themselves situated over a row of three consecutive "picture windows," the first of which is a panel subdivided into four quadrants, each of which is in turn broken down into further subpanels. The second, central panel depicts a man viewed from behind looking out a window onto nothing but cold, inky blackness; the window facing him is divided into eight individual panes of glass with the man's circular hat positioned over the central horizontal-vertical axis of the window frame. The third panel depicts a repetitive series of open bathroom stalls.

Whereas the words blocked out above the images in this row of panels seem at first to define the smallest "historiographic" unit as a panel— that is, as a kind of window with a picture on it—the images themselves call this definition into question. For not only can each window be broken down into individual panes, but these subwindows can in their turn be reworked into a mise-en-abîme structure of panes within panes. Through this comixing of words and images Spiegelman prompts one to see the panel as a picture *and* a window, as an oxymoronic "picture window" that must at once be looked at and looked through: *looked at* because its signifying surface does not simply efface itself, does not merely yield before the authority of a signified reality or become a transparent means to an end outside itself; *looked through* because such "picture windows" *do* open onto other windows, onto the abyssal depths of panes within panes. In an interview with Lawrence Weschler, Spiegelman remarks that what concerned him in MAUS was "not so much whether my father was telling the truth, but rather, just what had he actually lived through—what did he understand of what he experienced, what did he tell of what he understood, what did I understand of what he told, and what do I tell? The layers begin to multiply like pane upon pane of glass."[25]

The third panel in Spiegelman's mise-en-abîme structure provides a window onto a repetitive series of open bathroom stalls and seems at first to emphasize this movement of infinite regress. Yet, its scatological, "raw" humor subtly takes the movement one small but decisive step further.[26] For, as Spiegelman observes elsewhere, comics are "a gutter medium; that is, it's what takes place in the gutters between the panels that activates the medium."[27] Thus, it is ultimately not the panel itself, whether infinitely expanded in rows or infinitesimally broken down in a series of panels within panels, that constitutes the true unit of "historiographic" analysis for the comix artist. That unit, never directly named in this series of definitions, is instead the gutter *between* frames.

Yet to call this between-space a unit is also somewhat misleading. Not only is the gutter never unitary, never one with itself, but it "activates the medium" of the comic strip precisely by setting the seemingly self-contained, intact panels in motion. What I would describe as Spiegelman's art of the "slow-motion picture" may thus be said to fall somewhere between drawing and film; that is, once the medium is activated, the individual "picture windows" are no longer read primarily as positive meaningful units but rather as links in a signifying chain—which is to say that each panel itself becomes as a kind of gutter, an interspace, a self-different image whose relative value is determined only through its relation to other "interimages."

Although these strips may thus be said to set seemingly static images in motion, they obviously do so at a speed much slower than that at which normal moving pictures are typically projected. Indeed, whereas in the movies the illusion of continuous motion is produced by screening images at a speed of twenty-four frames per second, a speed that effectively effaces the "gutter between the panels," the activated medium of Spiegelman's comix slows things down enough to expose just these interspaces. If, as was suggested earlier, history becomes legible in the internal bleeding of the narrative tissue in MAUS, it may now be added that it also bleeds through the interspaces of the text, through the very gaps and gutters in the narrative that define, structure, and activate the comix medium. It must be emphasized, however, that these interspaces through which history bleeds are not merely positive breaks in the narrative but also and above all the cinematic movement of framed images repeatedly *breaking into* one another, a movement that not only splits each image from itself but, in doing so, effectively splices it into a chain of images open to and opened by the difference of the others. History bleeds, in short, through the slow-motion projection of these mutually reframing interimages.

The formal principle of the "slow-motion picture" is introduced at the very beginning of MAUS through the pointedly cinematic title of its first chapter. Taking its name from the silent-film classic *The Sheik*, first released in 1921, the chapter highlights Vladek's own star quality—his vaunted resemblance to the film's leading man ("People always told me I looked just like Rudolf Valentino") (1:13), his self-image as a real-life ladies' man, and finally his casting by Art as the protagonist of MAUS. The title also implicitly draws attention to important formal similarities between Spiegelman's comix and the medium of silent film, both of which rely heavily upon captions and speech bubbles to tell their stories.

As a way of suggesting that MAUS itself be read as a kind of silent film, Spiegelman casts his father not only as the star and narrator of *A Survivor's Tale* but also as its psycho-cinematic "projectionist." These two senses of the term are brought together in a single panel toward the beginning of the first chapter. In this frame an image of Vladek riding his exercycle is superimposed on a poster of *The Sheik* (fig. 3). At the bottom of the poster, in the portion covered by the figure on the stationary bike, one can just make out the generic subtitle "A Motion Picture." Though partially obscured by Vladek's frame, these words have a way of bleeding through; that is, the superimposition of fore- and background, of images and words, in this panel brings an altogether different kind of scenario into focus. Indeed, while Vladek may be going nowhere on his stationary bike, it is his pedaling that not only sets the text's own pictures in motion but, in doing so, generates a very different genre of silent "motion picture" from the one explicitly referred to in the poster behind him.

If, as Spiegelman says, "it's what takes place in the gutters between the panels that activates the medium," Vladek's pedaling here embodies

FIGURE 3

this activation process. Moreover, in contrast to film, where the projectionist is little more than an appendage to the machine that screens images at a constant speed, in MAUS the pictures set in motion through Vladek's cycling are projected at widely varying tempos. Obviously, the speed at which Vladek pedals is determined by the condition of his body. Yet, as the very embodiment of this activation process, of a process that sets seemingly static images in motion, his pedaling suggests different ways of reading these motion pictures in relation to one another. For instance, high-speed pedaling at an even pace evokes not only the cinematic illusion of continuous motion but also the continuity of a diachronic narrative read quickly row by row, from left to right, top to bottom, past to present. By contrast, a slower speed suggests frame-by-frame cinematic analysis or a breakdown of panels on the page which are to be read vertically as well as horizontally, in the time frame of the past as well as the present; a complete halt evokes the cinematic freeze-frame or photographic still, and suggests in narrative terms a reading of the entire page as one static, synchronic unit.[28]

While Vladek is in one sense a projectionist who repeatedly varies the speed of the images he sets in motion, in another sense he psychologically projects a little too much of himself into the motion pictures he screens. Telling in this regard is the way mouse faces have been projected onto the typically orientalized image of Valentino and his swooning European consort in the poster of *The Sheik*. It is as though the poster bearing the subtitle "A Motion Picture" had itself somehow become a kind of motion-picture *screen*, as though an overly identified projectionist had taken over the screen and filled it with images of his girlfriend and himself. Indeed, the poster of *The Sheik* ultimately bears a closer resemblance to Vladek and his old girlfriend Lucia Greenberg, dancing together in the adjacent panel, than to the Arab chieftain (who, it turns out by the end of the film, was actually educated abroad in England) and his "liberated" English mistress (who had fled the company of her compatriots abroad only to fall into the arms of a properly domesticated version of the Other). If, according to the conceit upon which MAUS is constructed, Jews are mice and Germans are cats, this panel of Vladek pedaling before a poster of *The Sheik* suggests that the human faces one expects to find hidden beneath the animal masks of the text are themselves less obviously but all the more irreducibly screens, masks, and projection surfaces.[29] As Spiegelman reflects elsewhere, "one thing that fascinated me, and it was a horrible fascination that I suspect I share with many non-religious Jews, was the fact that the people sent to their slaughter as Jews didn't necessarily identify themselves as/with Jews; it was up to the Nazis to decide who was a Jew. As Sartre pointed out in *Anti-semite and Jew*, a Jew is someone whom others call a Jew."[30] It is in just this way that the "projectionist," Vladek Spiegelman, eventually has a very different, much more literal kind of "stardom" projected on him.

Framing the Testimonial Contract

While MAUS may thus be described as a slow-motion picture, a narrative of words and images set in motion by Vladek's pedaling, it nevertheless has a hard time gearing up and getting started. "I went out to see my father in Rego Park," the first chapter begins. "I hadn't seen him in a long time—we weren't that close" (1:11). The real story, however, the story Art has really come for, must wait for the moment Vladek first mounts his stationary bike to begin. As his father slowly starts to cycle, Art begins to circle apprehensively about the true purpose of his visit. "I still want to draw that book about you . . . ," he stammers, "the one I used to talk to you about . . . ," "about your life in Poland, and the war" (1:12) (fig. 4). As though Art's tentatively phrased proposition carried with it more than he could put into words—namely, an unspoken desire *to contain the other*, to draw not just a book but a frame about his father—in the next panel he effectively proceeds to do just that. He takes up a picture that had been sitting on a table and, holding it by its frame, examines it more carefully as he describes his project to Vladek.[31] Not only is the question of the frame literally taken up here, but, as the visual language of the text suggests, it is still very much up for grabs at this point. Moreover, as if to emphasize the purely formal aspect of the situation—the question of the relationship between the framer and the framed—the panel provides no information to help the reader determine what the content of the picture might actually be. Thus, faced with Art's proposition and apparently sensing all that it implies, Vladek counters that "it would take MANY books, my life, and no one wants anyway to hear such stories" (1:12). His accentuation of the word *many* seems to shatter the unique frame of the book Art wants to draw about him. Furthermore, as Vladek voices this objection, his arms and the handlebars of the exercycle they grasp are depicted in such a way as to contain Art. They hold his head within the contours of *their* frame

FIGURE 4

while the framed picture once held aloft by the son is now shown sitting in its former place on the table. In a sense it is not just the picture but Art himself who is put back in his place here, a suggestion that is reinforced in this panel by a depiction of the paternal frame drawn about its would-be framer.

As the struggle over the frame continues, not only is the surrounding image of the paternal frame itself split up and spaced out in a triptych of three vertically contiguous panels, but in the lower left-hand corner of the page the son again takes up the framed picture he had just set down. The gesture suggests that Art is once again prepared to take up the challenge of drawing his father's many stories into a single book. In the same panel he verbally draws his father back in by contesting the claim that "no one wants anyway to hear such stories" with the emphatic attestation, "I want to hear it." Vladek's fear that his testimony will fall on deaf ears, that it too may die an anonymous death, is thus met and countered by Art's desire to be an exemplary listener, a live audience of one whose presence and integrity, he presumes, will be enough to stave off the indistinct specter of "no one."[32]

At this point a compromise is apparently struck between Vladek's fears and Art's desires. Yet, it is negotiated in a way that makes manifest the tenuous and provisional nature of the arrangement. Indeed, signs of its instability are legible at every point and in every position of the scene. Perhaps nowhere is this more apparent than in the place held by Art, whose I is itself a kind of pronominal placeholder, a displacement substitute, as Freud would call it, that only holds off the "no one" it stands in for by holding open a space for it, by having its own apparent identity compromised and haunted by the spectral anonymity of "no one." Indeed, as it turns out, Art becomes the audience he had hoped to embody for his father's "life" stories only through an act of self-division and supplementation—by becoming a "live audience" with a hearing aid, an audience, as it turns out, that can only listen with the mechanical ear of a tape recorder on hand. "Writing things down is just too hard," Art concedes midway through the first volume (1:73). Yet, what he fails to add is that the microphone he now wields is henceforth to be used not only as a writing supplement but also as a means of self-defense. Indeed, in a video appendix to the CD-ROM version of MAUS Spiegelman observes that "unlike other survivors, [Vladek] had no specific need to bear witness.

What he had a need for was his son to hang out and be around, and about the only way I could arrange for that to happen was with a microphone holding him at bay."[33]

Just as the microphone Art wields turns out to have a surprisingly double-edged quality, so too does the shift from handwriting to recording make manifest certain tensions touched on but not really played out in the scene in which the testimonial contract is first framed. Indeed, the belated introduction of the microphone, a writing supplement that seems, on the one hand, to add nothing to the testimonial dynamic and, on the other, to change it dramatically by highlighting its surprisingly conflictual nature, in the end leads one to reflect upon Art's own conflict-ridden status as a second-degree witness. It suggests that the struggles waged in this inaugural scene are played out not only *between* subjects but *within* them. By drawing attention to the particular way Art listens to his father's testimony, the shift from writing to recording prompts one to ask whether there might not be something uncannily and irreducibly mechanical, something *strangely dead* about the live audience he wishes to embody. In other words, one is led to question whether in defending himself in the act—and with the very instruments—of listening, there are not things he manages to hear only unconsciously and mechanically, taking them in without really hearing, without experiencing the full force of their impact. Indeed, perhaps the most unsettling question raised by the compromising situation in which Art initially finds himself is whether that which survives of the very excess of life stories—of that which cannot be drawn together and bound in a single book—and which "no one wants anyway to hear," perhaps least of all Art, will nevertheless have recorded and replayed itself, like a ghost in the machine, between the frames of MAUS.

Bearing these questions in mind, let us return to the moment in the initial negotiations when a compromise seems to be struck between the father's fears and the son's desires. For it is at this moment that Art again decides to take up the picture resting on the table. Yet this time he does so not in order to raise it as a question but simply and finally to indicate its content. He thus points a finger at the framed image and identifies the person depicted in it as his mother. "Start with mom," he suggests to Vladek. "Tell me how you met" (1:12). In a sense the testimonial contract that the father and son negotiate in this scene is framed in the name of the mother. Like the microphone already strangely on hand, the belated introduction of this supernumerary figure seems at once superfluous and oddly nec-essary. Even after being identified as the person in the photograph, the mother remains invisible to the reader. Although she is now in a sense on the scene, she is still very much out of the picture.

As a supplementary witness to the inaugural scene of witnessing, as a supernumerary both in the sense of a person serving no apparent function and of an actor employed to play the part of a walk-on, the mother appears here as a kind of testimonial specter whose mute presence haunts the entire telling of *A Survivor's Tale*. As though obeying a summons to appear at this pivotal moment in the text, the ghost of the dead mother bears witness in her very supplementarity not just to the start of the testimonial act per se but to the unstable limits of the scene of witnessing, to the way the testi-monial contract negotiated between Art and Vladek seems to raise more questions than it settles. The name of the dead mother, one might venture to say, lives on in the supplementarity of witnesses, in the interminability of the survivors' struggle to bear witness.

It goes without saying that Anja, Art's mother and Vladek's first wife, never bears witness in her own person in MAUS. Although depicted on the cover of the first volume in an image carefully centered over the words "A Survivor's Tale," the telling of that tale is left entirely to the hus-band and son who will have survived her. Conspicuously absent from the scene of narration, Anja, whose name first appears in a dedication placed between the title page and the opening of chapter 1, seems nevertheless to hover indefinitely at its limit precisely as the figure of a certain excess or remainder. She remains, in short, a figure of that which in *A Survivor's Tale* may be said to survive its telling by any or all of its more easily iden-tifiable survivor-narrators. If Spiegelman makes a point of invoking the name of a silent-film classic in the title of his opening chapter and of formally defining the text itself as a kind of slow-motion picture, it is, I would suggest, because MAUS is itself a silent film about silence, "a motion picture" in which the speech bubbles of its garrulous star/projectionist always threaten to eclipse the mother's silence in particular and that of those who died in the Holocaust in general. The challenge for Spiegelman in drawing MAUS was thus in a sense how to avoid silencing this silence, how to rehistoricize it by making a place for it in the telling of *A Survivor's Tale*, how, in short, to let it bleed through the words and images that his comix inevitably superimpose upon it.

Fatal Attachments

As in the frame narrative of *A Thousand and One Nights*, telling stories in MAUS is literally a matter of life and death. When, for example, Art finds out that his father did not simply misplace the diaries his mother had written after the war, but had in fact burned them, he experiences this revelation as an all-too-literal repetition of the Holocaust, a brutally ironic repetition in which the Auschwitz survivor, Vladek, now finds himself cast in the role of "murderer" (1:159). The burned diaries were to have been Anja's legacy to Art. As Vladek says, "only I know that she said, 'I wish my son, when he grows up, he will be interested by this'" (1:159). If Vladek can thus be called a murderer by a son whose maternal inheritance has been lost in transmission, it is presumably because he does to these texts what his own persecutors had done to the bodies of so many of their victims. That the incineration of Art's mother's writing can be experienced by him as the burning of a human being no doubt suggests his intense investment in whatever will have survived of his mother and his relation to her. It also suggests a certain investment in the matter of burning itself, an investment, moreover, that effectively keeps the term "Holocaust" (from the Greek *holocaustos* meaning "burnt whole") from ever establishing itself as a proper name used to designate a discrete, temporally circumscribed event. The uncanny resonance of this burning may thus be said to hold open a tenuous interspace in which the conflagration of bodies, lives, and texts are experienced as repetitions of one another.

The psychically interchangeable conflagration of bodies and texts is related to the notion of a smoke screen first introduced at the moment Art inquires into the fate of his mother's diaries. "I used to see Polish notebooks around the house as a kid," he says. "Were those her diaries?" "Yes," Vladek replies, "and also no. Her diaries didn't survive from the war. What you saw she wrote after: her whole story from the start." "OHMIGOD Where are they?" Art asks. "I need those for this book!" "Coff! Please, Artie," Vladek interjects, "stop with the smoking. It makes me short with breath." "I think it's all your pedaling," Art caustically responds, as he extinguishes his cigarette. "Don't be so smart!" says Vladek. " . . . What I was telling you? Yes . . . after the hanging I looked for another business" (1:84). Here the question of the burned diaries, which Vladek obviously wishes to avoid is dispatched—or at least deferred—by drawing attention to Art's smoking habit.

Although Art as a character appears to be taken in by Vladek's ruse, Spiegelman the artist uses the scene to introduce the figure of the smoke screen as a key to the structural principle of displacement operative in the text. Just as the smoke from the cigarette conceals that of the incinerated notebooks, so too does the revelation of the actual fate of the diaries later on lead Art to experience their incineration as a second Holocaust, as the burning not only of his mother's written remains, but also of her body, and moreover of a body that in its turn seems to stand in as a screen for countless others. All these issues come together in a panel in MAUS II, in which the mention of the mother's suicide is accompanied both by a drawing of corpses piled up at the foot of Art's drawing table and by the parenthetical mention of the fact that Anja left no suicide note (2:41). Insofar as the diaries would have been—or at least might have somehow filled in for—the note the mother never left, their burning not only returns Art to the traumatic moment of Anja's death, but deprives him a second time of the explanation or exoneration he had so desperately hoped to obtain from her.

That Art calls Vladek a "murderer" when he learns what his father has done to his mother's diaries suggests not only an identification of Vladek with his own persecutors, or a reexperiencing of the mother's suicide as a homicide, but also and above all a way of seeing the mother, who is clearly no longer alive, as still somehow at this point *not yet* dead. Indeed, if we now revisit the inaugural scene in which the testimonial contract is first framed in MAUS, a scene in which Vladek and Art fight to see who can frame whom and, in doing so, also implicitly battle over possession of the maternal frame, we may now begin to view their conflict not merely in adversarial terms but also in terms of a *joint struggle* to frame a question neither of them ever seems able to ask: the question, namely, of Anja qua specter.

Nancy Miller comes close to this view in her very perceptive essay on MAUS, one of the few readings that even thinks to raise the question of the mother in the context of "a survivor's tale" told by the father in collaboration with his surviving son.[34] "We should . . . understand the question of Anja," Miller suggests, "as that which will forever escape representation and at the same time require it."[35] Yet, whereas for Miller this question is primarily one of life, of its preservation or restoration—a matter, as she says, of keeping "the question of Anja alive," of "saving the mother by re-trieving her narrative," of "restoring the maternal body," of "reviving the link to Anja," or of keeping "the father as well as the mother alive"—my own reading seeks to frame the question of Anja in terms of a more haunted notion of sur-vival. Namely, it seeks to frame the question of that which is more than living and more than dead, of an experience so trau-matic that it exceeds the very opposition of life and death.

Clearly, neither Vladek nor Art is ever able to come to terms with Anja's death. Indeed, as Vladek remarks in the second volume, "Anja? What is to tell? Everywhere I look I'm seeing Anja . . . from my good eye, from my glass eye, if they're open or they're closed, always I'm thinking on Anja" (2:103). Yet, I would suggest that what *remains* to be seen in MAUS is not only the spectral presence of Anja per se but also, through her, a host of other haunting questions and persons that, in Miller's words, escape representation and at the same time incessantly demand it. It is no doubt telling in this respect that it was the trauma of the mother's suicide in 1968 that first prompted Spiegelman to engage explicitly with the related trauma of the Holocaust.[36] It is thus through the scene of the mother's death (whose limits remain to be defined) that one must proceed.

I begin then with the strangely corporeal terms in which Art figures his relationship to his mother in the section of MAUS entitled "Prisoner on the Hell Planet," which is explicitly framed as a text within the text. De-scribing his last encounter with his mother on the eve of her death, a sui-cide she committed by slashing her wrists in the bathtub, Art writes, "She came into my room . . . It was late at night . . . " "Artie," Anja stammers, "you . . . still . . . love . . . me . . . don't you? . . . " "I turned away," he says, "resentful of the way she tightened the umbilical cord . . . " (fig. 5).[37] Here Art literally turns his back on his mother, thereby turning her away for the last time. Such turnings graphically and verbally depict Anja's abandon-ment, her sense of having nowhere left to turn and no one left to turn to. Not only will Art remain bound to this traumatic scene, bound to repeat its tragically missed encounter long after his mother's death, but the very figure that continues to bind him to it is tellingly described as a potentially life-threatening link to the mother's body. The umbilical cord, introduced significantly in the penultimate moment before the mother's suicide, seems to function less like a nurturing lifeline than a tightening hangman's noose (and here it should be noted that the preceding fourth chapter not only

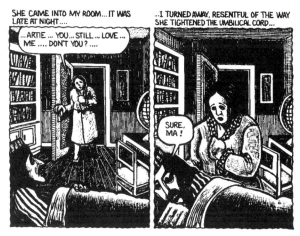

FIGURE 5

bears the title "The Noose Tightens" but is accompanied by a graphic image of hanging mice) (1:71). This life-threatening umbilical link to the mother's body functions in this particular scene as a tie that binds Art not only to the last fatal moments of his mother's life but also to the mother as a source of life and of death—and, moreover, to the mother as a *tainted* source of life-in-death.

That a mother's demand for love is described here as being so strong that it threatens to crush the very life out of her child is certainly nothing new. Yet while Art perhaps wishes the figure of the tightening cord to be understood in just this way, and perhaps only in this way, there is something else going on in the knotting of life lines and death lines. Something else, something unnameably and excessively other, is being transmitted through this equivocal link from mother to child that is specific to the Holocaust and the unconscious transmission of massive trauma.

In her 1995 essay "Images of Absence, Voices of Silence," analyst Louise Kaplan borrows the famous oxymoron of "black milk" from Paul Celan's poem "Death's Fugue" in order to describe how a survivor's child may be said to suckle the noxious nourishment of trauma. Such a child, she observes, "relishes and absorbs this 'black milk,' cultivates its bitter taste as if it were vital sustenance—as if it were existence itself."[38] In this article Kaplan discusses the notion of "transposition," first introduced by Judith Kestenberg to describe the psychological process of unconscious cross-generational transmission of trauma, noting that until the late 1970s therapists had regularly misdiagnosed the children of Holocaust survivors because their symptoms were often no different from those of other patients: "All were plagued by dreams and fantasies of body mutilation. All were beset by fears of bodily damage and illness. All complained of an eating disorder." Yet, "what made our experiences with children of survivors distinctly different," she continues, "was our own uncanny sensation of speaking with the dead." She further explains,

Our consulting rooms were filled with voices and gestures of the dead. The terrors in our patients' fantasies and dreams were only partially theirs. The children of survivors were living out and dreaming out their parents' nightmares. The children were enacting experiences and relating fantasies that could only come from a person who had actually been in a ghetto or extermination camp and actually observed the slaughters and deaths of her loved ones, her friends and neighbors, the strangers who became her cell mates—the murder of her own soul. Since the survivor parent had been unable to witness the horror, she could not remember it. And if she did remember, she remembered only fragments, and even these were rarely, if ever, put into words. The child of the survivor had been sheltered from the truth. But the child was living the nightmare.[39]

Spiegelman's figure of an asphyxiating umbilical cord, in which life lines and death lines not only pass through but also turn into one another, exemplifies the way the "black milk" of trauma is unwittingly transmitted from mother to child.

"Well, mom," Art cries from inside his cell in the concluding row of panels of "Prisoner," "if you're listening . . . congratulations! . . . You've committed the perfect crime . . . You put me here . . . shorted all my circuits . . . cut my nerve endings . . . and crossed my wires! . . . You MURDERED me, mommy, and you left me here to take the rap!!!" In this final twist of the cord, it is now Art himself who claims to be the victim of his mother's suicide—its true victim as well as its falsely framed perpetrator. Little wonder then that Art speaks here of crossed wires and shorted circuits.

If the parameters of the scene of the mother's death are difficult to delimit (despite its all too obvious confinement within the cell-like panels of "Prisoner"), it is because the pages of MAUS are haunted not merely by the traumatic loss of the mother but by the specter of her *repeated killing*.

Not only does Art's mother die more than once, each time in a different way, but she herself is cast at certain moments as a murderer. Her killing should thus be viewed simultaneously as a suicide ("MENOPAUSAL DEPRESSION"), an infanticide ("you MURDERED me, mommy . . . "), and a matricide ("It's his fault—the punk!"); as a suicide that is repeated in the form of a homicide (Vladek's "murderous" burning of the diaries); and as a suicide that is itself the repetition or belated enactment of the Genocide ("HITLER DID IT!").[40] As the painful question of who murdered whom becomes increasingly difficult to settle, and as the attachments between mother and son become more complex—as though fated by a strange logic to be even more fatal *after* the mother's death than *before*—the single thread of the umbilical cord initially used to figure such attachments gives way at this point to a language of shorted circuits, severed nerve endings, and crossed wires. In short, as the questions surrounding this fatal attachment grow in complexity, they not only become harder to answer but increasingly difficult to pose as such.

If the mother-child attachment is destined to be even more fatal after Anja's death than before, is it not perhaps because her untimely demise is also a kind of belated birth? In other words, does the introduction of the figure of the umbilicus, so obviously associated with life's beginnings, at the very moment in the narrative when Anja is about to take her own life not suggest a connection between the cutting of her wrists and the severing of the cord? Would not such a connection in turn imply that Art only really comes to life belatedly at the moment of his mother's death, that Anja in a sense dies in childbirth? Does the child born in this way carry not only his mother's death but his mother as a tainted source of death-in-life within him, bearing the one who had borne him as a noxiously nurturing womb turned inside out?[41]

The difficulty of the questions raised here is such that they should be left open. In endeavoring (in Friedlander's terms) to "withstand the need for closure," one should not just leave them hanging, however, but actively abide with them, *keep them open* through an examination of other related passages.[42] Of particular relevance to this matrix of issues is the series of panels in which Vladek recounts the circumstances surrounding Art's "first" untimely birth in 1948. Before turning to these frames, it is important to note the ways in which Spiegelman revised the initial layout of this scene. In an earlier draft of the page included in the CD-ROM version of MAUS, the story told is not Art's birth but that of his now deceased elder brother, Richieu. This account was to have been followed immediately by a description of Anja's ensuing postpartum depression. In its initial conception the narrative remains in the past and proceeds directly from the announcement of Richieu's arrival in the first row of panels to a phone call Vladek receives in the second instructing him to leave everything and come back to Sosnowiec ("Anja is sick and needs you!"). Only in the final, published version is an account of Art's own traumatic birth interpolated into this narrative sequence. Belatedly inserted into the second, third, and fourth rows of the page now set in the present, this narrative interruption is itself marked by a conspicuous series of verbal and visual breaks.

"But wait—," Art stops his father, "if you were married in February and Richieu was born in October, was he premature?" "Yes, a little," Vladek responds. "But YOU—after the war, when you were born—it was VERY premature. The doctors thought you wouldn't live. I found a specialist what saved you . . . he had to break your ARM to take you out from Anja's belly!" (1:30). In this revised version of the story the two births now appear to be so closely related in Vladek's mind that the memory of the second, more violent one in which Art's arm is broken is itself made to break through an account of the first. As always in MAUS, such abrupt shifts leave one to consider how the second story not only draws attention away from the first but, in so doing, becomes a screen through which to read it.[43] Moreover, the very violence of this narrative caesura suggests that the traumatic breach that *is* Art's birth, a trauma related through the break in Vladek's account not only to Richieu's *untimely birth* in 1937 but also to his *premature death* in 1943, is a rupture that cannot be safely contained as an object of narration.[44] Like the arm that had to be broken in order to save Art from Anja's womb, the story of his wrenching delivery is related here through a series of narrative dislocations.

Vladek continues, "And when you were a tiny baby your arm always jumped up, like so! We joked and called you 'Heil Hitler!' Always we pushed your arm down, and you would OOPS!" (1:30) (see fig. 1). The account again breaks off here, as Vladek spills over a bottle of pills while performing the act he is describing. Tellingly, at the moment Vladek plays himself and another, when his description of his own response to his son's "Hitler salute" is accompanied by a dramatic reenactment of those gestures, the performance itself becomes a scene of involuntary repetition. As the past spills into the present, the pills Vladek knocks over fall not just onto the table but out of the visual frame of the panel itself. Insofar as the effect of such spills is to leave neither the receptacle nor the relationship between contents and their containers intact—insofar, that is, as these spills *transform the very limits they transgress*—they turn the visual frame of the panel itself into a kind of overflowing pillbox.[45]

Underlying these visual and narrative disruptions is yet another connection to the maternal body. In his essay "Mad Youth," Spiegelman describes the Rego Park house in which he grew up as a "two-family brick pillbox."[46] While the pun on "pillbox" depicts the family residence as a place where drugs and the trauma of the war cohabited, this same house is figured elsewhere as a suffocating womb. "What happened to me the winter I flipped out was that I had gotten the bends; I had surfaced too quickly from the overheated bunker of my traumatized family . . . into the heady atmosphere of freedom."[47] Not only is the "pillbox" now an "overheated bunker," but Spiegelman's emergence from the oceanic depths of his home is a birth trauma inseparable from the trauma of his mother's death.

If, according to the strangely twisted logic we have been tracing, the attachment between mother and son is fated to be even more fatally binding after Anja's death than before it, it is because the mother, while clearly no longer alive after her suicide, is still somehow not yet dead; because her untimely end is in a certain sense also a belated beginning; because the trauma of her repeated killing is also that of an incessant birthing. It is no accident in this regard that an account in MAUS of one son's premature birth is made to interrupt and displace the story of another. Nor is it by chance that the account of Anja's first birth-related, suicidal depression ("But I don't care. I JUST DON'T WANT TO LIVE") (1:31) is placed on the page directly facing the one in which the tale of these untimely deliveries is told (fig. 6). As though to underscore the difficulty of contextualizing these relationships, the frame in which Anja first gives voice to this death wish is the only one on the page that visually breaks out of the horizontal-vertical grid in which the panels are plotted.

The thematic connection of the mother's suicide to her sons' premature births (and Richieu's untimely death), and the structural link tying

FIGURE 6

these related traumas to a series of visual and verbal disruptions, combine to suggest that MAUS is a text more generally conceived as a story of narrative ruptures, made up of tales (or tails) that are repeatedly broken off and prolonged without ever beginning or ending. As though to signal this circularly repetitive, nonlinear, and seemingly static movement, MAUS opens with an image of Vladek astride his stationary bike pedaling hard and going nowhere fast.

The Growth of a Relationship

In an audio appendix to the "Prisoner on the Hell Planet" section of MAUS, Spiegelman stresses that "it's important in these pages to think of them as complete pages. In the book there's a black border around the whole page that actually bleeds off the page. It acts as a funereal border. When the book is closed, on the edges you actually see that as a separate section inside the book."[48] The author's investment in having us view this text-within-the-text as a discrete, self-contained subsection of MAUS, as a kind of crypt in which the painful story of his mother's suicide is safely and securely buried, is understandable. The preceding analysis has tried to heed

Spiegelman's suggestion. Yet at the same time, the twisted logic at work in this section and elsewhere in the text has made it necessary to trace the various ways in which the story told here—like the black border surrounding it—bleeds off the page. In contrast to that ink, however, whose bleeding ultimately sharpens the edges it soaks through, the traumatic story of the mother's death spreads in a more insidious manner, so pervasively invading the narrative layers surrounding it that there is no visible point of effraction, no clearly definable break, wound, or hematoma in the text. In an attempt to trace this bloodless and inkless bleeding, the sheer imperceptibility of which is to be read less as an index of its immaculate absence than of its haunting ubiquity, it has been necessary to follow the faintest of leads, to allow oneself to be guided by the highly overdetermined and unstable figure of the tightening umbilical cord. The structural significance of this narrative "red thread" is highlighted both by its placement at the center of the last page of "Prisoner," where it is embedded like a page-within-the-page framed by the surrounding images, and by its close affiliation to the language of shorted circuits, severed nerve endings, and crossed wires used in the panel directly below. Following the twists and turns of this straitening cord, of a trope marking the last time Art was ever to see his mother alive, I have attempted to trace the complicated ties binding Anja, viewed here as a source of life and of death, as a tainted source of life-in-death, to a series of premature births and untimely deaths, the traumatic repetition of births *as* deaths.

In order to stay with the open questions raised in "Prisoner on the Hell Planet," questions that tend perhaps against the author's intentions to bleed off its pages and spread into other layers of the narrative, I turn now from the "crossed wires" of the mother-son relationship to Spiegelman's own fatal attachment to his rodent offspring, a work, as he told Lawrence Weschler, on which he'd spent his life. When asked in the course of this 1986 interview with Weschler "why he'd decided to publish the book version of MAUS in its current truncated form," Spiegelman's response was "Funny you should ask":

I'd never really had any intention of publishing the book version in two parts. But then, about a year ago, I read an interview with Steven Spielberg that he was producing an animated feature film entitled *An American Tail*, involving a family of Jewish mice living in Russia a hundred years ago named the Mousekawitzes, who were being persecuted by Katsacks, and how eventually they fled to America for shelter. He was planning to have it out for the Statue of Liberty centennial celebrations.

I was appalled, shattered. . . . For about a month I went into a frenzy. I'd spent my life on this, and now here, along was coming this Goliath, the most powerful man in Hollywood, just casually trampling everything underfoot. I dashed off a letter, which was returned, unopened. I went sleepless for nights on end, and then, when I finally did sleep, I began confusing our names in my dreams: Spiegelberg, Spielman. . . . I contacted lawyers. I mean, the similarities were obvious, right down to the title—their *American Tail* simply being a more blatant, pandering-to-the-mob version of my *Survivor's Tale* subtitle. Their lawyers argued that the idea of anthropomorphizing mice wasn't unique to either of us. . . . [W]hat I was saying was that the specific use of mice to sympathetically portray Jews combined with the concept of cats as anti-Semitic oppressors in a story that compares life in the Old World of Europe with life in America *was* unique—and it was called *Maus: A Survivor's Tale.*

I didn't want any money from them—I just wanted them to cease and desist. What made me so angry was that when *Maus* was eventually going to be completed, people were naturally going to see my version as a slightly psychotic recasting of Spielberg's idea instead of the way it was—Spielberg's being an utter domestication and trivialization of *Maus.* . . .

I mean, if Samuel Beckett had stolen the idea, I'd be depressed, but I'd be *impressed* as well. But Steven Spielberg! Oy!

Unfortunately, at the point in the story where Spiegelman presumably goes on to describe the actual publication of the first volume of MAUS, Weschler inexplicably breaks off the quotation, suddenly shifting to paraphrase and thereby uncannily perpetuating the movement of narrative rupture we have been tracing.

So . . . he decided that if he couldn't stop Spielberg, he might nevertheless beat him to the turnstiles, immediately publishing as much of the story as he'd already completed (he explained how all along he'd seen the arrival at Mauschwitz as the narrative's halfway point) and thereby at least establishing primacy. Pantheon was happy to go along, and Spielberg's production company obliged by running into difficulties and having to delay the film's release until around Thanksgiving.[49]

The circumstances surrounding the book's publication bear a striking resemblance to the conditions under which its author was born. Not only were both forced to appear prematurely due to a perceived life-threatening situation, but each "delivery" was in its own curious way a violent act of salvation. Just as Art had to have his arm broken by a specialist in order "to take [him] out from Anja's belly," so too was it necessary to break the spine of MAUS in order bring it out into the world "in truncated form" as a book.[50]

To pursue this curious link between text and body, parent and child, author and work, I turn now from Spiegelman's description of the circumstances surrounding the publication of the first volume of MAUS to an interview he gave upon completion of the second.[51]

Thirteen years ago I bet I'd live long enough to finish "Maus" and by God I did. On the other hand, insofar as I can tune in to these things, there's already a slight feeling of mourning. Somehow I got used to this large carcinogenic growth attached to my body and I feel sad that it's been cut away. . . . [A]lthough it was painful and difficult work, it was, in some ways, a staving off of a certain kind of other mourning. Even though it was on the battleground of a piece of paper, I was able to keep my relationship with my father going and was even able to have the illusion of having an effect. And so that was something, even though, like I say, it was difficult to keep going.[52]

Whereas the "crossed wires" of the mother-son relationship in "Prisoner on the Hell Planet" were originally figured in pointedly corporeal terms as a twisted umbilical tie, here the author's attachment to his own tainted offspring appears to be associated with a different kind of bodily connection—namely, with the inflamed tissue of what, for him, is not simply of the body or the text, but the very texture of his relationship to his work. If, as was suggested earlier, telling tales is a matter of life and death both for Scheherezade of *The Thousand and One Nights* and for the artist-narrator of MAUS, a significant difference between them now emerges. While the former tells stories in order *to defer* her own death, the latter seems to draw *A Survivor's Tale* precisely in order to accommodate it—or rather to make room for that which is more than living and more than dead. Spiegelman describes his relationship to his work and to what is commonly referred to as the "creative process" in pointedly uncreative and self-destructive terms. Indeed, in this interview the thirteen-year gestation of MAUS is depicted as a kind of antipregnancy, a time when the host body of the artist seems to accommodate itself not only to the unmourned dead who continue to inhabit it but moreover to the *monstrous vitality* of a deadly "carcinogenic growth."[53]

Through this unsettling image Spiegelman redefines the work of art and its extended process of labor and delivery as a work of mourning gone awry.[54] While the "painful and difficult work" of drawing MAUS no doubt provided a way for him to work through loss by reworking it into art (and Art), it also at the same time appears to have worked against itself, to have compromised and suspended itself in a way that made it possible to accomplish through the very work of mourning the task of "staving off a certain kind of other mourning." While this "other mourning" is presumably that which could not have been done so long as Art was able to keep alive his father and his contentious relationship with him by continuing to live it out on "the battlefield of a piece of paper," the notion of "a certain kind of other mourning" also seems to point more fundamentally to the inherent otherness of Spiegelman's *Trauerarbeit*, to how this work of mourning may not only have worked against itself, but, in so doing, may have worked open the space for another kind of survival.

What, then, is the space of this other survival? In an attempt to locate its unassimilated excess, the surplus of that which is more than body and more than text—and yet somehow (though not umbilically) linked to both the body and the text—one may be guided by the excessive language employed by the artist to describe his relationship to his work. MAUS is depicted not only as a growth attached to his body, as a cancer he "somehow got used to," but also as a text whose publication is experienced as an amputation that leaves him, as he says, "feeling sad." This surprisingly affectionate characterization of the text-as-tumor is, at the very least, a sign of ambivalence, an indication of Spiegelman's own potentially fatal attachment to a noxious growth attached to him. That this growth is described as being "carcinogenic" is all the more significant in light of the author's notorious nicotine habit. Indeed, I would suggest that Art's attachment to the cigarettes he so conspicuously and compulsively smokes throughout MAUS is no less desperate or ambivalent than his relationship to the work itself. Moreover, because these relationships themselves tend, as it were, to draw on each other, each may be read as the figure or symptom of the other.

This interaction between the draftsman's work and his drawing of smoke, between activities that sustain and contaminate one another, is further complicated by the artist's portrait of himself on the rear inner flap of the first volume of MAUS (fig. 7). He is shown sitting at his drawing table, cigarette in hand, while on the small shelf to his right reserved for the tools of his trade—ink, pens, correction fluid, and so forth—one notices a full ashtray and a pack of cigarettes. At first glance the cigarettes appear to be

FIGURE 7

Camels and yet on closer inspection the brand turns out to be "Cremo Lights." Where one might have expected to find a hump rising under the arch of the brand name, there are instead two fuming smokestacks. The cigarette pack is located in the lower left-hand corner of the self-portrait, while on the upper right one sees through the closed window of the artist's New York studio the barbed-wire fence, cat-patrolled guard tower, and smoking crematorium chimney of Auschwitz.

If one draws a line from the top of the chimney on the upper right to the lid of the cigarette pack on the lower left, it passes directly through the glowing tip of Art's Cremo Light. This diagonal connecting the smoking within to the burning without suggests that with each drag on his cigarette Art in effect draws in a breath of Auschwitz.[55] In other words, every drag seems to draw together inside and out, present and past, the inflamed airways of the living and the airborne remains of the dead. With each inhaling moment of concentration Art draws in the scattered ashes of the incinerated bodies of Auschwitz and buries them within himself only to witness their immediate disinterment and redispersion as he exhales. Each drag thus has the symbolic value of a burning desire fleetingly realized, a desire to draw two radically heterogeneous worlds together, to draw the one in with the other, and, moreover, to keep the contract of that double drawing safely encrypted within himself.[56] While the ensuing movement of exhalation may be said to vent the crypt, to atomize all that had just come together, and, thereby, to frustrate Art's desire just as it was being realized, it also at the same time guarantees through its very opposition the insistence of that impossible wish. In short, the cigarettes Art smokes do not so much satisfy his desire as exasperate it. Or rather they satisfy it in its very impossibility by frustrating and intensifying it. What keeps Art's desire aflame is thus this incessant oscillation between the two mutually constitutive, mutually inhibiting moments of aspiration and expiration, concentration and atomization, a pulse Richard Klein has described as the very "rhythm of smoking, tapped out in every puff on a cigarette."[57]

Any analysis of the rhythms of Art's smoking must be considered incomplete, however, if it does not in turn include an examination of the artist's depictions of smoke. For if the self-portrait of the artist-as-draftsman suggests nothing else, it is that the drawing of smoke is really no different from the drawing of smoke. Tellingly, this highly self-reflexive image is temporally focused around a momentary break in the drawing process, around an interval in which Art is shown staring off into space, abstaining both from putting pen to paper and from taking a drag on his Cremo Light. Such a pointed and pregnant pause no doubt accentuates a moment of artistic reflection within the already reflexive medium of the self-portrait. Yet, in making one see the suspended activities of drawing and smoking in their own mutual implication, the image also suggests that whatever compels Art to light one cigarette after another is the same thing that drives him to draw and redraw himself drawing smoke. His self-portrait is thus a *draft* in the further sense that it is but one in a series of provisional renderings, none of which may be said to constitute the final, definitive version of himself.

In order then to approach this seemingly self-contained image *as a draft*, it is necessary to read it first and foremost in relation to other drawings that appear to repeat and revise it. One such image—or rather series of images—is to be found in the bottom right-hand corner of a page in MAUS II, the very page on which Vladek begins a painstaking description of the operation of the gas chambers in Auschwitz ("For this," he says, "I was an EYEWITNESS") (2:69). As in the artist's self-portrait at the end of the first volume of MAUS I, the panel in question contains an image of a crematorium chimney with smoke coming out of it. Yet here the smoke is drawn in such a way as to appear quite literally to pour out of the past—out of a smokestack which itself appears to rise up out of its own frame and into the one above—into the present where it mingles with and loses itself in the smoke trailing out of Art's Cremo Light (2:69) (fig. 8).[58]

FIGURE 8

Whereas earlier the visual logic of the image suggested that Art drew in the air-borne remains of the dead with every puff on his Cremo Light, here it seems that Auschwitz is the very air he breathes. In other words, just as smoking tends in general to make one more aware of the rhythms of one's breathing, so too does the smoke from Art's cigarette tend to act as a kind of stain on the invisible air around it. Thus, far from simply filling the surrounding atmosphere with smoke, the fumes from Art's Cremo Light function instead to screen the smoke already there. They enable one to see that which is already so much "in the air," so massively and oppressively present, it cannot be seen as such.

While in a first moment it appeared that the rhythms of Art's smoking compulsively enacted an impossible wish to draw the past in with the present, to gather in the scattered remains of the dead and to bury them within himself, a wish whose repeated frustration was the perpetually renewed precondition for its ever-so-fleeting satisfaction, it now seems that those very same rhythms may play out another opposing, yet equally impossible, desire. Here the alternating movement of inhaling and exhaling, the pulse tapped out in every puff on a cigarette, may be read as the enactment of a desire to make that which is neither here nor there—a traumatic past which is all too hauntingly and pervasively present—return as if it were either here or there, now or then, present or absent. It is the coexistence of these mutually inhibiting moments of gathering in and separating out, each of which is in its turn internally contradictory, that makes the desires bound up with and compulsively played out in Art's smoking all the more impossible: both impossible to satisfy and impossible not to.

A Little Safe

The tensions inherent in such an impossible enterprise of double drawing are played out not only in the rhythms of Art's smoking (itself linked to the "carcinogenic growth" of MAUS), or in the redrafting of scenes of him drawing himself drawing smoke, but also in the rhythmic alternations of the narrative itself. Whereas MAUS has often been referred to as a "frame story" with an external narrative "enfolding" or "surrounding" an inner one, such static descriptions rarely do justice to the dynamic beating and bleeding of the tale.[59] Like Poe's story "The Tell-Tale Heart," Spiegelman's "survivor's tale" repeatedly oscillates between the level of the telling and that of the tale, between a scene of narration set in the present and a dramatic restaging of events from the past.

Often these shifts between the tale and the scene of its telling are motivated by some current distraction or disturbance. For example, there is a moment early on when Vladek suddenly breaks off an account of how, as a prisoner of war, he was forced by his German captors to perform the Herculean task of cleaning a stable in an impossibly brief period of time. He interrupts this account in order to reprimand Art for dropping cigarette ashes on, of all places, his living room carpet. "You want it should be like a stable HERE?" he asks (1:52). While such outbursts are clearly meant to destabilize the relationship between a still smoldering past and a smoke-free present, between the level of the tale and that of the telling, at other times the movement back and forth is more regulated and is made to accelerate in such a way that the focus gradually shifts from whatever is going on in either the past or the present to the pulsating, back-and-forth movement itself.

One such sequence significantly begins where "Prisoner on the Hell Planet" breaks off—as though it were intended to be read not simply as a new, relatively unrelated chain of events but also and above all as a continuation, in displaced form, of the embedded or encased narrative. In other words, even though this self-described "Case History" is clearly inserted in MAUS as a text-within-the-text drawn in a distinctly different style, it is, as we have seen, anything but a self-contained piece. The mention of shorted circuits, cut nerve endings, and crossed wires in its penultimate panel in fact suggests that the text does not so much end as reach a certain impasse. Indeed, insofar as Spiegelman's "survivor's tale" is quite explicitly a story of mice and their mutilated tails, it might be said that what *remains* to be read in MAUS is precisely the way these cut-off tails, these severed nerve endings, and violently interrupted narratives, are repeatedly restitched into a different kind of narrative structure—into a kind of "slow-motion picture" montage in which processes of interruption and displacement are no longer the exception but the rule.

The sequence following "Prisoner on the Hell Planet" thus tellingly begins with Art asking once again about the fate of his mother's diaries.

Whereas the last time the question was raised Vladek had managed to deflect it by drawing attention to the stifling fumes coming from his son's
cigarette, here, instead of trying to distract him again, the father simply
lies: "So far this didn't show up. I looked, but I can't find" (1:105). When
pressed by his son, who insists, "I've got to have that!" Vladek this time
literally plays for time by looking at his watch, announcing, "Another time
I'll again look. But now better we go to the bank" (1:105). The bank thus
becomes another kind of smoke screen, at once an ersatz destination toward which the frame story is ineluctably drawn and a roundabout way of
avoiding the inevitable question of the diaries. But the closer Art and his
father come to the bank, the larger the shadows of the dead mother and
her diaries loom.

To complicate matters even further, this tension *within* the frame
story is doubled by a tension between it and the embedded narrative it is
meant to frame and contain. This enframed, inner narrative recounted by
Vladek on the way to the bank is itself tellingly a story of progressive containment. It is the story, namely, of German efforts to confine Vladek,
Anja, and the remaining Jews of Sosnowiec within increasingly enclosed
and circumscribed living quarters inside the Stara section of town. At a
certain point in 1943 the Germans close this ghetto inside Sosnowiec and
move the remaining Jews to the nearby village of Srodula. At this point
the alternation between present and past, telling and told, begins to in-
tensify as the scene of narration rendered in an image of Art and Vladek
walking to the bank is superimposed on a drawing of the cat-guarded gate
of the Jewish ghetto viewed from without (1:105) (fig. 9). The ghetto is
then gradually emptied out as more and more of its inhabitants are deported to Auschwitz. By the end of 1943 there is almost no one left; those
who do remain are driven to find refuge in increasingly cramped hiding
places. Thus, Vladek tells of how he and his family were forced to move
from a basement bunker hidden beneath a coal bin into an attic bunker,
the entrance to which was hidden by a chandelier, and from there into another bunker in a shoe shop, which could be entered only by crawling
through a tunnel made of shoes.

As energies and spaces become increasingly compressed within the
enframed story, the pulse of the narrative accelerates, beating with greater
frequency between the story of Anja and Vladek's flight from one unsafe

AND THE POLES OF SRODULA, WE JEWS HAD TO PAY TO MOVE THEM TO OUR HOUSES IN SOSNOWIEC....AND HERE IN SRODULA WOULD BE OUR GHETTO TO LIVE EVER AFTER.

OUR FAMILY GOT A COTTAGE-LESS SPACE THAN BEFORE, BUT WE HAD AT LEAST WHERE TO LIVE. MANY LIVED ONLY IN THE STREET.

FIGURE 9

bunker to the next in the inner narrative and the story of Art and Vladek's stroll to the local bank in the outer narrative. The two stories finally converge at the point where Vladek and Anja are driven from the safety of their last bunker. "It was NOWHERE we had to hide," Vladek tells Art. At this point in the frame narrative the two men, having finally reached the bank, are about to visit a safe-deposit box. "Can I help you, Mr. Spiegelman?," asks a teller. "Yes, I have here my son, Artie. I want to sign him a key. So he can go also to my safety box" (1:125) (fig. 10). What then is the point of this narrative compression? Why is pressure being exerted on the reader to view the two converging stories in terms of one another? What is the connection here between unsafe bunkers and bank "safety boxes"? What might it mean in the context of these interpenetrating narrative frames to be "a little safe"?

While the phrase "a little safe" is initially used by Vladek to describe the precarious sense of security he and others felt upon completing their first bunker—"and there we made a brick wall filled high with coal. Behind this wall we could be a little safe" (1:110)—it also applies to the small "safety box" in which Vladek keeps valuables from before and after the war. That this trip to the safe is staged as a kind of rehearsal for the moment of Vladek's own death is suggested by the instructions he gives Art upon entering the vault: "in case anything bad happens to me you must run RIGHT away over here. Therefore I arranged for you this key. Take everything out from the safe. Otherwise it can go only to taxes or Mala will grab it" (1:126). The care with which Vladek seeks to secure the full transmission of

FIGURE 10

his legacy to Art stands in pointed contrast to the callous way he allowed his son's maternal inheritance to get lost in transmission. Little wonder then that Vladek takes Art to the bank instead of immediately revealing what he had done to Anja's diaries. While Vladek once again uses one scene as a kind of smoke screen to conceal another, and perhaps even seeks through this rehearsal of his own death and his promise of an intact inheritance to compensate his son for the loss of a maternal legacy he had failed to transmit, in the end the "little safe," to which he has given Art a key, comes to look more and more like a little coffin. Indeed, there is a striking resemblance between Spiegelman's depiction of Vladek lying prostrate over an empty safe-deposit box, crying, "ANJA! ANJA! ANJA!" (1:127) (fig. 11), in the very last frame of chapter 5, and a drawing of him sprawled across his wife's coffin screaming her name at the funeral home in "Prisoner on the Hell Planet" (fig. 12).

Whereas the coffin in the funeral home has apparently been closed for good, the one in the bank vault has obviously been reopened and its contents removed. That this trip to the bank is a visit to the family MAUSoleum is suggested not only by the visual resemblance between the depictions of Vladek in the funeral home and the bank, but also by his instruction to Art in the vault that this is the place he should run to "in case," as he says, "anything bad happens to me." It is at this point that one may begin to appreciate why the encased, inner story of Vladek and Anja's flight from one unsafe bunker to the next is made to dovetail with the frame story's account of a trip to the bank at the precise moment when Vladek and Anja are said to have nowhere to go and hide. Reading the two intersecting stories through each other at this point, the little coffin in which Vladek had hoped to find his wife "a little safe" turns out to be strangely open and empty, as though—like the couple starved out of its last bunker in the inner story (1:125)—she herself were now cast out in the open, unhoused, unframed, unsafe, en route with nowhere to go and "NOWHERE . . . to hide" (see fig. 10).[60]

In short, it is the very beating of this narrative rhythm back and forth between a bank safe and an unsafe bunker that in the end compels one to consider how Vladek's seemingly secure "safety box" is and is not safe, how it is a box that is at once "a little safe," a little coffin, an abandoned unsafe little bunker, and a broken heart. It should be recalled here that the trip to the bank and the story Vladek is telling on the way are themselves

FIGURE 11

FIGURE 12

suddenly interrupted by a potentially fatal seizure—"when HYAAK! mmy heart—Artie! Quick! Take from my pocket a nitrostat pill" (1:118).[61] A certain syncopation of cardiac and narrative beats thus seems to mark the location of a surprisingly unsafe little crypt in the text. In doing so, it effectively leads one back to the story of the mother's death framed by the strangely permeable "funereal border" of the "Prisoner" section, as well as to the rhythms of Art's smoking and the precarious little coffer located in his chest, which is filled up and aired out with each puff on a Cremo Light. As was suggested earlier, this hyperventilating little vault lodged within Art should itself be viewed as the space of something wanting—that is, as a lack which is repeatedly, futilely, and compulsively filled in, filled only by hollowing out an even greater lack which in turn demands ever more urgently to be filled. Like the carcinogenic growth of MAUS, this tell-tale little mausoleum to which Art remains so fatally attached through the chain of cigarettes he smokes is one he accommodates and maintains by putting his own life in danger. In other words, because the contents of *this* "little safe" are not just dead but deadly—as monstrously vital as a cancerous tumor—they always threaten to make over their living, breathing container in the very image of what it seeks to contain. To put it more cryptically, they always threaten to keep the keeper who seeks to keep them safe.

Crossroads

Before leaving this narrative juncture in MAUS, it is important to note the way this highly overdetermined textual intersection returns in Spiegelman's later work, in the form of a lithographic montage significantly entitled *Crossroads* (fig. 13).[62] It returns, however, not merely as a positive moment, as a particular image reworked into a new series of drawings, but also and above all as the locus of a problem, as the still unresolved question of how to frame the uncontainable, to accommodate the monstrous vitality of that which is more than living and more than dead. Whereas Spiegelman's redrafting of certain images often has the effect of teasing out latent problems and conflicts (as in his self-portraits drawing smoke, discussed earlier), it is also the case that he sometimes returns to particular images in order to stabilize and contain the energies and problems associated with them. In a work such as *Crossroads* he appears to do both.

FIGURE 13

Published by Tandem Press in 1996, *Crossroads* is a montage composed of three interrelated images. The drawing at the center, by far the largest of the three, and the one that functions as its pictorial ground, is a reworking of the panel in MAUS in which Anja and Vladek, forced to flee the last of their makeshift shelters, are depicted walking along a road drawn in the shape of a swastika. As was noted earlier, this pivotal panel not only shows Art's parents having nowhere to go and nowhere to hide on a path where all roads seem to lead inevitably to Auschwitz, but it also marks a narrative impasse, a point at which the story itself seems condemned to go nowhere, indefinitely suspended at the threshold between inner and outer narratives, crossing back and forth between the bank "safety boxes" of the one and the unsafe bunkers of the other. In Spiegelman's later redrafting of this thematic and diegetic dead end, the eye of the viewer is no longer made to follow Vladek and Anja from behind as they wander aimlessly along the branches of a swastika. Instead, we now see them head on, from an elevated perspective, as they stand frozen in place at the very crux of a *Hakenkreuz* (given the title of the piece it is important to recall that the German word for swastika literally means "hooked cross").

Wrenched out of its original context and pivoted 180 degrees around the central axis of this rotating cross (itself a traditional symbol of solar cycles), this image of Anja and Vladek in the open with nowhere left to turn is now associated with other depictions of Jews en route. Over the upper left-hand corner of this drawing Spiegelman has superimposed an engraving taken from Gustave Doré's *The Legend of the Wandering Jew*. The title character, whose face is covered by one of the artist's mouse masks, is shown passing under the oppressive shadow and vacant (yet strangely vigilant) stare of a roadside crucifix. Sight lines transmit this stare across the bottom edge of the engraving and onto the backs of Anja and Vladek in the drawing below, suggesting a historical and ideological nexus between Christian anti-Semitism and the Nazi persecution of the Jews.

These two depictions of Jews condemned to wander through desolate, inhospitable, rural landscapes in the top part of the montage seem to stand in sharp contrast to the third image centered at the bottom in which the artist and his two children (one of whom is wearing a Mickey Mouse T-shirt) appear to be very much at home in a distinctly urban setting. Yet, if we continue to follow the sight line that links the fate of the Wandering

Jew to that of Art's parents in the first two images, we see that it extends directly into the back seat of the taxi Art and his children are about to enter in the third. Working at cross-purposes with the prevailing vertical orientation of the lithograph, this diagonal unsettles the more obvious distinctions set up here between country and city, past and present, exile and asylum, as well as the less obvious split within the notion of exile itself between homelessness as a fate worse than death and diasporic existence as a positive way of life. At the risk of supplying a caption to the lithograph and thereby reducing its multiple cross-references to a single meaning, it is nevertheless worth citing a passage from Spiegelman's 1989 essay "Looney Tunes, Zionism, and the Jewish Question."

The Holocaust ought to have convinced the world that it must embrace the Diaspora Jew—that it must acknowledge, indeed, that it has become the Diaspora Jew. For me the romantic image of the Jew is . . . the pale, marginal, cosmopolitan, alienated, half-assimilated, International Stateless outsider Jew, existentially poised for flight with no place to run, eager for social justice since that might make the world a safer place for him to live, with nothing but his culture to hang on to.[63]

What then is one to make of the connection between Spiegelman's meditation on the fate of the Diaspora Jew in *Crossroads* and the panel in MAUS his lithograph redrafts? The artist's quotation of this particular scene in MAUS—and it is not just one scene among others—may be viewed as a way of highlighting it. Yet, the retrospective illumination of this vision of Art's parents, far from simply refocusing attention on it, instead redefines the drawing as the first in a series of drafts, remarking the way in which it will have already functioned in its initial context as an unfinished picture—that is, as one in a series of drawings intersecting with and circularly defined by others at a particularly volatile point of narrative and thematic impasse. If *Crossroads* may be said to place a supplementary *X* on this spot, it does so to remind us that the text it draws upon should itself already be read as a visual and verbal montage.

Read as an earlier draft of *Crossroads*, the moment in MAUS under discussion should be viewed as one in which the question of a certain diaspora, taken up and reworked in the later piece, is already at work. In MAUS, this question, which is never posed as such, tends instead to hover like the ghost of the mother over the entire scene. Moreover, related to the specific question of the mother-as-specter are a host of other haunting questions brought into focus through her representative spectrality: Where does one go to commemorate the loss of those whose ashes have been scattered? How does one mourn the supplementary loss of the missing remains (a question of particular relevance in a text where the mother's diaries have themselves been burned)?[64] As though Spiegelman himself had nowhere to go, nowhere to hide from these questions, as though the only way for him to continue to address them and for them in turn to go on speaking to him, were by means of a certain screen, he pieces *Crossroads* together as a montage in which the haunting question of a radical and irremediable dispersion returns in displaced form as the problem of the Diaspora Jew. That such a repetition is somehow calculated to harness and absorb the ambient energy of the initial scene is suggested in part by Spiegelman's uncharacteristic overgeneralization of the current predicament of the Diaspora Jew in the passage cited above. "The Holocaust ought to have convinced the world that it must embrace the Diaspora Jew—that it must acknowledge, indeed, *that it has become* the Diaspora Jew" (emphasis added). It is one thing to "embrace," quite another to assimilate and engulf through total identification.

Like the small cross embroidered by Kriemhild on Siegfried's cloak in *The Song of the Niebelungen*, the patchwork of images of which *Crossroads* is composed exposes a weak spot in the narrative fabric of MAUS in the very act of covering it, in the process of gathering its disseminating energies together under the rubric of a more stable and familiar notion of "Jewish Diaspora." Whereas this weak spot has been described primarily as a nodal or neuralgic point in the text, a point where otherwise distinct narrative strata are made to cut into and bleed through one another, it is now necessary to examine the way this all too literal *intersection* of the level of the telling with that of the tale marks a heretofore unsuspected cut within the very notion of telling, a small but decisive difference between telling as narration and telling as counting. It is therefore significant that it is the voice of a bank *teller* ("Can I help you, Mr. Spiegelman?") that jars Vladek out of the tale of the past ("It was NOWHERE we had to hide"), into the present of the telling ("Yes, I have here my son, Artie. . . ."), at the moment he enters the bank. This connection between numerical counting and narrative recounting, which marks and plays out a certain opening *within* the "telling" itself, is alluded to elsewhere in the first volume, most notably in the scene discussed earlier in which Vladek knocks over a bottle of pills while showing Art how his involuntarily gesturing arm always had to be pushed back down. "OOPS! Look now what you made me do!" "ME? Okay, I'll re-count them later." "NO! You don't know counting pills. I'll do it after . . . I'm an EXPERT for this" (1:30). In the second volume of MAUS, to which I now turn, this seemingly insignificant wordplay becomes a telling indicator of a structural principle organizing both the narration of the tale and its visual layout.

3

The Vanishing Point

SPIEGELMAN'S MAUS II

The first volume of MAUS concludes with a picture of Art leaving his father's house muttering, "murderer," after finally learning what happened to his mother's diaries, while the last image of the embedded narrative told by Vladek is a drawing of the truck in which he and Anja had been deported, stopping at the entrance to Auschwitz. Breaking off the tale at this point, at the threshold of the concentration camp, Spiegelman suggests that all roads in this volume will indeed have led to Auschwitz, that the camp is not only the telos of MAUS, volume I, but its dead center as well. That the volume leaves off at the gates of Auschwitz, the periphery of that dead center, suggests a radical disjunction between the outside of the camp and its inside, a fundamental discontinuity between the narrative paths that have taken us here and those that will follow.

In MAUS II Spiegelman does not so much invent new ways of telling the story of the inside as alter and dislocate established protocols of narration and depiction from within. In doing so, he suggests that there is telling and then again there is telling, that one mode of narration is at work within another, silently reworking it from the inside out. This homonymic practice, a linguistic staging of the very question of spectral doubling, places various burdens on the reader. First, it obliges one to be more attentive to the subtle differences, conflicts, and ghosts lurking at the heart of any apparent identity; second, it suggests that one begin translating not just *between* languages (as in the case of mouse and *Maus*) but *within* them there where translation seems unnecessary (as in the case of telling and telling); third, it makes the reader view "inside" and "outside" not simply as the symmetrically reversible terms they appear to be—as different sides of the same homogeneous space—but instead as radically heterogeneous, discontinuous realities. "I feel so inadequate," Art confides to his wife, Françoise, in one of the only scenes in MAUS in which he himself is shown being transported from one place to another, "trying to reconstruct a reality that was worse than my darkest dreams, and trying to do it as a COMIC STRIP! . . . There's so much I'll never be able to understand or visualize" (2:16).

". . . And Here My Troubles Began . . ."

At the beginning of MAUS II the question of how to tell the difference between telling as narration and telling as counting is posed as the very question of beginnings, of where an account broken off at the gates of Auschwitz begins again, of where this *recounting* actually begins counting from. The volume's subtitle, *And Here My Troubles Began*, suggests that these troubles—those of the father as well as the son—start at the entrance to the camp. Such an inference is complicated, however, by Spiegelman's use of the same words (apparently a quote from Vladek) as the title for the central third chapter of the volume, a chapter which opens with an image of Vladek counting crackers "27 . . . 28 . . . 29 . . . " (2:77) in the frame narrative as he recounts his *departure* from Auschwitz in the inner story. The second appearance of the citation thus seems not so much to specify the first as to revise it. Indeed, if anything, the troubles which began for Vladek upon his arrival in Auschwitz, instead of ending with his departure, appear to begin again—or rather to begin as if for the first time, this time in earnest, with the ensuing death march of "thousands of prisoners from all around . . . back into Germany" (2:84). The phrase "here my troubles began" then appears a third and final time later in this chapter, as Vladek describes his subsequent internment in Dachau where he contracts a nearly fatal case of typhus. "Yah—this was a camp—TERRIBLE! I had a misery, I can't tell you . . . Here, in Dachau, my troubles began" (2:91).[1] While it is certainly possible to interpret the repeated recontextualization of this same site-specific passage simply as an indication of escalating difficulties, as a way of saying "I didn't know what trouble was until . . . ," what truly seems to be at stake here, what is being marked and performed by this process of beginning over again, is a shift from linear to circular narration.

Yet precisely because this shift is itself not linear in nature, not a definitive transition from one mode of narration to another, the circularity that is silently at work here must be read as a process of narrative *self-alteration*—that is, as a process that begins repeatedly without ever simply beginning as such, as a stuttering movement of recitation and repetition that inwardly alters the telling without, however, turning it into something else—for instance, into a positively identifiable, straightforwardly cyclical narrative mode. One might say then that the chronologically ordered account Art gives of his parents' "troubles" in volume 2 is haunted not merely by the ghosts of the past but also and above all by the specter of its *own alterity*, by what Walter Benjamin refers to in his essay on translation and survival precisely as the original's "translatability [*Übersetzbarkeit*]."[2]

Spiegelman's repeated citation of the phrase "and here my troubles began" in the subtitle, in a chapter heading, and in an individual panel of MAUS II, ultimately leads one to read the second volume as a Benjaminian translation of the first—that is, not simply as its narrative continuation but also and above all as an ongoing attempt to meditate on—and actively keep open—the question of its limits. Indeed, in claiming in the subtitle of the first volume that "My Father Bleeds History," the cartoonist seems to suggest, if nothing else, that his father's story and the history of which he is a part are to be read precisely in the ways they overflow and exceed the parameters of any book one might venture to draw about them. Volume 2 not only leaves itself open to this overflow, to the excessiveness of an *Über-* which repeatedly *calls for Übersetzung*, but, in so doing, it participates in the process of self-alteration begun in the first volume of MAUS.

Telling in this regard is the way the second volume opens by doubling and displacing the very gesture with which the first begins. While at the outset of MAUS, volume 1, Art is shown circling hesitantly about his father ("I still want to draw that book about you . . . the one I used to talk to you about . . . about your life in Poland, and the war") as the latter starts to cycle—both apparently going nowhere fast—MAUS II: *And Here My Troubles Began* begins with Vladek's arrival in Auschwitz only to begin again when he departs, and then again when he enters Dachau. Beginning repeatedly without ever quite beginning as such, the narrative thus remains in a sense on the threshold. Like Vladek on his stationary bike, it moves in place. Yet, unlike him, the apparent stasis of this circular return to and of the beginning is also and above all a movement from threshold to threshold, a discontinuous movement from one limit-experience to another, leading us to confront the limits of representation at each and every turn.

The actual narrative of MAUS II, such as it is, begins by returning to a question of representation that apparently had already been settled in MAUS, volume I—the question, namely, of how to draw Art's converted wife, Françoise. Seemingly unaware of the fact that he had already depicted her as a mouse (rather than a French frog) in volume I (1:96–97), Art again takes up the question (as though for the first time) in the opening panels of volume 2. In doing so, he not only reflects explicitly on the representational choices made earlier, in effect turning those decisions back into questions, but moreover tests the very limits of representation when the particular question of how to draw a Jewish convert in turn raises the specter of the much larger issue of where *to draw the line* between Jews and non-Jews. The opening chapter entitled "Mauschwitz" (itself a double of the one following it called "Auschwitz") thus begins by asking who has the right to say who or what a Jew is. It opens, in other words, by reposing the Nazi answer, its Final Solution, to the Jewish question *as a question*. "One thing that fascinated me," Spiegelman confesses in a passage cited earlier, "was the fact that the people sent to their slaughter as Jews didn't necessarily identify themselves as/with Jews; it was up to the Nazis to decide who was a Jew."[3] In raising such questions in the frame narrative that directly precedes Vladek's eyewitness account of Auschwitz, Art suggests a link between the definitions of Jewishness imposed by the Nazis (the involuntary "stardom" thrust upon Vladek and others referred to earlier) and the policed boundaries of the camp itself. Confined within the parameters of these definitions, Vladek is in a sense already in the camp before actually entering it, "and here my troubles began."

The Vanishing Point

In contrast to Vladek, who comes "here to the concentration camp Auschwitz" knowing, as he says, "that from here we will not come out anymore" (1:157), Art brings the reader to the same point at the conclusion of volume I, knowing that *there is no way in*, no way for the story he is (re)telling to pass beyond this point. That the second volume begins by repeatedly beginning again bears witness precisely to this impasse. Indeed, while the gates of Auschwitz mark the literal endpoint of the first volume, they also prefigure the narrative dead ends one encounters at every turn in the second. In other words, the unresolved and perpetually unsolvable problem of how to narrate beyond the threshold of Auschwitz is rehearsed every time the narrative shifts from the present into the past.

The first time the text actually moves from the scene of narration, now set in the pseudotranquility of the Catskill Mountains of Upstate New York, to the interior of Auschwitz, the viewer is made to occupy the same place as Vladek and Anja. That is, the first time one comes face to face with an SS officer at the very gates of the camp, one is made to see him from the perspective of the couple still apparently inside the truck in which they had been deported—which is to say that the reader, like Vladek and Anja, is initially confronted not only with the officer's murderous gaze but also with the sight of two smoking crematorium chimneys in the background. Yet, while the viewer may be said to enter the camp with Art's parents, it is the officer's one-word command, "OUT!" (2:24) (fig. 14),[4] fired directly at the couple, that strikes the implicated reader—the interested bystander—as well, that turns one away in the very act of summoning them in. The force of this speech act that effectively polices the very threshold it straddles is such that it not only expels the reader as it orders Vladek and Anja to disembark, but it also and above all seems to drive out the *returning witness* at the very moment he is driven by his son's questions to recross the threshold of the camp. Vladek's return trip to Auschwitz, his painful attempt to reenter it in memory and in words addressed to Art, who now

FIGURE 14

returns with him as a second-degree witness, comes to an abrupt halt after just one panel. As though repulsed by the implacable face of death and afraid to face being separated once again from his beloved former wife ("I waved very fast goodbye to Anja"), Vladek immediately shifts back into the present ("But you understand, NEVER Anja and I were separated!" [2:25]). Thoughts of Anja lead him in turn to reflect on the current state of his second marriage ("Not so like Mala, what grabs out my money!" [2:25])—as though the present to which he returns through the evocation of Anja were not quite present enough.

That the ghost of Vladek's departed wife appears to hover once again over an important threshold of the text is certainly no accident. She returns to the narrative at the very moment Vladek returns to Auschwitz, only to be taken away immediately. Vladek now not only sees this first, temporary separation from Anja through the filter of the later, definitive one, but in the act of narrating it reexperiences the first in all its suddenness and brutality as if it were the last. Little wonder then that his painful account of the way he "waved a very fast goodbye to Anja" is broken off just as it starts. When Art later attempts to circle back to the question of his parents' separation ("What I wanted to ask you about though, is what happened to mom while you"), his father abruptly cuts him off and embarks instead on an all too literal narrative detour. "STOP! . . . ," he exclaims, "we must turn QUICK and go by THIS road to come to the Pines" (2:36). As was the case with the many smoke screens of the first volume of MAUS, the question Vladek refuses to answer directly here is addressed circuitously in the course of the ensuing narrative.

More important, however, than the particular answers one might hope to find by following these roundabout paths is the general problem of circularity in the text. Indeed, as the two central narrators of *A Survivor's Tale* repeatedly turn about one other, each seeking in his own way to frame the other as the "REAL survivor" (2:44) of the tale, both of these circling narrative foci may in turn be said to revolve around another center, the central silence, the "black sun" of Auschwitz.[5] MAUS II orbits around this dead center, returning repeatedly to the gates of Auschwitz, where it began, beginning there repeatedly without ever quite moving inside. When the returning witness urged on by his son's pressing questions ("Auschwitz, pop. Tell me about Auschwitz" [2:25]) does finally go back inside, the transition is marked by a strange break in the text, which I will now describe.

If, as Spiegelman observes in a passage cited earlier, "it's what takes place in the gutters between the panels that activates the medium" of the comic strip, and it is Vladek's pedaling that embodies this activation process, his cycling at various speeds suggests different ways of reading the "slow-motion pictures" generated and projected by him. It might be said that up to the point where Vladek crosses the threshold of Auschwitz in the text the images set in motion through his pedaling had been projected at a relatively fast and even pace, evoking the cinematic illusion of continuous motion.[6] In general, the foregoing narrative could be described as proceeding row by row, from left to right, top to bottom, past to present. Beyond this point, however, the projectionist slows down as though encountering resistance from some unspecified quarter. The space or gutter between panels, which one tends not to notice when the narrative moves more rapidly, becomes increasingly conspicuous both in and of itself and as an indication of silently emerging gaps, cracks, and discontinuities.

On the page where the narrative finally crosses the threshold of the camp, the panels are for the first time broken down into two vertical columns rather than four horizontal rows. The column on the left may still be said to precede the one on the right, which it introduces through a kind of cinematic fade: intradiegetic speech bubble, " . . . and now, I came again [to Auschwitz]"; to voice-over narration, "We came to a big hall and they shouted on us"; to intradiegetic commands, "GET UNDRESSED! LEAVE YOUR VALUABLES! LINE UP! SCHNELL!" (2:25) (fig. 15). While the movement from left to right suggests a transition from one scene to the other, the vertical descent of the columns invites one to read this narrative sequence, this apparent journey back in time, as a static juxtaposition of two strangely contemporaneous parallel universes. Father and son face each other exchanging words and discursive positions in the fresh mountain air of one column, while in the crowded interior of the other column defenseless new inmates are subjected to a monological barrage of shouted commands, as their papers, clothes, hair, and identities are taken away from them.

While the narrative at this point moves simultaneously from left to right, in a narrative sequence from the present to the past, and from top to bottom, in a static juxtaposition of two liminal moments, its double movement comes increasingly to be dominated by the deadly teleology and totalizing perspective of a certain vanishing point. Indeed, even on a page where the normal narrative flow is disrupted and altered by the vertical

FIGURE 15

orientation of two concurrently running scenes, ultimately the murderous perspective of the SS officer standing in the lower right-hand corner is what dominates the entire sequence. Drawn as a cat baring his teeth as he shouts out commands within this particular panel, the officer is the largest, most imposing figure on the page. Sight lines link the angle of his hat protruding out of the frame to the figures of Vladek and Art in the upper left-hand corner, just as the gaze he directs at the exposed prisoners standing before him seems to extend beyond the immediate confines of the panel—and the camp—to encompass within its field of vision Art and Vladek standing in the lower left-hand corner. It is not just that this particular officer oversees everything that goes on inside and outside the camp ("From Mauschwitz to the Catskills and Beyond" in the words of the volume's third subtitle), but, positioned strategically in the lower right-hand corner of the page, he stands at its narrative and visual endpoint as the embodiment of the vanishing point that organizes the Auschwitz chapters' entire field of vision and narration.

The organizing endpoint which the officer's gaze stands in for at this crucial turning point in the text is occupied in subsequent drawings in the "Mauschwitz" and "Auschwitz" chapters by a series of related figures: the smoking crematorium chimney standing at the end of a row of barracks drawn in one-point perspective and accompanied by the voice-over caption "Abraham I didn't see again . . . I think he came out the chimney" (2:27); the eyes of Dr. Mengele, whose gaze marks the focal point of a seemingly endless line of inmates queued up for "selektion" (2:58); the closed door at the end of a long row of identical bunkbeds, in which Anja hides from a female kapo who shouts, "I KNOW YOU'RE IN HERE SOMEPLACE, AND WHEN I FIND YOU, I'LL KILL YOU RIGHT HERE ON THE SPOT!" while wielding a club reminiscent of Mengele's baton (2:65); the smokestack drawn in the lower right-hand corner of the page, discussed earlier, where Vladek begins his account of the operation of the gas chambers (2:69); the words (again located at the extreme lower right-hand corner of the page) accompanying a perspectival drawing of the ovens used to burn bodies "2 or 3 at a time": "To SUCH a place finished my father, my sisters, my brothers, so many" (2:71); and finally even the nozzle of a can of pesticide that Art sprays at the very end of the chapter "Auschwitz (Time Flies)." "But these damn bugs are eating me alive!" Art exclaims, as the visual lines traced by the spray are relayed by those of the porch railing in the next frame, thereby connecting them to the literal endpoint of the chapter—the last panel in the lower right-hand corner of the page (2:74) (fig. 16).[7]

As the notion of a vanishing point takes on increasing structural and thematic significance in the course of these two chapters, the slow-motion pictures generated by the text's star/projectionist gradually grind to a halt. In other words, as this point—and the perspectival space organized by it—come to dominate the telling and drawing of the tale, the diachronic movement from one moment to the next, leading the eye from left to right, top to bottom, tends to give way to a synchronic stasis of visual and narrative lines drawn inexorably toward a dead center. The sense of stagnation associated with the rise of this "black sun" registers at every level of the text—most notably in the debilitating creative crisis Art suffers at this point in the frame narrative, which he describes to his "shrink" in one of their sessions. "So, how are you feeling?" asks the therapist. "Completely messed up. I mean, things couldn't be going better with my 'career,' or at home, but mostly I feel like crying. I can't work . . . even when I'm left alone I'm totally BLOCKED. Instead of working on my book I just lie on my couch for hours and stare at a small grease spot on the upholstery" (2:43). While the therapist attempts in good analytic fashion to relate Art's writer's block and overall sense of apathy to his father's death and its emotional aftershocks ("It sounds like you're feeling remorse—maybe you believe you exposed your father to ridicule" [2:44]), within the narrative logic of the volume it is telling that this moment of blockage should also coincide with the ascendance of a different, more saturnine gravitational center in the inner

FIGURE 16

narrative, a vanishing point which seems to surface in the outer one as the "small grease spot" that transfixes Art as he fixates on it. Moreover, the general loss of narrative momentum associated with the rising influence of this deadening center registers at this moment also as the disappearance of the text's cycling projectionist from the scene of narration. Insofar as Vladek's pedaling had come to embody the process of setting static images in motion, it is telling that Art chooses this particular moment of narrative deceleration to mention the fact that Vladek had died of congestive heart failure four and a half years earlier.

While the narrative thus appears to come to a halt at this point, as a different structural principle increasingly holds sway over the text, its stagnation also marks a transition in which "nothing takes place," in which telling becomes telling, and one sense of the term heretofore eclipsed by the other begins to make its occult presence felt. In short, what begins to count more and more here, on both a thematic and structural level, is the very question of counting. Numerical themes surface with increasing frequency in the frame narrative, still set at this point in the Catskills (a name that itself becomes eerily resonant) as Vladek spends his time counting days and matches (2:20), pills and crackers (2:77). He enlists Art and Françoise's help in preparing his bank papers ("Acch, Artie, AGAIN you made the wrong addition . . . It doesn't come out so as on the statement. We'll have now everything to do again" (2:23). Finally, he takes Art on a walk to the Pines Hotel, where, after numerous detours, the narrative reaches its (anti)climax as Art is invited to join Vladek and others in a game of bingo ("LOOK. They're giving NOW cards . . . you want we'll play?" [2:37]). Given the strictly teleological orientation of the narrative at this point, it is important to note how the chapter's last word, "BINGO!," (2:37), is used in a double sense by Spiegelman. Not only does it identify the winner of a game of chance involving letters and numbers but it also draws attention to a sudden or unexpected event.[8]

The occurrence alluded to here at the vanishing point of the first chapter, a point where parallel story lines appear to converge, itself has a double meaning. In narrative terms, the exclamation, "BINGO!," marks the advent of a different mode of telling—not just the sudden replacement of narrating by counting but the surprising *concurrence* of counting and re-counting in an entropic countdown to death. In symbolic terms, it marks the closely related death of the returning witness, who in a sense *does not survive* his testimonial return to Auschwitz. His failure to survive this return *to* the camp belatedly makes manifest the uncertainty of his return *from* it. Indeed, if Vladek, in the words of Art's therapist, Paul Pavel, is someone who "needed to show . . . that he could always SURVIVE" (2:44), it is because on some level he knew he hadn't. "I died in Auschwitz," Charlotte Delbo writes, "and no one knows it."[9] The unacknowledged death of the witness alluded to at the end of chapter 1, "Mauschwitz," is reflected in the opening words of chapter 2, "Auschwitz," which announces years after the fact that "Vladek died of congestive heart failure on August 18, 1982" (2:41). Beginning the chapter in this way, Spiegelman in effect has the returning witness die in Auschwitz, succumbing in the midst of the story he is telling—even though, chronologically speaking, Vladek had obviously finished the account before his death. As was mentioned earlier, this death announcement also marks the moment when the motion picture projectionist responsible for activating Spiegelman's comic strip disappears from the tale—the moment, that is, when narrative entropy sets in.

Countdown

The themes of counting and recounting that punctuate the frame narrative of the opening chapters of MAUS II are obviously much more pervasively present in the tale's inner story. Vladek's account of his arrival and initial "processing" in Auschwitz begins with a description of the way "they took from us our papers, our clothes and our hair . . . " (2:25), and culminates a page later with an image of him pointing to his left arm in the present and adding, "they took from us our names. And here they put me my number" (2:26). The numerical uniformity of which Vladek speaks here and elsewhere ("I looked like a million!" [2:33], he comments with unintended irony about his neatly fitting prisoner's uniform) finds its visual counterpart in these scenes in the drawings of endless rows of identical mice, of barracks (2:27), bunkbeds (2:65), toilets (2:67), columns (2:70), and ovens (2:71). While it is difficult to imagine drafting these rows of evenly spaced objects and objectified persons in some way other than in one-point perspective, it is important to note how these panels function not merely as perspectival drawings of particular things referred to in Vladek's testimony but also and above all as illustrations of that perspective itself.[10] Such a strategy is most apparent in the visual rendering of a scene in which

Vladek is shown working on the roof of a building as he carries on a secret conversation with a Hungarian woman named Mancie, who used to relay messages to and from Anja in Auschwitz-Birkenau (2:52). Here the drawing of the scaffolding he speaks through is skewed in such a way as to prompt the viewer to reflect upon the scaffolding of the drawing itself and moreover upon the question of perspectivally constructed space in general (fig. 17). In his famous study *Perspective as Symbolic Form*, first published in German in 1924–25, Erwin Panofsky writes,

> it is not only the effect of perspectival construction, but indeed its intended purpose, to realize in the representation of space precisely that homogeneity and boundlessness foreign to the direct experience of that space. In a sense, perspective transforms psycho-physiological space into mathematical space. It negates the differences between front and back, between right and left, between bodies and intervening space ("empty" space), so that the sum of all the parts of space and all its contents are absorbed into a single "quantum continuum." It forgets that we see not with a single fixed eye but with two constantly moving eyes.[11]

FIGURE 17

Panofsky's description of this space enables one to appreciate Spiegelman's interest in it as a privileged metaphor for the Nazi's totalizing point of view, a perspective that absorbs everything that falls under the purview of its fixed and transfixing eye into a single "quantum continuum." Elaborating on this highly schematized point of view, Shoshana Felman notes in a closely related context that the "essence of the Nazi scheme is to make itself—and to make the Jews—essentially invisible."

To make the Jews invisible not merely by killing them, not merely by confining them to "camouflaged," invisible death camps, but by reducing even the materiality of the dead bodies to smoke and ashes, and by reducing, furthermore, the radical opacity of the *sight* of the dead bodies, as well as the linguistic referentiality and literality of the word "corpse," to the transparency of a pure form and to the pure rhetorical metaphoricity of a mere *figure*: a disembodied verbal substitute which signifies abstractly the linguistic law of infinite exchangeability and substitutability. The dead bodies are thus verbally rendered invisible, and voided both of substance and specificity, by being treated, in the Nazi jargon, as *Figuren*: that which, all at once, *cannot be seen* and can be *seen through*.[12]

"*Perspectiva*," Panofsky notes in the opening line of his study, "is a Latin word which means 'seeing through' [*Item* Perspectiva *ist ein lateinisches Wort, bedeutet eine Durchsehung*]."[13] It is this radically objectifying perspective associated with the Nazi scheme of making itself invisible, while at the same time "seeing through" its victims by rendering them numerically interchangeable and formally transparent (negating, in Panofsky's words, the difference "between bodies and intervening . . . 'empty' space"), that is self-consciously evoked in the visual and narrative grid Spiegelman uses to plot the Mauschwitz-Auschwitz chapters of MAUS II. In doing so, he suggests that there is no clear view of the inside, no view that is not tainted by the disciplining perspective of his parents' oppressors, no way of bringing the story of the inside out without in some way opening and altering that perspective from within.[14] I would suggest that it is precisely in the necessarily ambiguous, circularly returning movement of the text that one may locate such an opening. As we have seen, this circular movement is never one with itself but instead uncannily double. It is a movement that repeatedly doubles back on itself, at once hesitant and insistent, tentative and probing. As such, it bears witness both to the relentlessly stifling hold of the perpetrators' perspective, to the deadening, inertial drag of its black sun, and to the returning witnesses' struggle to break the silence, to set back in motion static images frozen in time.

Breaking the silence, however, does not simply mean breaking into speech—at least not in a text in which Art seems to heed the words of his therapist, Paul Pavel, himself a survivor of Terezin and Auschwitz, who, in the course of one of their sessions, tells his patient that "the victims can never tell THEIR side of the story, so maybe it's better not to have any more stories." "Uh-huh," Art responds, adding, "Samuel Beckett once said: 'Every word is like an unnecessary stain on silence and nothingness.'" Even when Art points out an obvious exception to Beckett's dictum—noting (after a conspicuously marked silence in the ensuing panel), "On the other hand he SAID it" (2:45)—he does so not in order to invalidate that claim but rather to acknowledge the contradictory position in which it puts him. Spiegelman's way of negotiating this contradiction is to assume the task of working with the strange necessity of these "unnecessary" stains. He uses the verbal and visual language of the text as *contradictory* stains to *sustain* the very silence they taint, to allow that silence to "survive," in the Benjaminian sense, as a silence that lives on in its own self-difference, as a silence that first begins to resonate, to sound different from *mere* silence, only in being tainted and translated. Once again, it seems, one must begin translating not just *between* languages or even *within* them, where translation seems unnecessary, but also in those places where the silence that is never quite itself, never the same silence from place to place or from language to language, is kept.

The survival of this eerie stillness is closely and curiously related to the living on of Vladek's mechanically preserved voice in the narrative sequence that directly follows the announcement of his death. Indeed, while Art's

FIGURE 18   FIGURE 19

father disappears from the narrative at the beginning of chapter 2, he does so only to return a few pages later in the course of his son's therapy session with Pavel. In these panels the therapist is made to bear a striking visual resemblance to Art's father (cf. 2:36–37 and 2:44–45) (figs. 18 and 19). Moreover, the conspicuous mouse mask worn by Pavel functions as a *transferential screen* on which the former projectionist is himself now projected.

It is no exaggeration to say that Art uses these sessions with his therapist as a way of carrying on his interrupted dialogue with his dead father. As though to suggest what is at stake for Art in these sessions, why, as he says, they "somehow make me feel better" (2:46), he goes home right after this particular consultation and listens to a taped interview he had done years earlier with his father—in effect prolonging not only the shrink session but the séance he had just been conducting with Pavel.[15] On the tape Vladek is heard going on as usual about his second wife, Mala, until Art finally interrupts him with an outburst of such force that it seems almost literally to drive Vladek back into the camp. "ENOUGH!," he shouts, "TELL ME ABOUT AUSCHWITZ!" (2:47) (fig. 20). Upon hearing himself on tape, Art again shrinks down to the child-size he had assumed in the therapist's office—this time, though, more out of embarrassment than out of a regressive need to turn back the clock. As Vladek's account now returns to the time frame of Auschwitz in the very next row of panels, a tiny paternal "talking head" oddly appears just above it in the white space between the inner and outer narrative strata, marking not only the forced transition from present to past but also the spectral no-man's land between these time frames and narrative layers. The apparition of this phantom head moreover suggests that the foregoing efforts to conjure the ghost of Art's father were also and above all desperate attempts to summon the *departed witness* back into the scene of his testimonial return, to summon him, in effect, to return with Art to the very site of his annihilation. In short, Vladek returns as a ghost at this point in order to revisit the scene of his first death, which had essentially gone unwitnessed and unmourned the first time around.

Remaining at heart unacknowledged, this death in Auschwitz was to remain very much at the center of Vladek's life after the war, to abide there precisely as an empty center, a central numbness around which the survivor's afterlife, such as it was, revolved. This pivotal silence is itself silently inscribed in the scenes set at the Pines Hotel, scenes that paratactically frame Vladek's ghostly apparition in the text. It is inscribed there in the

FIGURE 20

figure of a seemingly innocuous umbrella pole about which father and son pivot as they speak about Vladek's experience in the death camps (see 2:37, 48, 49, 51) (fig. 21).[16] As though to emphasize the repetitive relationship connecting these rotations in the scene of witnessing to the death center of Auschwitz, Vladek later demonstrates for Art how he and others were made to stand before Dr. Mengele and repeatedly "FACE LEFT" (2:58). The last of the four quarter-turns he executes in this sequence is strategically positioned over the central axis of a crematorium chimney in the panel below (fig. 22).

Just as the words in the Beckett quote cited above function as strangely necessary stains, as words that keep the silence they taint by refusing to fill it in, by hollowing themselves into empty signifiers in which the stillness and nothingness they cover are given a chance to resonate and be heard as if for the first time, so too does Vladek's remarkable first-person narrative of courage, resourcefulness, luck, and survival increasingly make room for the deathly silence of those other "persons" that inhabit him and it. Indeed, if Vladek returns to the narrative at this point *as a ghost*, he does so as one who is himself haunted by a countless host of others, as one shadowed not only by the ceaseless press of a nameless and faceless throng but also by the oppressive silence with which the figure of the phantom crowd is bound up in modernist aesthetics.[17]

Nowhere is this haunting more apparent than in the place in Vladek's eyewitness testimony where the status of the first-person pronoun itself undergoes a literal change, the place where the capital letter *I*, used by the witness to refer not just to himself but also implicitly to his own uniqueness and irreplaceability, is redrawn to resemble and pun on the number *one*.[18] "Of the group when I arrived, only I remained . . . " (2:36) (fig. 23), Vladek tells Art in a cinematic voice-over. Before commenting on the manner in

FIGURE 21

FIGURE 22

which the **I** is strategically redrawn here, it is important to note first how the voice-over as a whole is made to hover not only at the limit between inner and outer narratives, as is usually the case, but also over the top of a panel that is the first one on the page in which Vladek is seen tutoring his Polish kapo in English.[19] Needless to say, Art's drawing of Vladek's *I* as a *one* here is itself another kind of language lesson. In this case, however, it is directed less at a nonnative speaker than at those who read English a little too well, those phonocentric readers who view writing exclusively as alphabetic script, as a servile transcription of the spoken word. It is no doubt telling in this regard that the play on *I* and *one* in question is a pun that must be seen rather than heard. Indeed, as a *silent* play on words Vladek obviously did not intend to make, it marks the opening of a space beyond the speaker's conscious control, a space we are invited to view not only as a hollow in the voice but also as an echo chamber in the self and in the narrative of the self, an interspace in which the doubleness of the "telling" referred to earlier is given a chance to resonate. In the clearing of this space, narrating and counting, the identity of the first-person *I* and the anonymity of the third-person *one*, the persons *I* and *one*, and the number *one* all seem to haunt, double, and pass through each other. Visually, the drawing of Vladek's *I* as a **I** connects it to the identical wooden match sticks he obsessively counts as well as to the innumerable cancer sticks his son compulsively smokes.[20]

   In an effort to make this play of numbers and letters resonate on every level of the text, Spiegelman returns on the page facing this scene set in Auschwitz to the outer narrative now located once again at the Pines Hotel, where the bingo game referred to earlier is being played. Here the organizer is shown drawing letter-numbers from a bowl and calling out "B-5 . . . G-22" in one panel as Vladek punningly informs Art in the row directly above that, "**I** WON here a bingo game *one* time. The winner got a prize over to his room . . . only it was, **I** HAD no room. Behind me sat a young lady what got so disappointed that she lost . . . she had just *one number away . . .* so **I** gave her MY card . . . " (2:37). In the central panel of this row Vladek is shown raising his left arm, on which his numerical tattoo is just barely legible, holding up a finger to indicate the number one.

FIGURE 23

In order to appreciate what is at stake in this scene, it should be re-called that MAUS begins in effect by playing on the relation between the pronoun *I* and the number *one*, the numbers *one* and *zero*, and the imper-sonal pronouns *one* and *no one*. Indeed, the effort to negotiate what I have referred to as the testimonial contract in the first volume is initially im-peded by Vladek's contention that "no one wants anyway to hear such sto-ries," a claim Art immediately counters with the emphatic attestation: "I want to hear it" (1:12). As was noted earlier, Art's I functions here as a dis-placement substitute, a mark of identity that staves off the anonymous specter of the "no one" it stands in for only by making a place for it within itself. In the present context the seemingly frivolous letter-number game Spiegelman is playing in both the inner and outer narratives becomes deadly serious when a remark made in the former—"of the group when I arrived, only I remained"—begins to resonate in the latter—"she had just one number away" (from winning at bingo). Read through each other, these passages suggest that Vladek is himself a survivor who will have re-mained in a sense always "just one number away" from death.[21] This jar-ring juxtaposition of scenes further suggests that the game of bingo itself be read as a figure for the randomness of death in the camps, as an "other scene," "*einen anderen Schauplatz*," as Freud calls it, in which Vladek's ter-rifying sense of having "won," of having survived in place of another, silently plays itself out. Haunted by this sense of guilt, Vladek unwittingly shares it with his son, on whom he takes out these unconscious feelings and to whom he delegates the task of surviving. As Pavel says, "he took his guilt out on YOU, where it was safe . . . on the REAL survivor" (2:44). What the therapist does not add, however, is that, as a surrogate survivor, Art is made to stand in not only for his father, but also for the brother who died as a child in Europe, a brother whose untimely death may in its turn be said to stand in for Art's own lost childhood spent in the confines of "the overheated bunker of [his] traumatized family."[22]

In allowing the play of the pronoun *I* and the number *one* in the em-bedded narrative to resonate in the letter-number game in the frame story, Spiegelman draws attention not only to the randomness of death and sur-vival, but also to Vladek's own status as a numerical and existential *re-mainder*. Through the superimposition of these scenes he comes to be viewed as being not just "one number away" from death, but moreover as a survivor constantly on the verge of annihilation. Having just returned from the dead always about to die, he is a survivor who is no longer/not yet *one*.[23] The "survivor's tale" told by him—or rather the tale told through a certain opening of the narrating **I**—is thus to be read not only as a teleologically driven countdown to the end, but also and above all as a circularly repeating movement back and forth across the threshold of death. Such a movement is poignantly summarized in a phrase that, it seems, could only have come from the mouth of a nonnative speaker of English: "so this next morning we were STILL again alive!" (2:109).

Endgame

If the "survivor's tale" told in MAUS II cannot be read simply as a linear countdown to the end, it is because this "tail-end," as Spiegelman elsewhere refers to it,[24] is in a sense already in its beginning; because its last word, its "last one," is "still again" its first. While the tale never moves beyond the vanishing point organizing the visual and narrative space of the first two chapters, *moving in place*, it nevertheless endeavors to distend and *displace* that point from within. Instead of simply moving in linear fashion from one point to the next, the tale proceeds through a *superimposition* of points. Thus, the death center of Auschwitz, the underground gas chamber first represented by its visible, above-ground counterpart, the crematorium chimney, returns at various points in the surrounding text as the centralizing perspective of the vanishing point; the vertical axis of the umbrella pole at the Pines; the pivotal silence and central numbness of Vladek's first unwitnessed death in the camps around which his "afterlife" continued to revolve; the quarter-turns performed by prisoners during "selektions," drawn as though the circle described were centered over the axis of a crematorium chimney; the central hollowness of the narrating **I** marking a space beyond the witness's control in which room is made for the mute and marginalized "nonpersons" of his story; and the grease spot on the upholstery that Art stares at during an acute creative crisis associated with the passing of the text's projectionist in particular and the entropic tendencies of the narrative in general.[25]

Moving in place like a broken record, the narrative not only remarks the point at which it is stuck but, moreover, through this very rescratching divides that point from itself. In doing so, it inscribes within the stasis of repetition the supplementary skip of a movement from threshold to threshold. Nowhere is this movement more apparent and nowhere is the question of the threshold itself more literally, or more paradoxically, posed than at the point in the text where Vladek's eyewitness testimony comes up against its own limits—the very moment at which it comes closest to the dead center of Auschwitz. The significance of this liminal moment is such that it merits a particularly close frame-by-frame analysis.

"You HEARD about the gas," Vladek says to Art and Françoise, who are sitting with him in the kitchen of his Catskills bungalow, "but I'm telling not RUMORS, but only what really I SAW" (2:69) (see Chapter 2, fig. 8). Since what is in question here is a certain privileging of seeing over hearing, of eyewitness testimony over rumors and hearsay, it is especially important to follow the witness's own gaze in this scene and, moreover, to pay close attention to what the beholder of the text is himself made to see.[26] At the moment Vladek mentions the gas and "what really [he] SAW" of it his gaze suddenly turns from Art, whose questions he had been answering, to the viewer on whom he now fixes a direct if somewhat vacant stare. While Vladek's look at this point in effect breaks through the invisible "fourth wall" of the scene opening it outward as it draws the spectator in, the reader also finds himself now verbally included in the "you" more obviously and directly addressed to Art and Françoise.

In the next panel, the last one on the page, the scene shifts back to Auschwitz, where a crematorium chimney is depicted in such a way that it appears to rise up not just out of the past but out of its own individual frame and to pour smoke into the panel directly above set in the present.[27] Below this image the caption reads, "For this I was an EYEWITNESS" (2:69). As in Magritte's *Ceci n'est pas une pipe*, the deictic *this*, which receives unusual emphasis here, points in at least two directions at once: at the drawing of the chimney (which itself points elsewhere) and at the word *gas*, just mentioned.[28] In doing so, it retrospectively suggests that Vladek, in looking directly at the viewer in the preceding panel, had already in a sense been training his empty gaze elsewhere. The surprisingly equivocal sense given to the word *this*, combined with the visual and verbal rhetoric of parabasis, seems calculated to raise the following questions: Why at the very moment Art's father identifies himself for the first and only time as an eyewitness, as one who claims to have direct, unmediated access to the experience he is about to describe—"I'm telling not RUMORS, but only what really I SAW"—does he find himself speaking through one audience to another? Why, in training his gaze directly on the reader, is he made to appear to be looking through him at something else? Why, in short, all this indirection through direction?

At the very least, these slight but decisive shifts have a way of refocusing attention on those aspects of the text that tend to be overlooked—namely, the "fourth wall" of the scene, the transparent "fifth side" of the cartoon frame, and perhaps most importantly the signifying surface of the tale itself. If the verbal and visual stains Spiegelman applies here may once again be said to be strangely necessary, it is because they help the reader to look *at* that which he or she is all too used to looking *through*. This is particularly necessary in a context where the focus has begun to shift from the silence and nothingness of the victims, of those who "can never tell THEIR side of the story," to the strategies of effacement employed by the perpetrators, strategies that are themselves, as Vladek explains, intended to be *self-effacing*: "When the Russians came near, the Germans made ready to run from Auschwitz. They needed tinmen to pull apart the machineries of the gas chambers. They wanted to pack it all to Germany. There they could take also all of the Jews to finish them in quiet. The Germans didn't want to leave anywhere a SIGN of all what they did" (2:69).

Coming back to this scene of erasure, this process of "undoing" or *Ungeschehenmachen*, as Freud calls it, a process in which Vladek initially had no choice but to participate as a tinman, the returning witness now makes it possible for the reader *to see through* the Germans' strategy, through a historical process consisting precisely in the "unmaking" of history. In "telling . . . only what really [he] SAW," Vladek now retroactively reconstructs the very "machineries" he had once been forced to "pull apart," thereby undoing the erasure and reinscribing it in history.

Ironically, this act of testimonial reconstruction performed by Vladek, an act which restores what was to have been erased at the same time that it makes visible the very traces of erasure, is one that will later be performed *on him* by Art. In this latter scene, set in a car driven by Françoise through the Catskills, Vladek is now telling his son about a French POW he had known in Dachau, with whom he had continued to correspond after the war. "Did you save any of his letters?" Art asks. "Of course I saved," says

Vladek. "But all this I threw away together with Anja's notebooks. All such things of the war, I tried to put out from my mind once for all . . . " As though to suggest the speaker's own absentminded absorption in the blank space he has just conjured, Vladek's voice trails off here.[29] Then suddenly catching himself, he adds, "until you REBUILD me all this from your questions" (2:98). While the word REBUILD is perhaps the most explicit point of contact between this scene and the one mentioned above, the two are also linked by movements of repetition and displacement. Here Art assumes the role of "rebuilder," a part played by his father in the first scene, at the very moment Vladek passes in his turn into the structural position of "active forgetting" formerly occupied by the Germans.

While this movement of repetition and reversal does not simply collapse or efface the difference between victims and perpetrators, it does suggest that Vladek's eyewitness testimony is "still again" somehow shadowed by its own blind spots, that it is itself not immune to the acts of effacement it depicts, that self-blindness, far from being an incidental or correctable aspect of his testimony, is precisely what distinguishes it as a performative act, as opposed to a merely constative report or historical description. Reading this testimony, then, both in terms of what it says and does, one comes to see Vladek not only as an eyewitness uniquely positioned to speak first-hand about the "unmaking" of history his captors had forced him to take part in, or as a witness who himself could not help but repeatedly engage in related acts of "forgetting" after the war, but also and above all as one who bears witness through such acts of erasure to the more insidious and enduring effects of the German will to silence.

That the second scene of "forgetting" and "rebuilding" is to be read not just in relation to the first but, moreover, as its unwitting prolongation is further suggested by the metonymic link connecting this scene to the one pictured directly below it on the page. In this panel Françoise is shown stopping the car to pick up an African-American hitchhiker only to hear Vladek respond with racial epithets that themselves rise to a panic-stricken crescendo: "PUSH QUICK THE GAS!" (2:98). As is often the case in MAUS, such juxtapositions seem calculated not just to underscore Vladek's blindness to the irony of his immediate situation, but also to suggest retrospectively (as though the car scene were itself the rearview mirror it contains) that the earlier, repeated scene in which it was a question of another, more lethal gas, be read not merely in terms of what the witness "really . . . SAW," but also and perhaps above all in terms of what he *failed to see*.

In approaching Vladek's eyewitness account of the death center of Auschwitz, one should therefore be prepared to read it as an exploration of the "limits of testimony" in a twofold sense: both as a constative account that takes one to the very threshold of the most unspeakable horror, to the door "closed hermetic" (2:71) of the gas chamber, and as a performative movement of witnessing that, in moving from threshold to threshold, steps off and plays out a series of testimonial impasses. While each of these dead ends may be said to mark a particular moment of breakdown, a point beyond which the act of witnessing seems unable to proceed, so too do the repeated efforts to restart the testimony, to find other, supplementary ways of moving on, seem in their turn only to highlight and exacerbate the original failure. Although Vladek initially promises an eyewitness account of the gas, the closer he comes to its dead center, the more the act of witnessing seems to turn back on itself—the more, that is, it seems fated to return as an "other scene" in which a traumatically *missed encounter* is compulsively acted out.

The page on which Vladek begins his eyewitness account of the gas chamber is unlike any other in MAUS. It is the only one in which there are no clearly discernible anthropomorphized animal figures depicted in any of the panels.[30] Guided only by the disembodied voice of the returning witness ("I came to one of the four cremo buildings") (2:70) (fig. 24), the reader has the sense of entering a ghostly postapocalyptic landscape. Not only does Vladek's voice-over narration appear to hover indefinitely over the scene depicted, but the point of view from which the "cremo building" itself is visually rendered makes one see it from a kind of floating, ungrounded, midair perspective; that is, one comes to view it first from an angle just above ground-level within the camp, and then in a second image from a point much higher up and apparently just outside the camp's perimeter. While this visual movement up and away from the gas chamber contrasts sharply with the ensuing narrative descent toward it, the opposition itself seems calculated to highlight the very moment of transition, to mark the shift from above to below not just as another spatial or visual threshold to be crossed, but as a point of no return. It is therefore telling that this particular moment is marked out in the topography

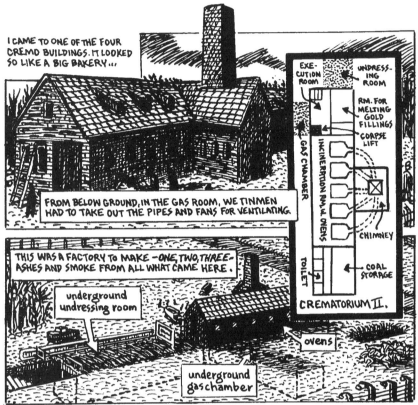

I CAME TO ONE OF THE FOUR CREMO BUILDINGS. IT LOOKED SO LIKE A BIG BAKERY...

FROM BELOW GROUND, IN THE GAS ROOM, WE TINMEN HAD TO TAKE OUT THE PIPES AND FANS FOR VENTILATING.

THIS WAS A FACTORY TO MAKE —ONE, TWO, THREE—ASHES AND SMOKE FROM ALL WHAT CAME HERE.

underground undressing room

underground gaschamber

ovens

EXE-CUTION ROOM

UNDRESS-ING ROOM

RM. FOR MELTING GOLD FILLINGS

CORPSE LIFT

GAS CHAMBER

INCINERATION ROOM OVENS

CHIMNEY

COAL STORAGE

TOILET

CREMATORIUM II.

SPECIAL PRISONERS WORKED HERE SEPARATE. THEY GOT BETTER BREAD, BUT EACH FEW MONTHS THEY ALSO WERE SENT UP THE CHIMNEY. ONE FROM THEM SHOWED ME EVERYTHING HOW IT WAS.

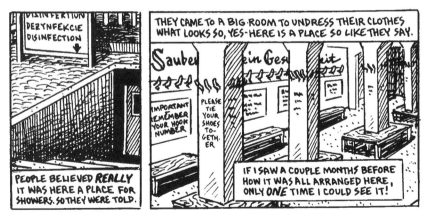

DISINFEKTION DEZYNFEKCJE DISINFECTION

PEOPLE BELIEVED REALLY IT WAS HERE A PLACE FOR SHOWERS. SO THEY WERE TOLD.

THEY CAME TO A BIG ROOM TO UNDRESS THEIR CLOTHES WHAT LOOKS SO, YES-HERE IS A PLACE SO LIKE THEY SAY.

Sauber in Ges it

IMPORTANT REMEMBER YOUR HOOK NUMBER

PLEASE TIE YOUR SHOES TO-GETH-ER

IF I SAW A COUPLE MONTHS BEFORE HOW IT WAS ALL ARRANGED HERE, ONLY ONE TIME I COULD SEE IT!

FIGURE 24

of the scene as a space *between frames*—as a space that does not belong, strictly speaking, to the scene depicted and that nevertheless marks the precise point in the depiction where one passes from a superficial view of things as they appear above ground to an insider's look at what was to have remained hidden below. The passage reads: "Special prisoners worked here separate. They got better bread, but each few months they also were sent up the chimney. One from them showed me everything how it was" (2:70).

This strategically framed visual transition also marks a crucial shift in the testimonial function. As though to suggest that the passage from above to below, outside to inside, surface to depth, light to darkness, were also and above all a movement from seeing to blindness, the eyewitness, who had heretofore helped us to see through the German strategy of efface-ment, through the camouflage of a building that "looked so like a big bak-ery" (2:70), appears from this point on as a guide himself in need of guid-ance, an eyewitness whose own limited vision must now be supplemented and prosthetically extended by the gaze and voice of another. With the sudden appearance on the testimonial scene of this other eyewitness, him-self a survivor of that grayest of zones, the Sonderkommando, the term "seeing through" begins to take on a very different sense.

As is the case elsewhere in MAUS, the introduction of such a wit-ness has the effect of transforming the testimonial scene in fundamental ways. First and most obviously, it draws attention to the limits of Vladek's own eyewitness account. Indeed, if "one of the special prisoners" is made to appear at the very point Vladek is about to proceed to a de-scription of the underground undressing room and the gas chamber ad-jacent to it, it is because, contrary to his initial claims, Vladek could never have spoken first-hand, could never really have testified "from the inside," about what went on there. His testimony remains in a certain sense stuck at this crucial point of transition. Indeed, if there is move-ment here, it is merely from one threshold to the next—from the space between frames, in which the "other eyewitness" is first introduced, to the closed door of the undressing room viewed from the top of the stair-way leading down to it in the panel below. The latter doorway marks the point at which Vladek's own eyewitness account ends and that of the other witness begins.

Yet, because this movement from threshold to threshold is never simply linear, this same doorway must be viewed both as a point of transition—an ending/beginning—and as an intransitive impasse where the process of ending begins again, begins ending, as in Beckett's *Endgame*, over and over again. Never quite ending or beginning as such, the eyewitness testimonies of these two survivors instead become increasingly implicated in one another. Thus, while the narrative perspective is henceforth implicitly that of the other unnamed witness, his point of view is not recognizably different from Vladek's own. Moreover, as these two perspectives gradually merge into one the closer they come to the gas chamber, the text's ultimate vanishing point, the term "perspective" itself (never used as such but structurally very much on the scene here) takes on an odd resonance. What is at stake at this point is not just the meaning of a particular word but the status of that which is effectively stained and brought into focus through a certain literalization of "perspective." Making one see this "perspective" as if for the first time *in its very opacity*, the text not only compels one to see seeing as a problem, but also and above all *to see double* when "seeing through" the all too transparent perspective of the "other witness." If it is through this witness's eyes that one is given to view that which few others would ever live to see or describe again—both the actual operation of the gas and the functioning of the Germans' self-effacing strategy of effacement—in looking through him one is also made to see the witness himself *as effaced*, that is, as a witness become thoroughly transparent in the utter collapse and total eclipse of testimonial perspectives that occurs here.[31] Consider then the "voice-over" narration (of one voice covering over another) that accompanies the series of panels leading up to the actual door of the gas chamber. "They came to a big room to undress their clothes what looks so, yes—here is a place so like they say. And everybody crowded inside into the shower room, the door closed hermetic, and the lights turned dark. It was between 3 and 30 minutes—it depended how much gas they put—but soon was nobody anymore alive. The biggest pile of bodies lay right next to the door where they tried to get out" (2:71) (fig. 25).

While it is clear that Vladek could not have known first-hand about the operations and struggles depicted here, he speaks at this point as if he did. In doing so, he not only effectively usurps the place of the other, but

FIGURE 25

does so at the precise moment in the text where what is being described is the Other's annihilation. This remarkable series of panels thus suggests that in recounting the death of the silenced witness in the darkened gas chamber, Vladek also in effect blindly reenacts it. As if to emphasize both the confusion of the voices in these panels and the fusing together in them of the object and act of narration, it is only after one has been brought up against the very limits of vision and the horizon of narrative impossibility, only after one has been made to see the dead end of the perpetrators' totalizing perspective in a dead-on view of the gas chamber door, that Vladek and the "special prisoner" from the Sonderkommando themselves appear on the scene, visible for the first time as separate individuals with Vladek now seen explicitly *in the position of listener*. Here it seems as though the first words of the "other witness"—"We pulled the bodies apart with hooks" (2:71)—were itself destined to be read as a description of the wrenchingly painful emergence of the witness himself from the dead. Like Toni Morrison's Beloved, this witness who has seen the "other side" does not, in returning, necessarily come back to life—which is perhaps one more reason why thresholds and borderline states are made to play such a conspicuous role in this scene.

Ultimately, Vladek's effacement of the "other witness" must be read not merely as the story of one voice covering over another but also in terms of the other witness's own relation to the silence of the others he himself speaks for. The movement from threshold to threshold is thus also a way of figuring a structure of substitution in which speech, as Beckett says, necessarily stains the silence whose place it takes. Yet, the particular manner in which that silence is tainted in MAUS has a way of covering it so as to make it perceptible in its very effacement. It is this central silence of the other witness's other witnesses, of those closed in on the other side of the gas chamber door "who can never tell THEIR side of the story," that is finally what resonates so powerfully in these passages. It is a silence that does not so much *come through* the door as carry from threshold to threshold, from impasse to impasse, resounding in the labyrinth of the listener's ear as the buzzing of "time flies," as the reverberating echo of a silent scream (2:39; 2:72).

At this point Vladek's "EYEWITNESS" account of the gas, which began with his privileging of first-hand seeing over second-hand hearing and ended literally at "death's door," is made to start over. In the panel immediately following a depiction of this door "closed hermetic," he is once again visibly present on the scene. Yet, he is now recast significantly in the role of listener. The juxtaposition of panels in this scene thus challenges us in effect to consider what it means to listen *at the door*, at the very threshold of our ability to hear. If the silence of the other witnesses, of the "drowned" (in Primo Levi's sense) as well as the *drowned out*, may be said to resonate in the shell-like hollow, the winding cochlea, of the survivor's ear, it does so, I would suggest, not because this space is one in which the others' silence finally becomes audible, but rather because it is a place where that which bears listening to, that which *demands a hearing* and yet cannot be heard as such, is perpetually stuck.

This is precisely the position Vladek now finds himself in vis-à-vis the prisoner from the Sonderkommando. In response to the latter's horrifying description of the bodies he was forced to remove from the gas chamber, of bodies whose "skulls were crushed," whose "fingers were broken from trying to climb up the walls" and whose arms "were as long as their bodies, pulled from the sockets," the listener cries, "ENOUGH," adding in a voice-over, "I didn't want more to hear, but anyway he told me" (2:71). While Vladek is still able to repeat years later to Art and Françoise what this other witness had told him as they "pull[ed] apart the machineries of the gas chambers" (2:69), the words themselves seem to have a delayed impact. It is thus only by *listening through* his own audience, through an audience which has in a sense been delegated the task not just of surviving but of listening on his behalf, that Vladek comes, if not to hear, at least to transmit the belated impact of his own survivor testimony.

It is no accident, then, that the scene of transmission is itself made to shift back and forth at this moment between the survivor's bungalow in the Catskills, where one sees Vladek speaking with Art and Françoise, and the site of his original traumatization, where the other witness and Vladek are shown conversing with one another. This alternating movement not only effectively relocates the latter, seemingly ancillary moment of transmission in the former, but also, conversely, makes that which was never really experienced first time around impact belatedly, as if for the first time, in the secondary scene of testimonial recounting. As the two scenes become increasingly implicated in one another, seemingly innocuous phrases such as "the time is flying . . . ," pronounced by Vladek at one particularly intense moment of transition, come to refer not only to their immediate context (" . . . and it's still so much to do today . . . ") (2:73), but also and above all to the *belated structure of temporal displacement itself.* At such moments the deferred impact of the initial trauma registers in the scene of its transmission merely as a kind of *acoustic disturbance*—that is, as the very sound of static interference heard variously in the final two pages of the chapter as the buzzing of signifiers in flight from any determinate context; as a certain breaking of the vessels ("oops!" CRASH! "Oi! You see how my head is? It's my favorite dish now broken!" [2:73] [fig. 26]); as the noise of

FIGURE 26

FIGURE 27

Vladek moaning in his sleep ("AAWOOWWAH!" [2:74] [fig. 27]); as Art's own painful outcry ("OUCH!" [2:74]) upon being bitten by one of the "time flies" hovering around his father's porch; as the sound of his self-wounding attempt at self-defense ("SLAP"); and finally as the "PSHT" noise the can of insecticide makes as Art points it blindly into the night (see fig. 16).

"As if There's a World After Auschwitz"

While the "time flies" so conspicuously present in the second chapter of MAUS II abruptly disappear by the beginning of the third, never to be seen or heard from again, the larger questions of temporal dislocation and traumatic repetition with which they are associated continue to haunt the text. Nowhere do these questions return more forcefully or in a more condensed manner than at a moment toward the end of the text that, once again, is less a positive place in the narrative than a liminal space between the frames: the point in chapter 5 where Vladek is telling Art about his journey home from Auschwitz. After surviving a combined bout of typhus and diabetes, Vladek is finally strong enough to travel. On the way back to Sosnowiec, where he and Anja had agreed to meet, Vladek stops in Belsen where he runs into two girls from his hometown. They have just come from Poland and warn him against going back, since, as they say, "The Poles are still killing Jews there" (2:132). Vladek interrupts their account of various persons who had returned to Sosnowiec only to be beaten and hanged, in order to ask, "Just tell me, did you hear anything about Anja?" "I SAW her," answers one of the women. "She didn't try to get her property back. The

Poles leave her alone" (2:132). At this point the scene set in the past in Belsen is interrupted by the gutter of the page only to resume on the top of the next one reset in Vladek's bedroom in Rego Park: "ANJA IS ALIVE! My heart jumped! I couldn't believe" (2:133) (fig. 28).

Whereas the scene of narration suddenly shifts from one place to another, the exclamation "ANJA IS ALIVE!" seems to remain somewhere in between. No longer exactly the words of the young woman, nor a phrase Vladek himself could pronounce in the present tense, the outburst "ANJA IS ALIVE!" is itself a small burst of life.[32] One imagines it lingering in the air for a fleeting moment, blown out of any determinate vocal, temporal, or narrative framework, before being reabsorbed and vanishing.[33] It should come as no surprise at this point to find the specter of Anja hanging once again in a kind of suspended animation, hovering like a "time fly," over an important moment of narrative discontinuity. Yet, whereas her suspension at such moments had heretofore tended to underscore the importance of the particular threshold she haunted, at a certain point the sheer accumulation of such liminal moments introduces a qualitative shift, a point at which it becomes less a question of ghosts hovering at the margins than of the repeated marginalization of the question of spectrality itself to such between-spaces of the text.[34] In other words, by focusing exclusively on the unlaid ghosts of the past, the text manages up to a certain point to avoid the more haunting question of our own spectral sur-vival, the question of whether ontology in the wake of the Holocaust has become more a matter of hauntology.[35]

FIGURE 28

FIGURE 28 (*continued*)

In his 1989 essay "Looney Tunes, Zionism, and the Jewish Question," Spiegelman describes the Holocaust as "a unique horror in the horror chambers of history," as an end to Western civilization, whose death, though already tolled, has yet really to register.

It can legitimately be argued that it is the watershed of human history, the death-knell of the Enlightenment, the proof that Western Civilization did not work. It's like the old Looney Tunes cartoons where the character runs past the edge of a cliff and keeps running through midair. It takes a while to notice there's no ground left to run on. Finally he notices and plummets earthward with a crash. So Western Civilization ended at Auschwitz. And we still haven't noticed. I include myself, sitting here, a picture of my one-and-a-half year old girl in my wallet, as if there's a world after Auschwitz.[36]

When Spiegelman compares the belated impact of the end to an animated figure's deferred awareness of the fact that "there's no ground left to run on," he asks the reader in a sense to contemplate the loony state of suspended animation in which we ourselves live—our way of living not only with the specters of the past but, even more precariously, with the uncanny reality of our own ghostly "as if" existence. He asks, in effect, how it is ever possible to wake up to such a reality, how it is possible to diagnose a state of radical self-delusion from within, a state from which the diagnostician himself suffers and knows that he suffers. If blindness in such a state is no longer simply a momentary lapse of consciousness, a temporary failure to see, but instead knowledge's very condition of possibility, how is it possible to "see through" our own blind spots? "So Western Civilization ended at Auschwitz. And we still haven't noticed." What would it mean then to *take notice*? What would the process of waking up to one's own survival, to one's own suspension in "midair," "past the edge" of any clear-cut opposition between life and death entail?

"Coming to Terms with the Past"

Such questions are at issue throughout MAUS, which opens by contesting the frame as a secure container and ends by finally erecting a tombstone over the grave of Art's parents (2:136). It is as though Spiegelman's survivors' tale had been struggling from the very outset not only to bury the dead, but to find a way of keeping them safely contained, buried in little safes, in little cartoon frames, that would not only stay shut, but keep their deadly contents from containing their containers, from making over the living in the image of the dead. While the tombstone appearing at the end of MAUS might lead one to conclude that the struggle is finally over and won, the next to last frame—which has such strategic importance throughout the text—troubles such reassuring conclusions. For here Art is quite literally made over in the image of the dead when his father mistakenly calls him by the name of his deceased brother. "I'm TIRED from talking, Richieu," Vladek says, "and it's ENOUGH stories for now . . . " (2:136) (fig. 29). Whereas the original three-page version of MAUS, published in 1972, is told explicitly as a bedtime story by a survivor to his little boy Mickey, at the end of the full-length version completed nineteen years later it is still the father who tells the stories, but he does so now *as a child* lying in his bed speaking to a son standing over him like a parent, whom Vladek mistakenly addresses as the other child who did not survive. Through this final slip the two brothers are made to trade places. While Art is effectively killed by his father's address, his dead brother is made to assume the role of listener to and addressee of Vladek's last words. Such role reversals suggest more generally that Vladek's testimony will have been addressed not merely to "the living *and* the dead," as Hirsch contends, but rather to the living *as* the dead.

The visual language of this panel further complicates the question of address. For here Vladek is shown lying on his deathbed, turning away from Art for the last time. The father's position and gesture evoke the structurally identical moment in "Prisoner on the Hell Planet," in which

Art, roused by his mother's own last words, turns his back on her in the penultimate moment before her suicide. "I turned away," he recalls, "resentful of the way she tightened the umbilical cord."[37] The pain of this earlier moment now bleeds through the scene of its belated reenactment, as siblings, parents, and generations once again trade places, passing in this uncanny space of sur-vival through and for one another.

The thirteen-year project of drawing MAUS was no doubt for Spiegelman a way of "coming to terms" with an all too hauntingly present and traumatic past, a way of engaging in a process Adorno referred to in a 1958 essay as one of *Aufarbeitung*. As Spiegelman himself observed in a 1986 interview,

in order to draw MAUS, it's necessary for me to reenact every single gesture, as well as every single location present in these flashbacks. The mouse cartoonist has to do that with his mouse parents. And the result is, for the parts of my story—of my father's story—that are just on tape or on transcripts, I have an overall idea and eventually I can fish it out of my head. But the parts that are in the book are now in neat little boxes. I know what happened by having assimilated it that fully. And that's part of my reason for this project, in fact.[38]

FIGURE 29

While Spiegelman's success at working through the past may in part be gauged in terms of his ability to bury it "in neat little boxes," to "know what happened by having assimilated it that fully," the true achievement of MAUS, I have argued, is instead to be measured in terms of another, much more literal, sense of the word *Aufarbeitung*, in terms, that is, of what is *worked open* (*aufgearbeitet*) in the text. For it is precisely in the way that MAUS works to open its neat little boxes, its safe little crypts, that it makes room for the excesses of its testimony, for that which it cannot contain in words or images, for that which it cannot draft or draw together in a single, bound volume.

Working itself open in this way, MAUS implicates the reader in an ongoing act of bearing witness. It positions such a seemingly innocent bystander as a supplementary witness, as one delegated the task of coming to terms with the very *unbound energies* of the text, of listening to the other tales that still remain to be told, of attuning oneself to the central silence of the mother's story, a story that in crucial ways will have survived its telling by the text's explicit narrator-witnesses. In making a place not just for the reader but for the silence of those who, in the words of Art's psychotherapist, did not survive to "tell THEIR side of the story" (2:43), MAUS asks us to hearken to these silences and, moreover, to attune ourselves to that which is silently and unconsciously transmitted in its own testimony. As a text that "comixes" words and images, MAUS invites us in the end to view its pictures not merely as illustrations or as visual counterparts to its verbal narrative, but also and above all as the nonverbal bearer of history's silences. Staining these silences and those of his father's story with the words of his text, Spiegelman screens them in such a way as to allow them all the more powerfully and hauntingly to bleed through.

4

Writing Anxiety

Like Spiegelman's MAUS, Christa Wolf's *Patterns of Childhood* is concerned with a past that will not pass away. An autobiographical novel written by a child of the Third Reich, *Kindheitsmuster*, as it is called in German, is a deeply searching, personal, and critically self-questioning text whose epigraph is taken, not by chance, from Pablo Neruda's *Book of Questions*.

> Where is the child I used to be,
> still within, or far away?
>
> Does he know that I never loved him,
> or that he never loved me?
>
> Why when we grew up together
> did we later grow apart?
>
> Why when my childhood years were dead
> didn't each of us die too?
>
> And if my soul fell from my body,
> why does my skeleton remain?
>
> . . .
>
> When does the butterfly in flight
> read what's written on its wings?[1]

Wolf's novel attempts to translate these questions into the specific context of postwar German society, where the separate states of the Federal Republic in the West and the German Democratic Republic in the East, to which she belonged, were each engaged in their own very different efforts at *Vergangenheitsbewältigung*, or "coming to term with the past." Published in 1976, *Kindheitsmuster* (translated initially under the title *A Model Childhood*, in 1980) raises questions that are simultaneously posed by the author to herself and her contemporaries, to *her* children as well as theirs, about the "child I used to be" and, more generally, about the unquestioned persistence in many quarters of a certain *infans*, the unspoken and seemingly unspeakable ties that continue to bind her generation to patterns of thought and behavior cultivated during the years of the Third Reich. While the word *Muster* in the title is meant to refer to such patterns, it also alludes more subtly, through its etymological affiliation with the Latin *monstrare*, to the unacknowledged *monstrosity* of those years of "innocence," to the belated sense of shock the narrator comes to experience in her autobiographical returns to a "model childhood" whose exemplarity is now understood in a very different way. The central metaphor in the novel for this movement of return is the journey home as a visit to a foreign place. It is a trip the narrator literally takes in the summer of 1971, traveling from her adult residence in the former East Berlin to her hometown of Landsberg on the Warthe, now the Polish village of Gorzów Wielkopolski.

As might be expected from a work so concerned with the bonds of silence that continue to hold the present in the grip of the past, with the very muteness of a tacit agreement to remain silent, and with the ways in which such silences are themselves passed on both consciously and unconsciously from generation to generation, the structure of address in *Patterns of Childhood* is anything but direct. Forced to circle about the silences with which it is concerned, the novel seeks to make its way through the necessarily indirect questions it asks both "toward an addressable you" (in Celan's phrase) and toward a dialogically reconstituted "I," neither of which is ever taken for granted in the text.

Without wishing in any way to minimize the differences between the generations of victims and those of the perpetrators or bystanders, my reading of Wolf seeks nevertheless to explore certain shared problems—particularly those related to the silences of the past and their often unintended transmission. In both Spiegelman's MAUS and Wolf's *Patterns of Childhood* it is the family that functions as the privileged locus of such scenes of transmission. On a more general level, the bonds of silence negatively holding each family together are associated with the issue of self-censorship, the gradual loss among the German population during the Nazi period of an ability to differentiate between dangerous and nondangerous subjects, a certain knack for knowing when to deflect one's "curiosity from dangerous areas."[2]

The effort to break this spell of silence is associated with the formal structure of the novel. Playing with the conventions of autobiography, Wolf replaces the narrating subject "I" with the pronoun "you" and the narrated object with the pronoun "she" in order to accentuate the cracks, distances, and elements of discontinuity at the heart of the *Ich*, in order to open a space of alterity in her writing in which a certain otherness of the ego may be given the chance to resonate. This opening toward the other associated with a particular disintegration of the "I" is repeatedly accompanied by a release of anxiety, a setting free of what the narrator calls "anxiety of the abyss."

Like Spiegelman's MAUS, Wolf's *Patterns of Childhood* takes very little for granted—least of all the question of beginnings. The novel literally opens with the words of another: "Das Vergangene ist nicht tot; es ist nicht einmal vergangen," a slightly altered translation of a line from Faulkner's *Requiem for a Nun*: "The past is never dead. It's not even past" (3, 9).[3] Lacking a proper opening and haunted by the specter of an unmastered and perhaps unmasterable past, the novel begins by questioning the very possibility of a clean break and a fresh start. This insistent question, raised in a variety of ways throughout the text, is posed at the outset as a kind of stutter, as a perseverating question rehearsed from the beginning—and in lieu of simply beginning—as a series of false starts, as repeated attempts to start over, as a desperate struggle to remobilize a narrative paralyzed by the anticipation of difficulties still to come. "You lay aside stacks of tentatively filled pages, insert a fresh sheet in the typewriter, and start once again with Chapter 1. As in so many times during the last eighteen months, when you were forced to learn: the difficulties haven't even begun [*die Schwierigkeiten haben noch gar nicht angefangen*]" (3, 9). Here the difficult question of how to begin is folded back on itself, turned inside-out, as it were, and reposed as a question of difficulties that apparently have not yet even started. Stammering from the start and repeating itself in lieu of simply beginning, the novel suggests both that the difficulties have *already* begun and that they have *not yet* even started.

Already-not yet: such is the split temporal framework of a difficult encounter, an encounter with difficulties that will never have been confronted as such.[4] The language of confrontation, of squaring off face-to-face, is particularly inappropriate in this context since the difficulties that force "you," the writer, to begin again are not simply identifiable or avoidable obstacles in the way of writing but rather irreducible and irreducibly conflicted aspects of the writing itself. They are what keeps the writing from ever having a self, ever being one with or self-consciously coming *to* itself.[5]

While it is tempting to describe *Patterns of Childhood* as a novel that is self-conscious in the extreme—difficult writing that writes about the difficulties of writing—one should bear in mind that it is a text that repeatedly calls into question the presumed authority and the capacity for self-knowledge of an instance derisively referred to in a passage deleted from the English translation as "His Majesty the Ego [*Seine Majestät das Ich*]" (83). In an apparent attempt to suspend the privileges usually accorded to—or rather autocratically arrogated to itself by—*das Ich*, the narrator makes a point of scrupulously avoiding the first-person pronoun when referring to herself in the text. (There is, of course, one important exception to this rule toward the end of the novel, to which I will return much later.) As was already evident in the passage cited earlier, "You lay aside stacks of tentatively filled pages, insert a fresh sheet in the typewriter, and start once again with Chapter 1," the narrator employs the second person rather than the first when speaking in the present—as though she could speak *of* herself at the moment only by speaking *to* herself. More significant still in this autobiographical novel that deals at length with the narrator's memories of growing up in a petit bourgeois family in the years of the Third Reich is her use of the third person when referring to the child she used to be.

Why this strange use of pronouns, this substitution of the second and third person for the first? In the latter case, the replacement of "I" by "she" and by the proper name "Nelly" could be read as an indication of the adult narrator's profound estrangement from the child, a sign of her reluctance, perhaps even refusal, to recognize anything of what she is now in what she once was. It is significant in this regard that the deferred opening of *Patterns of Childhood*, whose second sentence is in a sense its first, reads: "We cut ourselves off from [the undead past]; we pretend to be strangers" (3, 9). Is one to understand the narrator's substitution of the third person for the first in just this way—namely, as an attempt to distance herself from "a past that will not pass away" by cutting off linguistic and emotional ties to a "person" she pretends not to know? While such an interpretation is certainly plausible, one might also view this substitution of pronouns in a more sympathetic light—not as an act of severance and disavowal, but rather as the narrator's embarrassed acknowledgment of a certain numbness she feels with regard to the past, the distressing awareness of a growing inability—which is also that of her contemporaries, her readers, "you"—to connect with parts of herself that do indeed seem strangely and frighteningly remote, so remote in fact that they seem to belong to someone else. Obviously, one need not choose between these two possible readings, which, far from canceling each other out, give voice to contradictions and conflicts that drive the narrative.[6]

To these two ways of understanding the narrator's use of "she" rather than "I" when referring to herself as a child, a third interpretation might be added. For insofar as the text suppresses the self of this *Auto-* or *Selbstbiographie*, replacing the word "I" commonly used in such narratives with second- and third-person pronouns, it draws attention to the ways in which any sense of personal identity is both dependent upon and constructed through its emplotment in first-, second-, and third-person narratives, as well as through its location in a complex network of pronominal coordinates. In a novel that is very much concerned with forms of self-estrangement in the postwar period, this unconventional remapping of the pronominal grid of autobiography produces a Brechtian alienation effect, one that effectively denaturalizes any fetishized notion of personal identity. In short, the reader is never allowed to forget that the "persons" of the novel are narratively and grammatically constructed—functions rather than identities, pronouns whose most significant relations are not to particular proper names whose place they would temporarily occupy but rather to other pronominal placeholders. To put it a little differently, in *Patterns of Childhood* the second- and third-person pronouns do not so much fill in for a missing *Ich* as mark a movement of self-difference; each of these pronouns, in other words, is both open to and opened by the difference of the others.

It would therefore be less than accurate to say that the adult narrator uses the pronoun "she" and the proper name "Nelly" simply to refer to the child from whom she is now, for various reasons, cut off. The relationship among the different "persons" of the novel is in fact much more complex, since each of the pronouns marks a difference not just between "persons" but within them. If the text plays with the conventions of autobiography, it does so in order to draw attention to the unclaimed experiences and elements of discontinuity at the heart of the *Ich*, elements that are often eclipsed in first-person narratives couched in the present perfect tense. In such narratives, Wolf reminds us, "the present intrudes upon remembrance, today becomes the last day of the past" (4, 9). Here, past and present have the appearance of being seamlessly joined, an effect that in turn reinforces the impression that there is more than just a formal identity between the narrating "I" and the "I" whose story it tells.

Kindheitsmuster resists such facile identifications. In place of the present perfect tense and the sense of continuity associated with it, the multiple second- and third-person narratives of the novel are couched in the repetitive, discontinuous, overlapping, and belated temporal framework of the "already-not yet." It is through this disjointed time frame that the text puts into practice what is described at the outset as an attempt "to accord the tear that goes through time the respect it deserves [*ein Verfahren, dem Riß, der durch die Zeit geht, die Achtung zu zollen, die er verdient*]."[7] In short, rather than seeking to stabilize the uncertain relationship between the so-called "present" and a past that "is not dead," that "is not even past," and instead of minimizing the problems involved in coordinating these times out of joint, the text accentuates them. It does this in part through an unusual use of personal pronouns, a practice that effectively splits the presumed integrity of the autobiographical "I" along fault lines inherent in the genre. One consequence of this splitting is that the "I," far from simply dropping out when replaced by other pronouns, instead dis-integrates; it splits into something between an "I" and a "you"—speaking *of* itself as though it were speaking *to* itself and speaking *to* itself as though it were speaking to someone else. Given the fact that the written "you" of second-person narration does indeed address someone else, namely "you," the reader, the circuit described by these self-addressed "internal monologues" is never simply a closed circle. Similarly, the disintegration of the *narrated* "I" into something between a first and third person enables the narrator not only to treat the child, Nelly, as though she were in fact the stranger she appears to be, but also to accord her the respect such unknown persons usually have the right to expect.

Would it not be presumptuous, the narrative seems to ask, to behave toward this estranged child as though one were on the most familiar terms with her? Would it not in fact be an act of the most unmitigated narcissism to call her by one's own name and to treat her merely as a version of oneself, a less mature, enlightened, independent version of the adult I? Would such behavior not constitute a subtle form of child abuse? The ironic thrust of these questions is obviously twofold: for insofar as they demand consideration for the difference of the other, they also, particularly in this case, claim respect for the irreducible alterity of the *Ich*. The strategic disintegration of the autobiographical "I" and the related remapping of the pronominal coordinates of the novel open a narrative space for this otherness of the ego to emerge.

What emerges in this space, along the fault lines and interspaces of the narrative—"between the lines," as Leo Strauss would say—belongs, properly speaking, neither to the narrating subject nor to the narrated object, neither to the second- nor to the third-person narration. What emerges is uncertain, and yet signs of this uncertainty begin to appear precisely at the conclusion of chapter 1, where it is said that today a child "begins to stir, independent of certain promptings [*sich, unabhängig von gewissen Anweisungen, zu regen beginnt*]." These stirrings are accompanied by a feeling of fear that suddenly seizes the narrator—the feeling, she says, "that overcomes any living being when the earth starts moving underfoot" (24, 28).

Such passages, it should be noted, are relatively rare in *Patterns of Childhood*, a novel that generally devotes much more attention to the narrator's painstaking attempts to recall scenes from her childhood, to revisit "the terrain of the past" both literally, through a journey to her hometown in the summer of 1971, and figuratively, through numerous critical reflections on the language of memory and the privilege accorded geological metaphors of petrified remains, calcified imprints, and sedimented layers. It is therefore significant that the child who "begins to stir" at the end of chapter 1 does not answer the call of memory. Beyond conscious recall, she is said to "bestir herself [*sich . . . zu regen beginnt*], independent of certain promptings." It is only fitting, then, that instead of the child being summoned forth from the depths of memory, it is the narrator who feels as though an abyss were opening beneath her feet. And just as the narrator seems to lose her footing here, so too does it seem increasingly difficult to find grounds for maintaining any clear-cut distinction between the stirring child and the frightened adult. Indeed, it seems almost as though what begins to stir were but another name for the collapse of a stable narrative instance figured here as the feeling that seizes any living being when the earth begins to move underfoot, a seemingly groundless fear, one might say, that nevertheless threatens to engulf the narrating subject.

Much later in the novel, again in a passage omitted from the English edition, this fear returns condensed in the resonant phrase, "grundlose Angst," which one might translate as anxiety that is at once unfounded and unfathomable. It is perhaps for this reason that the narrator feels compelled to add immediately that such expressions are not only "ambiguous" but "treacherously" so ("Verräterisch der Doppelsinn der Wörter") (346). She further comments that any attempt to tackle taboo subjects, "to touch the untouchable and give voice to what has remained unspoken, will result in a release of anxiety. Anxiety will be set free," she says, "and in its freedom will imprison those who are prone to it."[8] Yet, "is it a question here," she goes on to ask,

merely of that banal anxiety, that fear of being punished for having broken some taboo—a question, that is, merely of a form of cowardice which could be met and overcome simply by a countervailing act of moral courage? . . . Or is it rather a question of *Grundangst*, a fundamental fear of finding out too much, of finding oneself driven into a zone of *Nichtübereinstimmung*, of dissonance and dissent, whose climate you haven't learned to tolerate? An old fear, one that has tormented you since childhood.

Yet, surprisingly enough, to be at the mercy of such fears, which are certainly debilitating in the extreme, is also, in the context of the novel, to be open to the possibility of a radically different mode of writing. "It is necessary to write otherwise [*Ganz anders muß geschrieben werden*]," the narrator reminds herself a number of times in the course of the text. Yet, in repeating these words she does not simply reaffirm her commitment to write differently, but, more radically, *to let* something else be written. It is an injunction, in other words, to open a space of alterity in one's writing, to *leave open* a space within it for another, for a certain otherness of the ego to resonate. This is in part what she means when she speaks at a certain moment of "living between echoes, between the echoes of echoes [*Zwischen Echos leben, zwischen Echos von Echos*]" (275, 255). This is also why it was a question earlier not simply of an overthrow of "his majesty the ego," but rather of his or its dis-integration into something between an "I," a "you," and a "she," something between first-, second-, and third-person narration. As might be expected, this disintegration does not occur without a release of anxiety, *grundlose Angst*, which floods through the very cracks and between-spaces of the splintering autobiographical "I," carrying along with it echoes of that which in the narrative never speaks for or as itself.[9] In short, to write otherwise, for Wolf, is to write not merely in a different voice, but through the very *différance* of echoing voices.

It is important to add, moreover, that these self-different, differentially articulated "voices" of the text are themselves inscribed in a kind of middle voice—a compromising suspension of the opposition between active and passive voices. As was suggested above, to write otherwise is not so much to open as to *leave* or *let* open a space in writing where the alterity of the ego might have a chance to resonate. If writing otherwise thus involves the courting of a certain risk, a way of leaving oneself open to that which is bound to sound differently, it also in this context means sounding the unfathomable depths of anxiety, an abyssal space which, one now realizes, is not unrelated to that zone of *Nichtübereinstimmung* whose climate the narrator finds so intolerable, in which dissonant, differently tuned voices, discordant voices out of tune with themselves and with the times, may be heard echoing through one another. If the child that begins to stir independent of certain promptings at the end of chapter 1 is but another name for a chasmic opening of the narrator, the opening within her of a greater susceptibility to fears of the abyss, it is precisely these openings that give the child room to bestir herself. This child is also a figure of writing otherwise, of writing that bestirs itself independent of certain promptings in the lapses and syncopes of authorial control. It is therefore telling that the narrator usually begins to worry at those points in the novel where she seems to have *too much control* over the story she is telling. For example, chapter 10 begins with the following reflection:

You expect the child Nelly to walk the plank for you. To prostitute herself. Aren't you fooling yourself by thinking that this child is moving on her own, according to her own inner laws? Living within preconceived patterns [*in vorgegebenen Figuren*]—that's the problem.

It's humming, Bruno Jordan [Nelly's father] used to say when things ran smoothly. On Saturdays, the store hummed. And so did the sale of bananas at reduced prices. Erwin, the apprentice, had to oil the store's delivery bicycle until it hummed.

Man is the product of his environment, says your brother Lutz. Don't worry, it'll hum: marionettes. The child is your vehicle the moment she starts humming. To what purpose? (210, 196)

Obviously, the child, who is compared here to a puppet on a string, is also a figure, a pointedly commonplace figure, for the author's own relation to her literary production. In an attempt to alter her relationship not only to this child or to the story she is telling, but also to such clichéd, *vorgegebenen Figuren*, it is significant that the narrator grows suspicious of her own motives precisely in those moments when the child seems to be her own person, totally self-motivated, "moving on her own, according to her own inner laws." At such moments, typically characterized by an audible absence of friction, the narrator knows the child has become merely a means to an end, a delivery bicycle, a vehicle used to convey neatly wrapped messages. In other words, she knows that it is not enough to pretend simply to sever the cords which bind an author to her literary offspring in order to produce writing that is more independent, spontaneous, "automatic," or self-generating. Such attempts seem, if anything, to produce mere parodies of liberation, which is why "writing otherwise" in this novel seems, by contrast, to be only as "liberated" as the free-floating anxiety with which it is so inextricably bound up, the anxiety which is released in a certain disintegration of the writing subject. To put it a little differently, "writing otherwise" seems to take its chances not in total independence of the author-narrator but rather in a certain suspension of her, not in an opposition between subjection and self-determination, between the living and the lifelike, the authentic and the parodic, but rather in the borderline states of the uncanny.

While much remains to be said about *das Unheimliche* and its unhomey place in the novel—for example, its relation to the word *secret* (*Geheimnis*) and what is described at a certain point as the *Geheimnis* that is *Geheimnislosigkeit* (the secret of secretlessness) (248, 231)—for now it may suffice simply to recall one of the central motifs of the text, namely, the return home as a journey to a foreign place.[10] This is literally what occurs in the summer of 1971, when the narrator now living in East Berlin returns along with her husband, brother, and daughter to her place of birth, her *Vaterstadt*, formerly the East Prussian city of L., now the Polish town of G. The motif of homecoming as a leave-taking, a return to and of a certain foreignness in the place of the familiar, recurs in various forms in the novel. As might be expected, such uncanny recurrences are accompanied not only by a release of free-floating anxiety, but also by a particular sense of anguish with regard to the act of writing.

Consider then a strangely familiar scenario of familial estrangement in postwar Germany. "Since when," the narrator asks, "is parental love so closely linked with anxiety [*so eng mit Angst verkoppelt*]? Did it start when each new generation felt compelled to refute the beliefs of its parents" (125, 119)? These anxious questions posed toward the beginning of chapter 6 are not only left unanswered, but are, as truly open questions, left to resonate in connection with related passages such as the following scene in chapter 2, in which the narrator catches herself surveying a group of family pictures mounted on chamois. "Pictures," she says,

you don't want to tamper with. The hand which shall wither or grow out of the grave if it is lifted against father or mother. Promptly you dream, exactly and in detail, all the stages of an operation in the course of which your right hand—the writing hand—is being expertly taken off, under local anesthesia, while you witness everything. What must happen must happen. You're not putting up any resistance. But it's hardly pleasant. What do you think when you wake up? In the semidarkness you lift your hand, you turn it this way and that, study it as if you were seeing it for the first time. It looks like a fit tool, but you could be wrong. (30, 33)

This nightmarish scene seems to suggest some of the consequences of taking up the pen in revolt against the past. To attempt to distance oneself from the beliefs of one's parents is also apparently to run the risk of losing the ability to write—that is, so long as a severed hand is incapable of writing otherwise. Yet, what would it mean in this context to write otherwise, to write, not simply as a different generation, but rather, "between the lines" of familial descent, in the suspension of intergenerational difference? At the very least, such writing would involve not only a shift from the straight line of parent-child-grandchild, past-present-future to the overlapping, repetitive texture of the "already-not yet," but also a reinscription of seemingly direct, unmediated relationships in a more complex network of indirect intertextual allusions. As the narrator remarks at the beginning of chapter 13:

Ideally, the structures of experience should coincide with the structures of narrative. This should be the goal: fantastic precision. But there is no technique that permits translating an incredibly tangled mesh, whose threads are interlaced according to the strictest laws, into linear narrative without doing it serious damage. To speak about superimposed layers—"narrative levels"—means shifting into inexact nomenclature and falsifying the real process. (272, 251–52)

If a family, according to the narrator's husband referred to only by his initial, H., is defined as "an agglomeration [*Zusammenrottung*] of people of different ages and sexes united to strictly conceal mutually shared embarrassing secrets" (78, 77), the only way to penetrate this web of secrecy, it seems, is by weaving together an equally intricate network of indirect questions. As the narrator says of her fourteen-year-old daughter, "You've learned that Lenka never answers a direct question unless she wants to, and you're secretly hoping that you'll find out about Lenka by way of Nelly" (20, 24). Here one might say that writing between family lines involves an attempt to gain access to aspects of one's own child by indirectly approaching her through the mediation of another, through the irreducible otherness of one's own childhood, which can itself only be accessed in a roundabout way. It is telling in this regard that the sixth chapter of the novel opens with the observation that "it is the person who remembers—not memory. The person who has learned to see himself not as 'I' but as 'you'" (118, 113). It is all the more telling that these remarks, which stress the necessity of using the second person to approach areas of the self unavailable to the first, are themselves expressed in the third person.

Given the extremely circuitous nature of this ineluctably "interpersonal" approach, how does one ever know when one has in fact found what one had secretly hoped to find out? What, for example, does the narrator finally learn about Lenka by way of Nelly? However legitimate such questions may be, they are in the end somewhat beside the point. For the ultimate success of these oblique interrogations is to be gauged not in terms of the answers or knowledge arrived at, but rather in terms of the difficulty of the new questions generated. For what is self-censorship, the novel asks, but the acquired inability to generate questions? If self-censorship is always in some sense a question of secrets and secret revelations, "the secret we're looking for," the narrator confides in a rare use of the first-person plural, "is the blatant lack of any secrets [*Das Geheimnis, nach dem wir suchen, ist die platte Geheimnislosigkeit*]. Which is perhaps why it can't be revealed" (248, 231–32). If, as was noted earlier, a *Geheimnis* like the word *unheimlich* is etymologically of the home, *Geheimnislosigkeit* like *Heimatlosigkeit* is perhaps the condition of a wandering, homeless question, the stateless and un-stated condition of a question one never even thinks to ask.[11] The narra-tor's search for the secret of such conditions leads her immediately to re-flect on a scene which is said to have taken place in fall 1943.

Nelly was crouching on the fields of the estate, digging up potatoes, together with a row of Ukrainian women. The feeling aroused in her by these strangers wasn't pity, but rather a shyness, a strong sense of being different [*ein starkes Gefühl von Anderssein*], a notion which was not based on any secret, but on [her teacher] Julia Strauch's history lessons: her being different made her more valuable [*Anders heißt wertvoller*]. Nelly wasn't allowed to put her potatoes into the same basket as one of the foreign workers. Did she think about the soup which was being dished out for the Ukrainians from a separate pot? Would it have occurred to her to get up and walk the thirty steps across the separating abyss, over to the foreigners, who were sitting along the same edge of the field, and hand one of them her own bowl, which had pieces of meat swimming in the soup?

The horrible secret: not that one didn't dare, but that the thought didn't oc-cur to one. All attempts to explain stop at this fact. The usual thoughtlessness of the well-fed with respect to the hungry doesn't explain it. Fear? Certainly, if there had been such a temptation. But the temptation to do the natural thing no longer occurred to her. Nelly—innocent [*unschuldig*], so far as she knew, even exem-plary—was sitting there, chewing her meat. (249, 232)

"Innocence" in the all too natural setting of this episode thus comes to signify the acceptance without question of a dehistoricized, "natural-ized" distinction between them and us, a distinction this child of the Third Reich ironically learns in history class. It seems, then, that just as the per-sons of this novel are to be read in quotation marks as narratively and grammatically constructed "persons," functions rather than identities, so too must this story of a small-town child learning to live in the world of adults be read as an allegory of adult "innocence," a story about adults learning how to pass for "human beings" in the new world order of Na-tional Socialism.[12]

"Every sentence, almost every sentence, in this language," the narra-tor laments, "has a ghastly undertone" (48, 49). To this, one might add the further observation that every question in this novel, almost every question concerning the child, Nelly, has a kind of false bottom—at least insofar as each one seems to apply not only to her but also and especially to the faceless crowd of adult "innocents" who are indirectly addressed through her. Consider in this regard the following series of questions:

Had her curiosity meanwhile diminished? Does curiosity diminish if it remains unsatisfied for a long time? Is it possible to numb a child's curiosity completely? And could this perhaps be one of the answers to the question [raised] by the Pole Kasimierz Brandys about what enables human beings to live under dictatorships: that they learn to restrict their curiosity to realms that are not dangerous to them? . . .

Would Nelly then gradually lose her ability to differentiate between dangerous and non-dangerous subjects—"instinctively," as people like to say, deflecting her curiosity from dangerous areas—and cease asking questions altogether? (67, 67)

The question for the narrator, one might say, is ultimately not whether or how much people actually knew about forced sterilization and "euthanasia" programs, about concentration camps, and the systematic destruction of European Jewry—all issues touched on in the course of the novel. The question is rather at what point did people know enough not to ask any more questions about what they might have begun to suspect was going on. At what point, as the narrator says, does one lose the ability to differentiate between dangerous and nondangerous subjects and cease asking questions altogether?[13] If the adult narrator secretly hopes to find out about her own child by way of Nelly, she also seems to use this strangely familiar third person as a way of focusing the questions raised here and, moreover, of addressing them (however indirectly) to those who, like Lenka, "never answer a direct question unless they want to."[14]

Among the questions raised in the passage cited above, the issue of self-censorship is obviously of pivotal importance. For if the narrator speaks of the gradual loss of an ability to differentiate between dangerous and non-dangerous subjects, such losses, she adds, are more than offset by the development of a compensating "second sense," a certain knack for knowing when to deflect one's "curiosity from dangerous areas." Elsewhere in the novel the development of this "instinctive" sense of "what goes without saying" is related to an entire network of unspoken cues: a play of "glances, a fluttering eyelid, a turning away, a change of inflection in the middle of a sentence, a stopping short while talking, an unfinished or falsely finished gesture: in short, those numerous details which determine more strictly than laws [*die strenger als Gesetze regeln*] what must be said, and what must be irrevocably held back, and by what means" (135, 129). If the rule of self-censorship may indeed be said to be stricter than that of the law, it is because self-censorship never rules as such. "Instinctively" ruling itself out, it rules as that which goes without saying. Self-censorship, in other words, is the rule of "instinct," the "naturalized" innocence of the self-evident, the anonymous voice of what is ironically referred in the novel as *Übereinstimmung*.

While this term is usually rendered in English as conformity, agreement, accord, or harmony, what is lost in such translations is precisely the sound of the voice, the *Stimme* that resonates within the word and that is so crucial to its functioning in the novel. When, for example, Nelly's father, Bruno Jordan, joins the Navy storm troops, the narrator begins to mimic the self-exonerating voice of the one who claims that "membership in this comparatively harmless organization . . . could not have been refused without consequences. What consequences?" she asks, suddenly switching into a more skeptical tone. "That's too precise a question: *Übereinstimmungs-glück*," she continues, "(it isn't everybody's thing to be an outsider, and when Bruno Jordan had to choose between a vague discomfort in the stomach and the multi-thousand-voice roar [*dem vieltausendstimmigen Geschrei*] coming over the radio, he opted, as a social being, for the thousands against himself)" (43, 45).

Übereinstimmungsglück is thus not just "the bliss of conformity," as the English edition would have it, but more precisely the happiness that comes from losing oneself in the crowd of a "multi-thousand-voice roar." In contrast to that zone of *Nichtübereinstimmung* whose climate the narrator finds so intolerable, *Übereinstimmung* is the "instinctively" self-regulating realm of climate control—not a space in which dissonant voices out of tune with themselves may be heard echoing through one another, but rather one in which differences are drowned out in the anonymous roar of *eine Stimme über alles*. It is not by chance that the only Nazi song cited at length in the novel is Heinrich Annacker's "Vom Ich zum Wir" (From the Me to the We). Not only does this verse celebrate the constitution of a collective identity as a movement in which the individual ego "becomes the great machine's subservient wheel [*wird zum kleinen Rad an der Maschine*]" (191, 179), but the song is designed to realize through its communal performance the very movement of which it sings. If the novel takes great pains to avoid both the "me" and the "we," the *Ich* and the *Wir*, employing in their stead other personal pronouns and practicing a strategic disintegration of the first person, it does so in a context in which terms like *Übereinstimmung* seem ironically to give voice only to a certain voicelessness, to what might be described as the very silence of a tacit agreement to remain silent. *Übereinstimmung* is thus in a strange way the voice of the people, *die Stimme des Volkes*—at least insofar as this people is, as the narrator imagines, a *"Volk von Schläfern*, a nation of sleepers . . . whose dreaming brains are complying with the given command: Erase, erase, erase. A nation of know-nothings," she continues, "who will later, when called to account, assert as one man, out of millions of mouths [*wie ein Mann aus Millionen Mündern beteuern wird*], that they remember nothing" (149, 141; trans. modified). The oneiric syntax of this secret order of erasure calls for a reading which respects its overdetermination and treats it as a complex dream-thought—as, in other words, a command secretly issued as though in a state of oblivion, a state of sleep and dreams in the course of which the secret order to erase and to erase all traces of erasure is secretly and obliviously carried out, thereby keeping both the secret and the secret of its erasure a secret even and especially from oneself—a *Geheimnis* the narrator elsewhere describes as that of *Geheimnislosigkeit*, the secret lack of any secrets. This secret command of erasure is moreover linked to another kind of "secret order," to a *secret* and secretly tongue-tied *society* "of know-nothings," to a nation "unknowingly" bound by a bond of silence, by the always already forgotten dream of forgetting, a dream that as such obliviously and pervasively invades the sleeping nation's waking life, haunting it in the form of a dream from which it will have forgotten to awaken, a dream that uncannily makes over the present in its own image—in the *afterimage* of a haunting past "that is not dead, that is not even passed."[15]

What then can give the lie to this dream of self-presence and the tongue-tied cult of silence with which it is tacitly tied up? As in the tale "The Emperor's New Clothes," in *Patterns of Childhood* it is the voice of a child. Yet, unlike the boy who in the children's story so innocently breaks the rule of silence, loudly proclaiming the truth of nakedness as if it were the naked truth, the child of Wolf's novel speaks not as a single dissenting voice, but rather as the *Nichtübereinstimmung* of a number of discordant voices speaking—or rather echoing—through one another. Whereas in Andersen's tale the puerile innocence of the emperor is mirrored in the voice that recognizes and reflects it, in Wolf the accent falls on the moment of *non-recognition* in any encounter, on the return, that is, of an uncanny strangeness in (the) place of the self-same. This is precisely what occurs toward the end of the novel when Nelly's mother goes to the local train station to meet her husband who had been taken prisoner by the Russians at the conclusion of the war. Telling the story of her husband's return, Charlotte Jordan is said to have been distraught. As the narrator recalls,

she kept repeating, always with the same foolish expression on her face, that they hadn't recognized one another. Several times they had passed each other on the station platform. Only now—since she rarely looked in a mirror—only by her husband's vacant glance, which went right through her, did she learn of her own transformation into an unrecognizable person, together with the realization that the one whom she expected, whom she described to others as somebody special, whose picture she had shown around, that this person would not return. With a single blow she had lost herself and her husband. (398, 369)

Here as elsewhere in the novel an anxiously anticipated homecoming turns into an alienating scene of mutual nonrecognition, a missed encounter in which one is driven to confront one's "own transformation into an unrecognizable person." To appreciate the larger significance of this scene, however, it is necessary to bear in mind the pointedly theatrical language used to introduce it, language which not only turns the scene into a play entitled *The Return of the Father* (397, 368), describing his appearance as the *Auftritt der Hauptfigur* (the appearance onstage of the main character), but also effectively puts the scene of narration itself on display. In doing so, it places the third-person narrator—by definition outside the scene—into it, that is, into a scene in which she is forced to confront her own transformation into an unrecognizable person. Yet, when exactly will this metamorphosis have taken place? Will it not have occurred already at the very outset in the disintegration of the autobiographical "I" into something between a first, second, and third person? Or is it perhaps still happening, since, as the narrator reflects near the end of the novel in a passage once again omitted from the English translation, "this girl, still called Nelly, grows more distant instead of gradually coming closer. You ask yourself, what has to happen—what did happen—to turn things around [*sie zur Umkehr zu bewegen*]?" (375).

To return to the theatrical language that introduces this scene of mutual nonrecognition, it might now be said that such language not only effectively reframes the relationship in this particular instance between the narrated scene and the scene of narration, but also foregrounds the issue of narrative framing itself. In a related context, Shoshana Felman explores such issues in her subtle reading of Claude Lanzmann's film *Shoah* (1985). The film, she contends,

> testifies not merely by collecting and by gathering fragments of witnessing, but by actively exploding any possible enclosure—any conceptual frame—that might claim to *contain* the fragments and to fit them into one coherent whole. *Shoah* bears witness to the fragmentation of the testimonies as the radical invalidation of all definitions, of all parameters of reference, of all known answers, in the very midst of its relentless affirmation—of its materially creative validation—of the absolute necessity of speaking. The film puts in motion its surprising testimony by performing the historical and contradictory double task of the breaking of the silence and of the simultaneous shattering of any given discourse, of the breaking—or the bursting open—of all frames.[16]

In describing the ways in which Lanzmann's film actively resists containment, radically invalidating all ready-made parameters of reference, Felman implicitly challenges her reader to think more carefully and creatively about the issue of framing itself. For if the film does indeed perform the task of bursting open all frames, it does so only insofar as it forces each particular "parameter of reference" to break into and through another. In other words, the force of the "explosions" described by her causes the shattering frames not merely to fly apart in any simple *centrifugal* sense but rather to fly through one another in a more decentered, *fugal* manner, complicating, displacing, and counterpointing each other in flight.[17]

Wolf's novel, with its system of *ineinandergreifender Schichten*, its "interpenetrating layers" (164, 154), as the narrator calls them, approaches the question of framing in a strikingly similar manner. Indeed, if, as was mentioned at the outset, the novel begins fitfully with a number of false starts, one might now view this initial stuttering not merely as an attempt to restart a narrative paralyzed by the anticipation of difficulties still to come, but also as a way of introducing the multiple "voices" of a strategically decentered fugal composition. It is no doubt telling in this regard that Wolf chose the name "Ein Satz" as the title of a speech she delivered on the occasion of her reception of the 1977 Bremen prize, presented to her in honor of *Patterns of Childhood*. As the performance of this talk makes clear, the title "Ein Satz" (A Sentence) is itself a kind of *Einsatz*, the entry of a musical voice into a speech artfully composed in the manner of a fugue. Like the voices of *Patterns of Childhood*, Wolf in her acceptance speech repeatedly interrupts herself as she circles anxiously and obsessively around "a simple sentence," which, it turns out, is anything but one ("ein Satz"), or rather only "one," insofar as it is an *Einsatz* written asunder ("auseinandergeschrieben") as a sentence ("ein Satz") riddled with cracks and fissures against which and through which the speaker's "own" voice tremulously breaks.

"I thank you." A simple sentence, appropriate to the occasion, with a subject, a predicate, and an object. So what is wrong with it—or with me? I don't know if you can hear it, too. It rattles. As if it had a fine crack running through it.

Now the thing is spreading. There are cracks in the words, fissures running through the sentences, fractures shooting across the pages, and the punctuation marks—periods, commas—are opening up like clefts and trenches. Not to mention the grimaces the question marks make, the mysterious way that the exclamation marks vanish into nothing. Language starts refusing to perform its customary services.[18]

In both the Bremen address and *Patterns of Childhood* there is no speech that is not broken speech, no voice that does not crack in breaking through the fissures of another. In other words, each of these self-interruptive and inter-irruptive voices—like the grammatically and narratively constructed "persons" of the novel with which they are associated—bears the mark of self-difference and as such is contrapuntally open to and opened by the difference of the others. What might be described as the differential articulation of these voices is alluded to at the very beginning of the novel in yet another passage left out of the English edition: "I, you, and she, which pass through each other in thought, are supposed to become estranged from one another when pronounced in a sentence [*Ich, du, sie, in Gedanken ineinanderschwimmend, sollen im ausgesprochenen Satz einander entfremdet werden*]" (9).

If these "persons" are indeed estranged from one another at the very beginning of this text without beginning, what is one to make of their apparent reunification at the novel's end? If, in other words, the autobiographical "I" can be said to have disintegrated into something between a first, second, and third person, does the sudden appearance of the pronoun *Ich* in the last paragraph provide an answer to the question posed only a few pages earlier: "When will you and she coincide in me [*Wann werden du und sie im Ich zusammenfallen*]" (368; my trans.)? Given the fugal structure of

Kindheitsmuster, such facile reconciliations seem difficult to imagine. Indeed, I would argue that the appearance of the first-person pronoun, far from signaling the return of a lost voice, marks instead the site of musical stretta, of what in German is called an *Engführung*.

The term *Engführung*, Peter Szondi notes in his reading of the Celan poem bearing this name, "means 'temporal constriction,' i.e., bringing together the themes of a composition in the most simultaneous contrapuntal manner possible. In the narrowest sense, the *Engführung* is the ... last part of a fugue, in which the rapid succession of the canonic entry themes [*Themeneinsätze*] of the different voices produces an especially intense, interlaced contrapuntal pattern."[19] Before turning to the final passage of Wolf's novel, it should be noted that the term *Angst*, which plays such a crucial role in the text, has the same derivation as the *Eng* of *Engführung*: both terms carry the sense of a certain narrowing.[20] To describe the conclusion of the novel in terms of a musical *Engführung* is thus to suggest not only a sense of temporal constriction, but also a passage through the straits of anxiety, through the very straits in which I, you, and she might be said to pass anxiously through one another—*ineinanderschwimmend*.

The closer you are to a person, the harder it seems to say something conclusive about him; it's a known fact. The child who was hidden in me—has she come forth? Or has she been scared into looking for a deeper, more inaccessible hiding place? Has memory done its duty? Or has it proven—by the act of misleading—that it's impossible to escape the mortal sin of our time: the desire not to come to grips with oneself? And the past, which can still split the first person into the second and the third—has its hegemony been broken? Will the voices be still?

I don't know.

At night I shall see—whether waking, whether dreaming—the outline of a human being who will change, through whom other persons, adults, children will pass without hindrance [*den Umriß eines Menschen sehen, der sich in fließenden Übergängen unaufhörlich verwandelt, durch den andere Menschen, Erwachsene, Kinder, ungezwungen hindurchgehen*]. I will hardly be surprised if this outline may also be that of an animal, a tree, even a house, in which anyone who wishes may go in and out at will. Half-conscious, I shall experience the beautiful waking image drifting ever deeper into the dream, into ever new shapes no longer accessible to words, shapes which I believe I recognize. Sure of finding myself once again in the world of solid bodies upon awakening, I shall abandon myself to the experience of dreaming. I shall not revolt against the limits of the expressible [*mich nicht auflehnen gegen die Grenzen des Sagbaren*]. (406–7, 377–78)

In contrast to the self-effacing dream of erasure cited earlier, a dream which in many respects effaces the limit between dreaming and waking states and moreover expunges the very traces of this process of erasure, thereby leaving this limit *seemingly* intact, the last lines of the text are poised to be read, "whether waking, whether dreaming," as a liminal discourse on the limits of the discourse. Thus, the text respects in its own way "the limits of the expressible" against which it claims not to revolt. It does so, however, not merely by remaining safely within those limits (or by surreptitiously transgressing them), but instead by working creatively at and on them, *writing otherwise* in the interspace *between speech and silence*. The first-person narrator's pointed recourse to figures of liminality in the concluding passage seems designed to draw attention to just such a strategy—which, one might add, in turn redirects our attention to the liminality of the *Ich* itself.

What then is the status of this "I" that finally appears on the last page of the text? Like the "nation of know-nothings" "unknowingly" bound by a bond of silence who, "when called to account [*zur Rede gestellt*] will assert as one man, out of millions of mouths that they remember nothing," the first utterance of this "I" is the all too familiar phrase "I don't know." Yet, the "I" who claims not to know or at least not to know with any certainty ("*Ich weiß es nicht*") speaks not as one voice among millions, or, for that matter, as a single dissenting voice, or even ultimately in its own voice, but instead merely as a certain echo bound (like its mythical namesake) by a bond of silence, bound to speak through another's voice as the return of an otherness *of* the voice—or in this case as the return of a certain otherness of the silence, of the *infans*. Like the anxious writer who begins to panic precisely at those moments when the child seems to be "moving on her own" and everything seems to be humming along—"Das schnurpst, sagte Bruno Jordan, sobald etwas von alleine lief" (210, 196)—the echo makes both the silence and the silent autonomization of the act of (self-)silencing strangely audible.

The return of the "I" at the end of the novel, like the pointedly theatrical staging of the "return of the father" recounted a few pages earlier, thus enacts another scene of nonrecognition, another missed encounter in which one is driven to confront one's "own transformation into an unrecognizable person." Yet, it is precisely the acknowledgment of this uncanny alteration, of the narcissistic wounds which echoes embody and inflict, that opens the "I" in the end, that lets it open in its wounded uncertainty, its uncertain assertion, "Ich weiß es nicht." It is important to add, moreover, that such acknowledgments are themselves necessarily uncertain—which is why the "I" who in the end says "I don't know" still seems strangely bound to repeat the language of denial from which it would have wished to distance itself.[21] To write otherwise, the text again seems to suggest, is not simply to speak another tongue, but rather to echo the language of denial in such a way that its bonds and boundaries are altered and displaced from within.

Like the staged "return of the father," the return of the "I" involves a certain performance of self-difference. Thus, while the "I" who says "I don't know" may be said to give voice to a sense of uncertainty, it also at the same time uncertainly opens itself *to* the unknown. It leaves itself open to the series of questions that precede it, questions for which there are (as yet) no known answers. Accommodating itself to these questions that are thereby given room to resonate as truly open questions, the *Ich* in a sense makes itself over into a kind of echo chamber.[22] It is from this perspective, I would suggest, that one should approach the overly accommodating language of the novel's concluding vision: "the outline of a human being who will change, through whom other persons, adults, children, will pass without hindrance. I will hardly be surprised if this outline may also be that of an animal, a tree, even a house, in which anyone who wishes may go in and out at will" (377–78, 407). It is no coincidence that this fugal vision of flighty figures passing through one another as they pass unhindered through the permeable borders of a human being who is herself passing through a series of fluid transitions ("in fließenden Übergängen") into different states of being should eventually come to rest, however fleetingly, on the image of an open house. This utopian vision of an *Ich* incessantly making itself over in an effort to make room for the open, unresolved questions, the dissonant voices and incompatible "persons" which inhabit it, is in a sense an image of the text itself—or rather an outline of its idealized self-image. Indeed, for all its apparent fluidity, the textual ego-ideal captured in this image remains strangely static—as though all the free-floating anxiety with which the disintegration of the *Ich* had heretofore been bound up were now suddenly drained from the text. "Sure of finding [itself] once again in the world of solid bodies upon awakening," the narrative in the end seems to abandon itself not merely "to the experience of dreaming" as such, but, more specifically, to the dream of accommodating the various internal pressures which drive it as well as those imposed upon it from without, (internalized) outside pressures which will later become the subject of Wolf's controversial narrative *What Remains*, a text which opens significantly with the (self-)admonition, "Don't panic [*Nur keine Angst*]."[23]

An eerie serenity thus pervades the dream of accommodation with which *Patterns of Childhood* ends. And yet precisely because the ending rings false, it remains to a certain extent open, at least to the supplementary entry or *Einsatz* of Wolf's Bremen speech, "Ein Satz" (A Sentence). It is here, in the speaker's angst-ridden, obsessive circling about the seemingly simple sentence "I thank you," that one might finally locate the belated *Engführung* of Wolf's contrapuntally constructed novel. It is also here that one may situate with greater precision the straits in which I, you, and she pass anxiously through one another. Whereas in the novel these "persons" are said to float through each other only in thought ("Ich, du, sie, in Gedanken ineinanderschwimmend"), before becoming "mutually estranged when pronounced in a sentence [*im ausgesprochenen Satz einander entfremdet*]" (9; trans. mine), in the Bremen speech this *Engführung* comes to be embodied in the speaker's throat.

There is no language to follow or shore up the paths where our most necessary and riskiest thoughts and feelings must travel. . . . There is no sentence that stays open, open like a wound. Instead, we have an increase of sentences that stick in our throats, or are rammed back down them—which seem to depend on our increasing indifference. The sentences which are left unspoken [*Die unausgesprochenen Sätze*] are those for which there is not an urgent enough demand. Their place is taken, more and more often, by ersatz sentences, additive sentences, alloy sentences, whipped-up sentences, tune-in-next-week sentences [*An ihrer Stelle immer häufiger Er-Sätze, Zu-Sätze, Bei-Sätze, Auf-Sätze, Fort-Sätze*].[24]

The throat thus becomes the privileged locus of a certain impasse, a clogged and congested passageway in which throttled, unpronounceable sentences are anxiously choked back and broken up. Yet this throat is also in the end a kind of strait through which these wounded, open sentences continue to reverberate, insistent in their very fragmentation. Unpronounceable as such, what remains to be said remains bound, bound to stammer in fits and starts at the narrow "limits of the expressible."

5

Toward an Addressable You

OZICK'S 'THE SHAWL' AND THE MOUTH OF THE WITNESS

> hör dich ein
> mit dem Mund
> Paul Celan, "Die Posaunenstelle"[1]

The more general issue raised by Wolf's association of the "limits of the expressible" with the narrows of the throat and by Spiegelman's related assertion "My Father Bleeds History" is the place made for the body—its gestures, languages, and symptoms—in the act of bearing witness. Traditionally, the verbal act of swearing an oath as a witness "to tell the truth, the whole truth, and nothing but the truth" is accompanied by the physical gesture of raising one's hand or of placing it on a sacred text. The linguist Émile Benveniste discusses the origins of this gesture in an entry on "*Ius* and the Oath in Rome," in *Indo-European Language and Society*.

In Oscan the verb for "to swear" is known to us in the verbal form *deiuatuns* "may they swear"; the verbal root *deiua-* in Latin would appear as *divare*, the proper meaning of which would be "take the gods to witness", a clear expression but actually not found in Latin.

In other Indo-European languages the expression for the oath *reflects the way in which one swears*: Irish *tong* corresponds to the Latin *tango* "to touch"; similarly in Old Slavonic *prisegati* and *prisegnoti* mean etymologically "to touch". The primary sense of Skt. *am-* is "seize". This correlation is explained by the custom of touching the object or the living thing by which one swears. For to swear by someone or something is to bring a divine curse on this person or thing if he should be false to his oath.[2]

Whereas the physical gestures accompanying an oath traditionally serve as a guarantee of the witness's pledge to remain faithful to the truth of what has been seen or experienced first-hand, in the case of survivor testimony it is often the language of the body that *betrays* the truth of experiences to which the witness himself does not have access. How then does the body of the traumatized survivor bear witness? In what ways can it bear and impart truths which the speaking subject, the conscious witness, himself does not possess? How, in betraying the conscious intentions of the speaker, does the body unintentionally reveal—or at least give way to—that which is beyond the witness's ability to grasp? If the body is in this sense the bearer of unconscious testimony and itself an unwitting witness, how can one respond to its address? How can one assume co-responsibility for that which speaks otherwise in its gestures, symptoms, and compulsive acts? How, in short, can one learn to listen to this singular idiom of the body and its modes of address, to a language of testimony foreign to any and all mother tongues?

To address these questions, I turn now to Cynthia Ozick's two-part fictional narrative *The Shawl*, a text in which the Holocaust survivor Rosa Lublin's struggle to bear witness is repeatedly frustrated. Not only does she—like so many actual survivors in the immediate postwar years—fail to find an audience willing and able to listen to her story, but her story is one that in fundamental ways she herself does not possess. On the contrary, it is a story that inhabits and possesses her. The unsuspecting bearer of this secret story, Rosa carries it like an undeliverable dead letter inscribed upon her flesh—inscribed there in and as the very foreignness of her own traumatized body. In *The Shawl* the desire to bear witness is enacted as a struggle to deliver this dead letter, to "deliver" it not only in the postal sense but also through a laborious act of belated parturition.

"The Arena of the Mouth"

First published in 1980 and 1983 as two separate narratives in the *New Yorker*, *The Shawl: A Story and a Novella* appeared in book form with an epigraph taken from Paul Celan's famous poem "Todesfuge" (Death Fugue) in 1989. Like so much of Ozick's work, this text turns obsessively around the opening of the mouth, around an orifice that is a perpetual site of conflict and a privileged locus of abjection. In her 1984 essay "The Question of Our Speech" the author recalls a humiliating scene of voice training and speech repair which no doubt fueled this obsession. "When I was a thirteen-year-old New Yorker a trio of women from the provinces took up, relentlessly and extravagantly, the question of my speech."[3] The aim of these women was to reform the New York voice, notoriously situated in the throat and having to descend, "pumping air to this nether site," so that the phrase "young Lochinvar came out of the WEST" might, in Ozick's words, "come bellowing out of the pubescent breast" (146). These well-meaning elocutionists from the Midwest also took aim at the New York palate. "*T*'s, *d*'s and *l*'s were beaten out against the teeth, European-fashion—this was called 'dentalization'—while the homeless *r* and *n* went wandering in the perilous trough behind the front incisors. There were corrective exercises for these transgressions, the chief one being a liturgical recitation of 'Tillie the Toiler took Tommy Tucker to tea,' with the tongue anxiously flying up above the teeth to strike precisely on the lower ridge of the upper palate" (146–47). Finally, there was "the arena of the mouth where vowels are prepared. A New Yorker could not say a proper *a*, as in 'paper'—this indispensable vibration was manufactured somewhere back near the nasal passage, whereas civility demanded the *a* to emerge frontally, directly from the lips' vestibule" (147).

Ozick goes on to compare her tutors to Shaw's Professor Higgins, catching in herself something of Eliza's degradation. The elocutionists' zeal, evangelical in inspiration, demanded of its potential converts the will "to be born again . . . to repudiate wholesale one's former defective self" (147). Having been put "into the wringer of speech repair" (148), Ozick's voice in the end came through neither reborn nor naturalized, as her teachers might have hoped, but instead orphaned and adrift. "Like a multitude of other graduates of my high school, I now own a sort of robot's speech—it has no obvious native country" (148). "Effectively made over: these noises that come out of me are not an overlay. They do not vanish during the free play of dreams or screams. I do not, cannot 'revert'" (148). While her mentors perhaps saw themselves as "democratic noblewomen" (149)—without recognizing, as Ozick observes, the obvious contradiction in terms—who sought to provide their pupils with the wherewithal to rise to a higher station, for Ozick what seemed to lurk behind their good intentions was a repugnance. "The speech of New York streets and households soiled them:

you could see it in their proud pained meticulous frowns. . . . Trolander, Davis, and Papp saw us . . . as tainted with foreignness, and it was the remnants of that foreignness they meant to wipe away: the last stages of the great turn-of-the-century flood" (149) of immigration.

The specter of this gentle scene of instruction returns thirteen years later in the opening chapter of *The Puttermesser Papers*. Fresh out of law school, the protagonist, Ruth Puttermesser, takes a job at a blueblood Wall Street firm. "Three Jews a year joined the back precincts of Midland, Reid. . . . Three Jews a year left—not the same three." There was no quota per se, the narrator later adds. "They left of their own choice; no one shut them out."

Puttermesser left too, weary of so much chivalry—the partners in particular were excessively gracious to her, and treated her like a fellow-aristocrat. Puttermesser supposed this was because *she* did not say "a" in her nose or elongate her "i," and above all she did not dentalize her "t," "d," or "l," keeping them all back against the upper palate. Long ago her speech had been standardized by the drilling of fanatical teachers, elocutionary missionaries hired out of the Midwest by Puttermesser's prize high school, until almost all the regionalism was drained out . . . [4]

Ozick's female American protagonists are not the only ones subjected to such sanitizing regimens. In *The Cannibal Galaxy* the child of Jewish immigrants, Joseph Brill, is inspired by his French University "to alter his diction—fumy . . . with the odors of the shops on the Rue des Rosiers. His friends, new ones from *arrondissements* to the west and north, did not sound their vowels as he did; it was humiliating to be an immigrant's child and fill one's mouth with the wrong noise. Every night Joseph scrubbed the fish smell off his hands with an abrasive soap that skinned his knuckles mercilessly."[5]

As this brief survey suggests, the oral cavity for Ozick is always an embattled space in which remnants of foreignness are made to contend with and ultimately give way to more standardized, accepted ways of voicing the mother tongue. It is the place where the so-called "naturalness" of native speech is at once asserted and contested, where the taint of a foreignness that was to have been "wiped away" continues to bleed through like a return of the repressed. A privileged locus of interlingual conflict, the mouth is itself a wounded and injury-prone orifice in the Ozick corpus. Ruth Puttermesser suffers from periodontal disease. "'Uncontrollable pockets,' the dentist said" (25). Rosa Lublin's suitor in *The Shawl*, Simon Persky, has false teeth. "Two whole long rows of glinting dentures smiled at her," Rosa notes as she sizes up her new acquaintance in the course of their first meeting.[6] Even when the word *mouth* is used only in a meta-phorical sense, the bodily connotations and violence associated with this organ tend to carry over. In *The Messiah of Stockholm*, for example, the mouth in question is that of an amphora into which a lost manuscript has been deposited. "With both hands Dr. Eklund took hold of the brass am-phora and raised it above the table. There it was, high up, traveling at a de-cent steady speed—a torpedo; a whale with its mouth wide; a chalice. Midway he tipped it over, until the mouth hung upside down, vomiting disorder, chaos."[7]

Here and elsewhere in Ozick's work the upside-down mouth stands as a figure of bodily inversion. Turned on its head, the tipped-over am-phora is transformed into an upright womb with its mouth now doubling as a vaginal opening.[8] In *The Cannibal Galaxy* such an opening is referred to as "the pocket-mouth of the uterus" (40). In *The Messiah of Stockholm* what is disgorged from the mouth of the womblike amphora in this scene of displaced parturition is not a child, as one might expect, but only an umbilical cord that the orphaned protagonist of the novel, Lars Andemen-ing, hopes will tie him finally and definitively to the body of his lost par-ent's work, giving him the proper name, lineage, and patrimony he so des-perately desires. In Ozick's short story "The Shawl," published seven years before *The Messiah of Stockholm*, an umbilicus may again be seen to pour from the oral cavity, taking shape this time as the cry of "Maaa—" de-scribed by the narrator as "a long viscous rope of clamor" (8) spilling from the infant Magda's mouth.

In the book-length version of *The Shawl*, a text that combines the earlier short story with the novella *Rosa*, the mouth is at once a source of life and a locus of death. Or to be more precise, it is a fluidly unstable and painfully embattled between-space of life-in-death. Telling in this regard is the way Rosa's strangely mute child, Magda, comes to life belatedly in an unnamed concentration camp, emerging from her deathly silence and giv-ing voice to the plangently animated cry of "Maaa—" at the very moment of her impending death. The moments of birth and death are so densely intertwined here in large part because the child's life begins, in effect, with the unacknowledged death of Rosa, who was left pregnant and mortified by a rape—pregnant, that is, not merely with a new life but with a virulent new strain of life-in-death. There is remarkably little discussion of the circumstances surrounding Magda's conception in the critical literature devoted to *The Shawl.* This is not surprising, given Rosa's own version of the story. "Your father was not a German," she writes in an undeliverable letter addressed to her deceased daughter after the war. "I was forced by a German, it's true, and more than once, but I was too sick to conceive. Stella has a naturally pornographic mind, she can't resist dreaming up a dirty sire for you, an S.S. man! . . . Never believe this, my lioness, my snowqueen! No lies come out of me to you. You are pure" (43).[9]

The violent circumstances surrounding Magda's conception are never explicitly spelled out in the text, and Rosa herself repeatedly dismisses any allusion to them as "excretions" of another's "pornographic mind" (43). Yet it is impossible to read *The Shawl* without taking this state of affairs into account. Not only do fragments of this traumatic scene continue to wash up on the shores of Miami and the edges of Rosa's consciousness forty years after the fact, but the rape itself is silently and unwittingly acted out in a number guises and on a variety of stages throughout the text—most notably in a scene on the beach outside a Miami hotel, to which I will return at length below: "Her pants were under the sand; or else packed hard with sand, like a piece of torso; a broken statue, the human groin detached, the whole soul gone, only the loins left for kicking by strangers" (48).

The question of Magda's paternity is raised early on in "The Shawl." In the opening scene Rosa and her niece, Stella, are being marched along a road leading to an unnamed camp. As the protagonist walks with her infant daughter hidden away in her shawl, she dreams "of giving Magda away in one of the villages" (4). Weighing her options in a rhetoric of "if she . . . if she . . . " which will be encountered at every turning point in this seven-page story, she reflects: "She could leave the line for a minute and push Magda into the hands of any woman on the side of the road. But if she moved out of line they might shoot. And even if she fled the line for half a second and pushed the shawl-bundle at a stranger, would the woman take it? She might be surprised, or afraid; she might drop the shawl, and Magda would fall out and strike her head and die" (4).

As though kept in line by the competing pull of equally impossible alternatives, Rosa trudges on with Magda in her arms and her fourteen-year-old niece at her side. The two women take turns studying the child's face until Stella at one point "says in a voice grown as thin as a string," "Aryan" (5). Rosa's reaction is telling, for at the moment Stella blurts out the unspeakable truth of the child's paternity, her mouth seems to meta-morphose before her aunt's eyes from an organ of speech into an omnivo-rous oral cavity seemingly bent on consuming the very person spoken about: "and Rosa thought how Stella gazed at Magda like a young canni-bal. And the time that Stella said 'Aryan,' it sounded to Rosa as if Stella had really said 'Let us devour her'" (5).

The anxious mother no doubt hears in the single word uttered by her starving niece both the threat of future violence—"She was sure that Stella was waiting for Magda to die so she could put her teeth into the little thigh" (5)—and the traumatic return of a violent past. Or to be more pre-cise, she now experiences the return of her violation coming to her through Stella's mouth as the threat of injury "still again" to come. While this vio-lence may in the future be directed at Magda rather than herself, at another who is at the same time an extension of herself, the present evocation of the moment of conception also returns Rosa to a scene in the past in which the woman being raped is never acknowledged to be the same person as Magda's mother.[10] When the word "Aryan" passes Stella's lips, the physical space of her mouth is transformed, in Rosa's eyes, from an organ of speech into a rapacious instrument of destruction. In addition to suggesting the murderous thrust of Stella's surprisingly blunt remark, this sudden trans-formation draws attention to the mouth as such—or rather to the mouth *as other*, to an organ that, no matter how clearly it appears to speak, cannot help but be heard as saying something else: "'Aryan,' it sounded to Rosa as if Stella had really said, 'Let's devour her'" (5).

Such a moment would hardly merit close scrutiny, were it not for the fact that the specific opening of the oral cavity serves throughout *The Shawl* as a privileged point of focus for Rosa. Indeed, it is around this opening that the survivor's anxieties tend to cluster—anxieties not only about the foreignness of her own body or the presence within it of other "foreign bodies," but also about the betrayal of secrets, the telling of stories better kept to and from oneself. Often appearing to the protagonist as a lo-cus of abjection, the mouth is a place where outside and inside incessantly commingle, the outside prosthetically taking the place of the inside—as it does quite literally in the case of Simon Persky's "long rows of glinting den-tures" (19). It is a place where the inside itself at times spills out in the very process of taking the outside in, as when Magda, turning to the shawl for sustenance after Rosa's breasts have dried up, is said to have "sucked and sucked, *flooding* the threads with wetness" (4–5; emphasis added). No longer simply an opening *in* the body, but a privileged point at which its contours and "seamless continuity" (28) appear to dissolve, the mouth also and above all marks the site at which life and death bleed into one another.[11] "Every day Magda was silent," the narrator observes, "and so she did not die" (7). Yet, in remaining silent she is, if not already dead, still in her mother's eyes not yet really alive.

> Ever since the drying up of Rosa's nipples, ever since Magda's last scream on the road, Magda had been devoid of any syllable; Magda was a mute. Rosa believed that something had gone wrong with her vocal cords, with her windpipe, with the cave of her larynx; Magda was defective, without a voice; perhaps she was deaf; there might be something amiss with her intelligence; Magda was dumb. Even the laugh that came when the ash-stippled wind made a clown out of Magda's shawl was only the air-blown showing of her teeth. Even when the lice, head lice and body lice, crazed her so that she became as wild as one of the big rats that plundered the barracks at daybreak looking for carrion, she rubbed and scratched and kicked and bit and rolled without a whimper. (7)

It is hard to know how to begin to address passages such as this. Let me at least start by acknowledging the difficulty of doing so. It is a passage in which a mother's fears initially focused around the malfunctioning of her child's mouth begin to spread to other parts of the body. Anxiously moving from one organ to another, from the mouth to the throat to the chest, ears, and brain, her specific fears gradually seem to dissolve into a more diffuse, unfocused, and panic-stricken sense of anxiety. It is as though the mouth itself were dissolving here, and with it the distinction between mother and child, inside and out, as though the mute writhing of the daughter had become the embodiment of the inexpressible torment of the mother.[12] "But now," the passage abruptly continues,

> Magda's mouth was spilling a long viscous rope of clamor.
> "Maaa—"
> It was the first noise Magda had ever sent out from her throat since the drying up of Rosa's nipples.
> "Maaaa . . . aaa!"
> Again! (7–8)

With incredible economy the oral cavity now suddenly comes to life transformed into a kind of vaginal opening around which the rest of the body reforms itself. Or to be more precise, it is the amorphous mass of mute and writing pain into which mother and daughter had dissolved a moment ago that is now remolded into two distinct bodies joined by the umbilicus of "a long viscous rope of clamor." That this clamorous rope is meant to be read as an umbilical cord is suggested first by the burst of vitality, the outbreak from deathly silence, with which it is immediately associated; second, by its evocation of Stella's "voice grown as thin as string," which had earlier betrayed Magda's unspoken (and for Rosa unspeakable) ties to her paternal line; third, by the way the sound "Maaa—," in hovering equivocally between an appeal to "Mama" and a first annunciation of "Magda," itself links these two nascent bodies together in their "viscous" ambiguity. In addition to the possible meanings one might attach to this incipient cry, one should note that the very utterance of "Maaa—" involves the movement of lips opening.

Magda's "long viscous rope of clamor" may thus be said to function as a kind of tie among ties, a figure through which three different modes of connection are interwoven: the tenuous attachment of mother and daughter in the process of separating; the conjunction of the lips above and those below at the moment of parting; and the sounding together of an infant's first cry and its last. Having Magda's last cry sound and resound at this moment as though it were her first, the text suggests that the child comes to life many months after the fact, that she is born again, as though for the first time, at the very moment she is about to die. Moreover, insofar as this coming to life-in-death may itself be said to repeat in inverse form Rosa's own silent death at the moment of Magda's conception—at the moment, that is, when "the physiological fact" (41) of motherhood was first inflicted upon her—the "long viscous rope of clamor" linking parent and child should also be read as the belated cry of the silenced mother erupting through the lips of the daughter.

The outburst "Maaa—," ostensibly a cry for the shawl, is enmeshed in this complex fabric of relationships. The fact that the shawl itself turns out to be missing at this particular moment suggests that this other fabric has in a sense taken its place, that the shawl has in its turn been inscribed in this movement of substitution and—precisely in its not being where it should be—is the very figure of this movement.[13] Upon discovering that her shawl, her "baby, her pet, her little sister" (6), has disappeared, Magda wanders off in search of it. "Scribbling on . . . pitiful little bent shins," she staggers out of the barracks into "the perilous sunlight of the [roll-call] arena" (8). Rosa does not immediately follow her, in part because she knows the shawl is back inside the barracks, in part because she "does not know which to go after first" (8), but mostly because the cry "Maaaa . . . aaa!" itself means so much to her. "If she jumped out into the arena to snatch Magda up, the howling would not stop, because Magda would still not have the shawl; but if she ran back into the barracks to find the shawl, and if she found it, and if she came after Magda holding it and shaking it, then she would get Magda back, Magda would put the shawl in her mouth and turn dumb again" (8).

If nothing else, the terrible bind in which Rosa now finds herself (marked again by the repetition of the phrase "if she . . . ") underscores the fatal equation suggested earlier between a last and a first cry. Throughout the rest of the narrative Rosa will remain bound to this moment of indecision, bound to hear the one cry through the other (and still others through them), bound to repeat in the very mode of hesitation the murderous scene that led to Magda's conception as one in which the daughter dies in the process of coming (back) to life.

That the latter scene of coming to life-in-death is to be read as a displaced repetition of the former is suggested by the particular prominence of two motifs: the theme of silence and the figure of the double bind. If Rosa hesitates before running back to the barracks and retrieving the shawl, it is ostensibly because she is afraid that it will be used to turn Magda "dumb again." Yet, not only do such fears (centered once again around the opening of the mouth) seem unfounded, but their very groundlessness suggests their displacement from another context, in which the person being reduced to silence (if not literally gagged) was presumably Rosa herself. The figure of the double bind seems also to allude to this earlier scene. As a figure that in the present context explicitly links mental paralysis to physical immobility ("she did not know which to go after first, Magda or the shawl" [8]), it implicitly conjures another situation of being helplessly pinned down, a scene of deathly immobilization which Rosa in a sense never moves away from. While her current feeling of being caught in a double bind may thus be said to reenact crucial aspects of this earlier scene, the added layer of retrospective narration through which one reads both the former and the latter suggests that what is ultimately being repeated "here" is not simply Rosa's entrapment in any particular moment but rather her suspension *between scenes*, between two life-and-death situations, each of which seems uncannily to mirror and repeat the other.

As this sense of suspension (already alluded to at the outset: "Rosa, *floating*, dreamed of giving Magda away . . . " [4]) becomes increasingly prevalent in the text, the appearance of narrative progression itself gradually gives way to a more hesitant and faltering rhythm of discontinuous leaps from impasse to impasse, from threshold to threshold. It is telling in this regard that when Rosa finally makes up her mind to retrieve the shawl and then go back out after Magda, she emerges from the barracks only to pause once again at a point described as "the margin of the arena" (9). Whereas her hesitation initially seems only temporary ("She stood for an instant at the margin . . . " [9]), it soon becomes clear that she remains rooted to this spot for the rest of the narrative. Indeed, given the fact that the term *arena* itself derives from the Latin *harena* meaning sand or sandy place, it might be said that Rosa never moves from it even and especially when she later relocates from New York to Miami Beach. It is not by chance, then, that a crucial reenactment of this scene (itself the repetition of another) will be set on the shoreline outside a large beachfront hotel. "How simple the night sea; only the sand is unpredictable, with its hundred burrowings, its thousand buryings" (48). Wavering on the water's edge, Rosa will find herself once again stranded at "the margin of the arena."

Yet even before its return in another scene, there are indications that this "margin" is from the very first already a space between scenes. Ostensibly a point at which Rosa comes to a standstill midway between the darkness of the barracks and the "perilous sunlight of the arena," the margin is also and above all a place where the very opposition between inside and outside no longer holds. It is therefore telling that Rosa undergoes a radical change in appearance at the moment she comes to occupy it. Not only is her skin now said to be "greased" "with a bitter fatty floating smoke" (9)—obviously the incinerated remains of other deportees—but, coated in this way, her outside turns out to be an exact replica of Magda's inside. Described earlier as being "fat with air, full and round" (5), the child's empty belly is now referred to as being "air-fed" (9). This grotesque depiction of the mother's outside as a refolding of the daughter's inside not only reinforces the sense that each one's story is a version of the other's turned inside out, but also that Rosa is somehow fated to view the ensuing scene of Magda's death as a traumatic repetition of her own.

The "margin" at which these changes occur is thus to be viewed not just as a point of transition in an otherwise homogeneous space, but instead as a locus of radical inversion, a space in which an abject maternal body once again in the process of dissolution seems to lose its contours only to find itself still held together by the "second skin" of actual bodily remains. It is a space, moreover, in which bodies seem to lose their contours only to become contours without bodies—in other words, the merest outlines of hollow selves, tracings of lost souls in a forsaken place.

While the margin first appears as a positive midpoint between darkness and light, inside and outside, and then, more radically, as a locus of inversion, ultimately it comes to mark the edge of an abyss, the very limit of localizability as such—which is to say that Rosa is no longer at this point simply a person distinct from the space through which she moves. Instead, in coming to a standstill at this margin, she is henceforth entirely defined by it. Not only does this space now mark the point at which she will remain fixated, the gaping wound around which any future sense of self will have to be reformed, but, as a marginal space perpetually on the brink of dissolution, it is what gives the abyss, the wound, the unspeakable itself its edge. At the very limit of localizability the margin thus comes to define a negative space or emptiness whose contours it traces. Outlined in this way, emptiness itself is maintained as the space of an elementary separation. "Might narcissism be a means for protecting that emptiness?" the psychoanalyst and critic, Julia Kristeva, writes:

But against what?—a protection of emptiness (of "arbitrariness," of the "gaping hole") through the display of a decidedly narcissistic parry, so that emptiness can be maintained lest chaos prevail and borders dissolve. Narcissism protects emptiness, causes it to exist and thus, as lining of that emptiness, ensures an elementary separation. Without that solidarity between emptiness and narcissism, chaos would sweep away any possibility of distinction, trace and symbolization, which would in turn confuse the limits of the body, words, the real and the symbolic.[14]

The "margin" thus marks the very limit of (in)distinction, the point at which a certain emptiness may itself be said to stand in for and protect against the ever-present threat of chaotic dissolution. As such, it is also a point of marginal disorientation, at which the vanishing coordinates of space and time become instead, in the interim, mere functions of one another. It is therefore telling that time itself seems to come to an abrupt halt when Rosa pauses at the margin. Remaining there "for an instant" that never ends, she now stands silently transfixed by the sound of "grainy sad voices" humming inside the electrified fence into which Magda is about to be thrown. These voices tell her to hold up the shawl and wave it at Magda. As she does so, she sees her daughter in the distance "reaching out with the rods of her arms" (9), carried away on the shoulders of a camp guard. Although Rosa is clearly an eyewitness to what follows, the ensuing description is so abstract and aestheticized that it reads less like an actual account of Magda's last moments than a depiction of Rosa's own distance from the scene.

All at once Magda was swimming through the air. The whole of Magda traveled through loftiness. She looked like a butterfly touching a silver vine. And the moment Magda's feathered round head and her pencil legs and balloonish belly and zigzag arms splashed against the fence, the steel voices went mad in their growling, urging Rosa to run and run to the spot where Magda had fallen from her flight against the electrified fence; but of course Rosa did not obey them. She only stood, because if she ran they would shoot, and if she tried to pick up the sticks of Magda's body they would shoot, and if she let the wolf's screech ascending now through the ladder of her skeleton break out, they would shoot; so she took Magda's shawl and filled her own mouth with it, stuffed it in and stuffed it in, until she was swallowing up the wolf's screech and tasting the cinnamon and almond depth of Magda's saliva; and Rosa drank Magda's shawl until it dried. (10)

In addition to evoking the particularly aestheticized violence of the concentration camp, Maidanek, to which I will return below, phrases like "swimming through the air," traveling "through loftiness," and touching down "like a butterfly" on "a silver vine" suggest that this description of Magda's horrific flight through the air and into the fence is also at the same time an account of Rosa's own psychical flight from the scene, an indication of her *failure* to bear witness. Indeed, the peculiarly overwrought style of this passage makes it read less like a faithful rendering of what actually transpired than a description of what will have taken its place in the survivor's memory. The point of such displacements is not only to draw attention to the screens through which such unspeakable events are inevitably filtered, but also to suggest that the event described here may itself be just such a screen memory. In other words, the fact that one is given such a highly mediated, pointedly revised account of Magda's death suggests that this event may be a distorted and belated repetition of another.[15]

More than any specific detail in the description, it is the insistent rhetoric of "if she . . . if she . . . ," in which this particular scene and the narrative as a whole culminates, that draws attention to this movement of repetition. Appearing three times in the course of the story, the locution is first used to describe Rosa's "dream of giving Magda away," of "pushing the shawl-bundle at a stranger" (4). It then returns at the moment she finds herself forced to choose between Magda and the shawl, a choice made all the more impossible by the fear that, once recovered, "Magda would put the shawl in her mouth and turn dumb again" (8). In its third and final appearance the rhetoric of "if she" marks a moment of multiple displacements, whereby Rosa now is turned dumb when she stuffs the shawl into her own mouth. Each mention of this phrase thus confronts the protagonist with an impossible choice. As these impossibilities multiply, Rosa finds herself increasingly paralyzed: in the first instance she walks while weighing her options; in the second she pauses momentarily while deciding "which to go after first, Magda or the shawl"; in the third she stands completely immobilized "at the margin of the arena" looking on helplessly as her daughter is murdered. As the possibility of taking positive steps to avoid the inevitable becomes increasingly circumscribed, Rosa's internal agitation grows and the repetitive rhetoric of "if she," the very index of inhibited action, rises like a surging wave of nausea toward her mouth. The "wolf's screech ascending . . . through the ladder of her skeleton" (10) should thus be read not merely as a discrete content, as a mounting cry of pain about to "break out," but moreover as a movement of revulsion about to turn Rosa—already in a sense little more than an empty contour—once again inside out.

Early on in the story Rosa suspects there is magic in Magda's shawl for it somehow has the capacity to "nourish an infant for three days and three nights" (5). By the end, however, its special powers appear ironically to have more to do with its miraculous ability to arrest a stomach-turning movement of inversion, to keep Rosa quiet and intact. Indeed, not only does the shawl inserted in her mouth effectively silence her, it also "magically" turns the grieving mother into a nursing infant. Moreover, it is precisely Rosa's overidentification with Magda at this point that enables her to screen out and seal off the more violent connotations of "gagging." While it is certainly no accident that "The Shawl" draws to a close around the opening of the mouth, what is surprising is the way this orifice, heretofore a privileged locus of abjection, is metamorphosed in the end into a remark-ably stable space of containment. As though its contours were reinforced by the overidentification of mother and child, it is a space now able to con-tain the explosive energy of the swallowed up "wolf's screech." Not only is this screech (and all that it stands for) negatively held in check here, but through its contact with Magda's own reabsorbed gastric juices ("she was swallowing up the . . . screech and tasting . . . the saliva" [10]) it appears to be positively broken down into a more quiescent form of energy. What keeps Rosa quiet, then, is not merely the fear of losing her own life ("if she let the wolf's screech . . . break out, they would shoot" [10]), but also, more enigmatically, the regressive oral "pleasure" of sucking the lost child back in. Whereas Magda had previously used the shawl as a surrogate breast, sucking on it "for the taste of the drying nipple" (4), Rosa now milks it for the savor of her daughter's own overflowing mouth, for "the cinnamon and almond depth" of the saliva which had oozed out of her, "flooding the threads with wetness" as she sought in vain to drink the shawl in.

It has been suggested that in "swallowing the 'wolf's screech' . . . [Rosa] internalizes both the child's cry and the child's muteness."[16] But can one describe what occurs at this point simply as a process of internaliza-tion? I would argue instead that just as Magda's own saliva is said to ooze out onto the shawl in the very act of drinking it in, so too at this moment does Rosa draw Magda back into herself only by overflowing her own fluid boundaries, only by in effect becoming the child. It is telling in this regard that Magda is herself now described in the strangely fluid language of swimming and splashing (even as she is being "splashed against the fence" [10]). Dissolving into the child Magda was *before* being dismembered into individual parts ("Magda's feathered head and her pencil legs and balloon-ish belly and zigzag arms splashed . . . " [10]), Rosa seeks not only to can-cel the child's death and thereby restore her to life, but to do so by retract-ing her birth, by drawing them both back into a prenatal state in which mother and child are wholly dissolved in one another. Such a solution, however, amounts to nothing more than a restatement of the initial prob-lem of when and where to locate the moment of birth. For, as we have seen, Magda comes to life repeatedly in "The Shawl," her belated birth be-ing always at once a return from and a return to her premature death. Lit-tle wonder then that Rosa is said to witness the scene of Magda's murder from the "margin of the arena," a liminal space in which the oppositions between inside and outside, before and after, victim and witness, no longer seem to hold.

It is important to note in this context that "the long viscous rope of clamor," employed earlier as a figure of the umbilical knotting of Magda's first cry with her last, reappears at this point as the disembodied "electric voices" of the fence. "'Maamaa, maaamaaa,' they all hummed together" (9). The displacement of the umbilical "Maaa—" from the mother-and-child to the meshwork of the fence into which Magda is thrown thus marks a significant shift, which does not change the initial situation so much as belatedly tease out its latent complexities. Whereas Magda's first—and last—cry had to be read in its viscous ambiguity both as an appeal to "Mama" and as a first annunciation of "Magda," the return of this cry in the "humming together" of the fence's "electric voices" now bears witness to the collapse of a tenuously vital ambiguity into a fatal identity; it bears witness, in short, to the silent dissolution of Mama into Magda.

Rosamunde

In many ways the traumatized mother, Rosa Lublin, never leaves this scene, which concludes the first part of *The Shawl*. Indeed, Ozick herself seems to have been so haunted by it that she felt compelled to return to it, to rewrite it as the much longer narrative "Rosa," published three years later. "Rosa" is less a sequel to "The Shawl" than its belated repetition. As such, it bears witness to the protagonist's ongoing marginalization between scenes—between the trauma of her own rape and that of her daughter's murder. Yet, the two scenes together seem also to be haunted by a third, in which it is not simply a mother or her daughter who is "turned dumb" when something is stuffed in her mouth. In this other scene it is instead the mouth itself, a particularly Aryan version of Rosa's *Munde*, that is used as the silencing agent.

On November 3, 1943, 18,400 Jewish men, women, and children were shot by the SS in ditches near the crematorium of Maidanek. As these mass executions were carried out, camp loudspeakers played the popular German tune "Rosamunde, Give Me a Kiss," in order, in the words of the historian Konnilyn Feig, "to muffle the sounds of the shooting and the cries of the dying."[17] The SS code name for this action, the largest single mass execution in the history of the camp, was *Erntefest* or Harvest Festival; inmates called it Bloody Wednesday.

Readers of *The Shawl* have sought to trace the name of its protagonist to the *Song of Songs*, in which Shulamith (mentioned in the text's epigraph taken from Celan's "Todesfuge") is associated with the "Rose of Sharon," in Hebrew "Shoshana," which is also Cynthia Ozick's Hebrew name. I would suggest, however, that the name "Rosa" and the *Mund* or mouth to which it is so closely and anxiously linked throughout the text be read as residues of the aestheticized violence of this mass murder.

There was only one Jewish survivor of the events of November 3, Pinkhas Lazarovitch Trepman. He was able to remain alive, thanks, as he says, to "his false 'Aryan' identity," as Pawel Kolodziejczyk, and his "non-Jewish appearance."[18] I reproduce the following excerpts from his "testimony against Hitler," *Among Men and Beasts*, in order, first, to suggest it as a possible source for Ozick's narrative and, second, to draw attention to the way his account of the mass execution is scanned by the repeated mention of "Rosamunde," a song which returns in it like a revenant—like the ghost of a haunting refrain. As though to accentuate this acoustic dimension of his eyewitness testimony, Trepman begins his account with the chorus of a song—not the German tune which prisoners were forced to hear repeatedly on November 3, but a song of the inmates' own making, the so-called "Maidanek Song," composed by an unknown Polish poet in the camp.

> There never has been,
> Nor will there ever be,
> Anywhere on earth,
> A sun like that which shines
> Upon our Maidanek . . .

According to Trepman, this song became the unofficial anthem of the camp inmates. "We sang it everywhere we went, all day long: at work, at mealtime, before going to sleep, and even while we were kicked and beaten by our jailers. At night, as we lay on our bunks, our stomachs hollow, our spirits despairing, we would hum the 'Maidanek Song' and see visions of peace and contentment. And for a little while the heavy burden pressing on our hearts dissolved into healing tears of hope and yearning." Set against the background of this song, which seems like Magda's "magic shawl" to have the power to nourish and invigorate, Trepman's account of the executions begins.

The day began like any other, but somehow the mood was different. Roll call had been completed, but the Camp Elder had not yet given the usual order for the labor details to line up.

Why this deviation from the regular camp routine? All sorts of conjectures were whispered up and down the countless rows of inmates standing at attention. Suddenly we became aware that we were surrounded by a cordon of S.S. men, their loaded rifles pointed at the inmates, ready to shoot. . . . And then the charged silence was broken by the Camp Elder's sharp command: "All Jews report at once to the camp office!"

What followed can only be described as chaos. The massed rows of inmates arranged according to barracks split into two, three and four separate parts. Jews poured out of the kitchens and infirmaries; typhus patients, half dead, were carried on stretchers and loaded onto wagons. As loudspeakers blared forth the strains of a popular German song: "Rosamunde, Give Me a Kiss and Your Heart," the wagons moved off in the direction of Camp Five. . . .

On the other side of our barbed wire fence, in the far part of our camp, was Maidanek's main road. Lined up in a double row along the full length of that road were members of the "death's head squad" who comprised the "Jew extermination detail." As these men and dogs stood at attention, waiting for the action to begin, Jewish women appeared on the thoroughfare, marching toward Camp Five and the ovens. . . . They walked quietly, their heads lowered, accompanied by obscenities, guffaws and blows from their torturers. The loudspeakers continued to belt out their merry song and the sun shone more brightly than ever as the procession moved on.

Shortly thereafter, the men began to march. . . . And all the while, the loudspeakers kept on playing "Rosamunde." . . .

The death march and mass slaughter of Jews on September [*sic*] 3, 1943 was the largest single operation of its kind at Maidanek. It began at seven o'clock in the morning and continued without pause until six o'clock that evening. All that day we saw Jews march away to a place from which there was no return. It was a breathtakingly beautiful day on God's earth but we did not see the beauty. We only saw that the sun was beaming merrily from a large patch of blue sky while thousands of Jews below were being taken to their death as the German loudspeakers played "Rosamunde, Give Me a Kiss." . . .

The next morning the chimney of the crematorium began to belch smoke. It smoked for a long time, scattering the ashes of 22,000 Jewish men, women and children across the face of the smiling golden sun and the cloudless blue sky so that both sun and sky turned black.[19]

Toward an Addressable You

It is difficult to read Trepman's testimony in which strains of the "Maidanek Song" are set in ironic counterpoint against the refrain of "Rosamunde" without hearing echoes of Celan's "Todesfuge," the last two lines of which form the epigraph to *The Shawl*:

> dein goldenes Haar Margarete
> dein aschenes Haar Sulamith
>
> your golden hair Margarete
> your ashen hair Shulamith

Like Trepman's testimony, Celan's fugal composition repeatedly juxtaposes two songs of yearning, Goethe's *Faust*, represented by the figure of Margarete, and the biblical Song of Songs, personified by the beloved Shulamith. The parallel structure of the poem's last lines makes the two yearnings resonate with one another. And yet, as has often been noted, a bitter difference and a shocking irony resound from within this echoing resemblance.[20] The strategy of ironic displacement so evident in these concluding lines is at work in the poem from the very beginning.

> Schwarze Milch der Frühe wir trinken sie abends
> wir trinken sie mittags und morgens wir trinken sie nachts
> wir trinken und trinken
>
> Black milk of daybreak we drink it at evening
> we drink it at midday and morning we drink it at night
> we drink and we drink

Here the figure of drinking, traditionally a metaphor for yearning, for romantic thirst and desire, for poetry and poetic intoxication, is turned into the abusive figure of an endless torture, of having to endure, absorb, and continuously *take in* that which one is powerless to resist. In Trepman's testimony the refrain of "Rosamunde" functions in a similar way to transform a song heard over and over against the background of mass executions carried out on the other side of the barbed wire fence into a kind of "black milk"; that is, this song of romantic yearning ("Rosamunde, Give Me a Kiss and Your Heart") is itself now contaminated by the sounds of the shooting and the cries of the dying its playing was meant to muffle and drown out.[21] Trepman's testimonial repetition of this seemingly innocent song thus has the effect of corrupting it, of ironically turning it against itself, of making it bear witness precisely to the violence it was supposed to silence as well as to the violent act of silencing itself. Moreover, in juxtaposing "Rosamunde" with the "Maidanek Song," also a song of longing, a song whose singing, it was claimed, could dissolve "heavy burdens" into "healing tears of hope and yearning," Trepman makes the inmates' own song now resound as a cry of lamentation. This unofficial anthem of the camp, which had formerly invoked the restorative powers of sunshine, is heard henceforth as an evocation of the morning after the executions, when "the chimney of the crematorium began to belch smoke" and "both sun and sky turned black."

The Celan translator and biographer John Felstiner notes that the author of "Todesfuge" once remarked that the poem arose from something he read about Jews playing dance tunes in a Nazi camp. He goes on to suggest that Celan might have seen a pamphlet dated 29 August 1944, on "The Lublin Extermination Camp" (Maidanek). "In July 1944 the Red Army took Maidanek, and what they discovered was publicized worldwide, as propaganda. This pamphlet, issued by Moscow's Foreign Languages Publishing House, appeared in various cities and languages. Written by Konstantin Siminov, it reports that tangos and fox-trots were played during camp functions, and it contains other details suggestive of *Todesfuge*."[22]

There are many reasons why Ozick chose the last two lines of Celan's poem, cited in German, as the epigraph of *The Shawl*. Not only does the poem thematize and interrogate questions of aesthetic pleasure and artistic mastery, but it also focuses on the question of address. The double apostrophe with which "Todesfuge" ends no doubt locates the poem in a complex web of cross-cultural intertexts which have been meticulously analyzed by Hana Wirth-Nesher.[23] Yet, the lines "dein goldenes Haar Margarete/ dein aschenes Haar Sulamith" (your golden hair Margarete/your ashen hair Shulamith) also, more immediately, point back to the writing done in the poem itself, to Margarete's status as the actual addressee of letters written by "a man"—possibly the camp commandant—"when dusk falls to Germany."

> Ein Mann wohnt im Haus der spielt mit den Schlangen der
>   schreibt
> der schreibt wenn es dunkelt nach Deutschland dein goldenes
>   Haar Margarete

> Dein aschenes Haar Sulamith wir schaufeln ein Grab in den Lüften
>   da liegt man nicht eng
>
> A man lives in the house he plays with the serpents he writes
> he writes when dusk falls to Germany your golden hair Margarete
> Your ashen hair Shulamith we dig a grave in the air
>   there one won't lie too cramped[24]

Here one man's ability to address his golden-haired German beloved is juxtaposed with the predicament of another subject, a "we" whose collective—or rather collected—identity has been forcibly imposed upon it. The formal symmetry linking the phrases "he writes" and "we dig," both of which are couched in the active voice, thus serves merely to underscore the actual asymmetry of their respective positions. Not only is the "we" a grammatical subject defined precisely by its lack of agency, but it is one for whom the impossibility of addressing *its* beloved, the ashen-haired Shulamith, is reflected in its inability to speak directly to the "man who writes." The vexed relationship between mastery and addressability touched on here is further developed in the following famous lines, the only two in the poem to end in a rhyme:

> der Tod ist ein Meister aus Deutschland sein Auge ist blau
> er trifft dich mit bleierner Kugel er trifft dich genau
>
> death is a master from Germany his eye is blue
> he shoots you with shot made of lead shoots you level and true

The possibility of a face-to-face encounter, of a reciprocated gaze, of an exchange of discursive positions between an "I" and a "you," all of which are suggested by the symmetry of the rhyme, is not only frustrated here but contrapuntally reframed as a fatal encounter in which the "you" is seen through the sights of a gun as nothing more than a target, an annihilated subject become death's own reflection. The sole grammatical subject in these lines, *der Tod*, "death" sees only itself as it reduces everything else to its own mirror image. Moreover, if this sovereign Subject is said to be a German *Meister*, it is not only because it brings death and totally controls its "collected subjects" or even because it plays the *maestro* or the *Meistersinger*, the master of arts who strives to produce death as an artistic *masterpiece*, but also because it has assumed the status of a *master teacher*. "Death," Shoshana Felman observes in a discussion of this passage, "has taught a lesson that can henceforth never be forgotten. If art is to survive the Holocaust—to survive death as a master—it will have to break, in art, this mastery, which insidiously pervades the whole of culture and the whole of the aesthetic project."[25]

Insofar as the master's teaching is inextricably tied up with a certain structure of address in Celan, in endeavoring to break its insidiously pervasive hold, the poem suggests, the question of address must itself be radically reopened and strategically displaced. In other words, it is not enough simply to wish to restore a more reciprocal, equal, or mutually respectful dialogical relationship between subjects, cultures, or literary traditions. Indeed, the contrapuntal movement of the poem repeatedly deconstructs the lure of such aesthetically pleasing formal symmetries. In his 1958 Bremen address Celan explicitly takes up the question of address in a passage whose further relevance to *The Shawl* will be discussed below. "A poem," he asserts,

as a manifest form of language and thus inherently dialogue, can be a message in a bottle, sent out in the—not always greatly hopeful—belief that it may somewhere and sometime wash up on land, on heartland perhaps. Poems in this sense are always underway: they are making toward something.

Toward what? Toward something standing open, occupiable, . . . toward an addressable you perhaps, toward an addressable reality.[26]

In Search of Lost Pants

Like Celan's poem, the protagonist of Ozick's novella, "Rosa," is herself something of a message in a bottle. A perpetually displaced person irremediably cut adrift from the refined and genteel world of assimilated Polish Jewry she knew as a child, driven in a state of ever-increasing disorientation from cosmopolitan Warsaw to its embattled Ghetto, and from there to an unnamed *Lager*, which, I have argued, may well be Maidanek, to Brooklyn, New York, she washes up on a Florida beach at the opening of the second part of *The Shawl*. "Rosa Lublin, a madwoman and a scavenger, gave up her store—she smashed it up herself—and moved to Miami" (13).

While it is initially unclear whether this movement of repeated displacement will have brought Ozick's protagonist any closer to "a 'you' that can perhaps be addressed" or to "an addressable reality," what is clear is that the very question of addressability imposes itself so massively and with such urgency in "Rosa" that it seems to pervade every level of the narrative. Not only does the protagonist now spend much of her time writing impossible letters to her dead daughter, but, having just moved from New York, she anxiously awaits the belated arrival of Magda's "magic shawl," which her niece, Stella, had promised to send her. In the meantime—and obviously in lieu of the expected delivery—she receives first a "university letter" from a certain Dr. Tree with "five, six postmarks on the envelope. Rosa imagined its pilgrimage" (35), and then a package she mistakenly identifies as the one Stella was to have put in the mail, which instead contains a book on "Repressed Animation," also sent by Tree. While these postal exchanges literalize the question of address and thereby bring it into sharper focus, they also significantly complicate the question both by introducing various modes of in- and misdirection and by reintroducing through the motif of "delivery" all the issues of belated parturition discussed earlier. As a medium of telecommunication, the mail system is also related in the second part of *The Shawl* to the telephone used by Rosa not just to speak with her niece in New York but to conjure the dead. It is telling in this regard that one such conversation with Stella is suddenly interrupted when Magda is said to "spring to life" at the very instant the phrase "long *dis*tance" (64) is pronounced. To these more explicit—and explicitly *directed*—forms of address employed in the text should be added a much less certain movement of stuttering, whose tentative yet insistent cadences are reminiscent of those heard in Celan's own speech about the "other heading" of his messages in a bottle. I cite his Bremen speech again, this time in German, in order to draw attention to those rhythms: "Gedichte sind . . . unterwegs; sie halten sich auf etwas zu. . . . Auf etwas Offenstehendes, . . . auf ein ansprechbares Du . . . , auf eine ansprechbare Wirklichkeit."

While Celan's repetition of the term *auf,* translated above as "toward," no doubt suggests the uncertain and erratic movement of his poems, their ever-renewed struggle to find a heading, to make their way "toward something standing open," it also implies (particularly when one takes into account the juxtaposition of *auf* and *zu*) that these poems endeavor to make the very openings they are said to be making toward, that in addition to being bottled up messages they are also and above all *performative acts*. In this sense the act of stuttering should itself be viewed not merely as a movement in place, but instead as the making of another place, as the echoing return of a self-difference within the "same" place, a movement of *displacement* performed in Celan's own speech in the silent return of *auf* (open) within *auf* (toward).

In Celan this stuttering manifests itself in the self-altering repetition of a single word. In the second part of *The Shawl* it may be heard, more minimally, in the insistence of a perseverating *p* sound related both thematically and metonymically to the protagonist's search at one point for a pair of lost underpants, a search which is accompanied by—and painfully evocative of—the sound of a certain "panting." In view of the increasingly hallucinatory quality of this search and the nightmarish landscape through which it proceeds, it should be noted that the verb *to pant*, according to the *Oxford English Dictionary*, derives, via the Old French *pantoisier*, from the Vulgar Latin *phantasiare*, meaning "to be oppressed with nightmare, to gasp or pant with nightmare," from *phantasia*, "phantasy, nightmare." In current usage *to pant* means: "1. To breathe hard or spasmodically, as when out of breath; to draw quick labored breaths, as from exertion or agitation; to gasp for breath. 2. To gasp (for air, water, etc.); hence figuratively to long or wish with breathless eagerness; to gasp with desire; to yearn. 3. To throb or heave violently or rapidly; to palpitate, pulsate, beat. . . . 5. To utter gaspingly; to gasp out." Bringing these various senses of the term into play in the second part of *The Shawl*, Ozick gives the verb and the acoustically related nouns *pants* and *underpants* tremendous resonance.

In "Rosa" the protagonist's search for the panties she suspects her new acquaintance Simon Persky of having taken begins in a local laundromat five blocks from her hotel. "In the laundromat she sat on a cracked wooden bench and watched the round porthole of the washing machine. Inside, the surf of detergent bubbles frothed and slapped her underwear against the pane" (17). The sense of violence hinted at in this spectacle of underpants being beaten against the glass is reinforced not only by the pun on "pane" but, more generally, by the ties connecting this scene to two others around which it itself seems to revolve. While already anticipating a later moment set literally at the edge of the surf in which Rosa's pursuit of her missing underwear will gradually dissolve into an hallucinatory reenactment of her rape, the scene also echoes a description at the end of "The Shawl" of Magda "swimming through the air" before being "splashed against the fence" (9–10). Rosa's view of underpants being churned in the machine as though in the wash and backwash of the surf thus becomes a nightmarish vision through which the two related traumas of the first part are brought together again in the second.

While waiting for this infernal machine to finish, Rosa first notices Persky, who had been sitting cross-legged on the bench beside her reading a Yiddish newspaper. He now strikes up a conversation with her, in the course of which it is revealed that both are originally from the same place— even though, as the banker's daughter informs the retired button salesman, "My Warsaw isn't your Warsaw" (19). After helping her fold her laundry, Persky invites his new acquaintance to have tea with him in a local cafeteria, Kollins Kosher Kitchen. At a certain point during the meal Persky sticks his finger in his mouth in order to remove what is described as "an obstruction from under his lower plate" (26). While dislodging an eggplant seed caught under his denture, he notices something white on the floor near Rosa's laundry cart: ". . . a white cloth. Handkerchief. He picked it up and stuffed it in his pants pocket" (26). When Rosa returns to her hotel room, she unloads her laundry only to find that she is missing one pair of underwear.

> Degrading. Lost bloomers—dropped God knows where. . . . Again Rosa counted. A fact, one pair of pants lost. An old woman who couldn't even hang on to her own underwear. . . . Then it came to her that Persky had her underpants in his pocket.
>
> Oh, degrading. The shame. Pain in the loins. Burning. Bending in the cafeteria to pick up her pants, all the while tinkering with his teeth. Why didn't he give them back? He was embarrassed. He had thought a handkerchief. How can a man hand a woman, a stranger, a piece of her own underwear? He could have shoved it right back into the cart, how would that look? A sensitive man, he wanted to spare her. When he came home with her underpants, what then? What could a man, half a widower, do with a pair of female bloomers? Nylon-plus-cotton, the long-thighed kind. Maybe he had filched them on purpose, a sex maniac, a wife among the insane, his parts starved. (33–34)

A short time later, after spending the afternoon immersed in disjointed flashbacks of "darkened cities, tombstones, colorless garlands, a black fire in a gray field, *brutes forcing the innocent, women with their mouths stretched and their arms wild, her mother's voice calling*" (emphasis added), Rosa convinces herself that "whoever put her underpants in his pocket was a criminal capable of every base act" (45). Toward sundown she decides to set off in search of her lost undergarment. "To retrieve, to re-prieve" (45) is now her own alliterative motto.

As in the first part of the text, where Magda's shawl functions as a kind of surrogate for the child it had previously covered and concealed, here the "stolen" underpants come increasingly to stand in for that part of Rosa which had been taken from her when Magda was conceived. It is in this way that her search for the underpants gradually dissolves into an uncon-scious restaging of her violation. Indeed, as the sun goes down over Miami, the house lights of the present and of the world of consciousness seem to dim, and the narrow strip of hotels and beaches along which Rosa walks slowly appears to shade into a kind of dreamscape. As this theater of the un-conscious fades in, the nouns *pants* and *underpants* start to sound more and more like the verb *to pant*, used a number of times in the preceding pages to describe Rosa's own actions. In order to appreciate the full resonance of this acoustic shift it is necessary to examine not only the various contexts in which the verb first appears but, moreover, the way it gradually drops out and is itself replaced by other terms, as well as by a more diffuse perseverat-ing *p* sound, as the activities, rhythms, and scenarios associated with a cer-tain panting come increasingly to dominate and pervade the text.[27]

The verb is first used in a context in which the protagonist's heavy breathing is linked by a series of mediations to the area of her crotch. While waiting for Persky to bring a platter of food to the table, Rosa "sat and panted. . . . The air-conditioning was on too high; she felt the cooling sweat licking from around her neck down, down her spine into the crevice of her bottom. She was afraid to shift. . . . If she moved even a little, an odor would fly up: urine, salt, old woman's fatigue. She left off panting and shiv-ered" (24). In addition to drawing attention to the sense of shame now at-tached to her lower parts as well as to an internalized imperative to remain still (both of which are implicitly related to her rape), the passage evokes Rosa's visceral—and nearly eviscerating—response to the related trauma of her daughter's murder by tracing the movement of the "wolf's screech" in reverse. In place of this screech, described earlier as "ascending . . . through the ladder of her skeleton" (10), it is now a trail of sweat that seems to leave Rosa suspended in time and frozen in place as it trickles down from her neck along her spine and into the crevice of her bottom. Little wonder then that she leaves off "panting" at this point and starts to shiver.

The panting, however, soon returns as Rosa and Persky leave the cafeteria and head toward her hotel. "She toiled away from him," the narrator observes, gradually shifting into Rosa's voice. "The handle of the cart was a burning rod. A hat, I ought to have worn a hat! The pins in her bun scalded her scalp. She panted like a dog in the sun" (28). Not only does the simile foreshadow a later moment in which this "dog in the sun" will be brought into contact with other animals "in heat," but, more immediately, it anticipates the overly familiar form of address used by the hotel receptionist to greet Rosa upon her return: "'You a lucky dog, Lublin,' the Cuban girl said, and tossed an object into the pile of wash" (30). The "object," Rosa assumes, is the long-awaited package containing the shawl Stella had promised to send her. Clutching it "tight against her bosom," she goes directly to her room where the panting starts again. "She breathed noisily, almost a gasp, almost a squeal, left the laundry askew in the tiny parody of a vestibule, and carried the box and the two letters to the bed. It was still unmade, fish-smelling, the covers knotted together like an umbilical cord. . . . She turned the box round and round—a rectangular box. Madga's shawl! Madga's swaddling cloth. Magda's shroud" (30–31).

Like the little package arriving in the mail, a delivery which seemed destined to remain incomplete so long as it was not supplemented by another related act of parturition, by the other "delivery" it presumably should have been in the first place, the second attempt to "bring it to term," though accompanied here by the sole mention of an umbilical cord in the text, is itself quickly aborted. Indeed, far from being associated with a moment of birth, the mention of the cord instead seems to mark a certain knotting of life and death lines, as though the child's belated birth were already—or rather once again—preempted by her premature death, as though in returning from the (un)dead she were fated to be delivered repeatedly without ever quite coming to life as such. It also seems that Rosa's failure to bear witness to her death was destined to return here as a failure to actually bring her (back) to life, as though the one were condemned to return as the other: "Magda's swaddling cloth" *as* "Magda's shroud." If Rosa decides at this point to postpone opening the package, it is because she knows on some level that the only way to prevent Magda's being born dead again is to defer her imminent arrival.

In the interim, she goes off in search of her lost underwear. Had Rosa opened the package when it first arrived, she would have found in place of the expected shawl an unsolicited tome bearing the uncannily appropriate title *Repressed Animation: A Theory of the Biological Ground of Survival.* The point of these numerous substitutions is to suggest that the shawl will already have been a text—not the one received from Dr. Tree, in which the phenomenon of psychic numbing or "nonattachment" observed among camp survivors is perversely transfigured into a Buddhist position of "consummated indifference" (38), but a text inscribed on Rosa's own estranged body as the indecipherable enigma of her own survival. As such, it is a text that does not wait to be opened like a package or a book to begin reading its addressee, to begin inscribing her in its own wanderings toward another possible "you," toward "an addressable reality" which cannot possibly be known in advance. In order to follow this text making its way blindly, erratically, and unconsciously "toward something standing open," it is necessary to begin by tracing Rosa's own movements while in possession of this undeliverable "dead letter."

Such movements are already under way long before Rosa ever sets out to recover her lost underpants. Yet, they appear to take a decisive turn, something seems to open, in the course of her search. That opening is not by chance related to the resurfacing of the figure of an open mouth, a figure which had played such a crucial role earlier in the text and which returns at this point only to open in a very different way.

If someone wanted to hide—to hide, not destroy—a pair of underpants, where would he put them? Under the sand. Rolled up and buried. She thought what a weight of sand would feel like in the crotch of her pants, wet heavy sand, still hot from the day. In her room it was hot, hot all night. No air. In Florida there was no air, only this syrup seeping into the esophagus. Rosa walked; she saw everything, but as if out of invention, out of imagination; she was unconnected to anything. She came to a gate; a mottled beach spread behind it. It belonged to one of the big hotels. The latch opened. At the edge of the waves you could look back and see black crenellated forms stretching all along the shore. In the dark, in silhouette, the towered hotel roofs held up their merciless teeth. Impossible that any architect pleasurably dreamed these teeth. The sand was only now beginning to cool. Across the water the sky breathed a starless black; behind her, where the hotels bit down on the city, a dusty glow of brownish red lowered. Mud clouds. The sand was littered with bodies. Photograph of Pompeii: prone in the volcanic ash. Her pants were under the sand; or else packed hard with sand, like a piece of torso, a broken statue, the human groin detached, the whole soul gone, only the loins left for kicking by strangers. (47–48)

At the edge of the waves Rosa now finds herself doubly marginalized, closed out, on the one side, by the towered hotel roofs' black "merciless teeth" biting down on the city and, on the other, by the forbiddingly open expanse of the sea across which the sky is said to breathe a starless black. Between these clenched teeth and the gaping void they mirror, in an infinite reflection of black on black, nothing is heard but the resounding of a certain panting. No longer coming from the mouth of a single, identifiable individual or suggested by the use of a specific verb, this panting is now associated with a more diffuse and pervasively insistent *p* sound: "a pair of underpants, where would he put them?" "Photographs of Pompeii: prone in the volcanic ash. Her pants . . . under the sand . . . packed hard with sand, like a piece of torso" (48). Thematically linked to Rosa's blind and groping search for a piece of her shattered self, the sound's own painfully probing rhythms are ones to which the reader has become gradually attuned through the repetition of phrases such as the following: "Persky had her underpants in his pocket. . . . Pain in the loins. Burning. Bending in the cafeteria to pick up her pants . . . " (35). "The pants were not necessarily in Persky's pocket . . . he had come down for an afternoon paper, her pants in his pocket . . . " (46).

The sound of panting is also very much a part of the sexually charged atmosphere of the beach onto which Rosa has strayed. Indeed, the bodies with which the sand is said to be "littered" are those of naked gay couples she nearly steps on, "double mounds in the sand" (48), whom she later taps with her shoes in order to ask for directions out. Finding herself thus stranded on the beach surrounded by indistinct panting noises which seem to come from everywhere and nowhere at once, from the present as well as the past, Rosa herself begins to pant, "to be oppressed with nightmare, to gasp . . . with oppression," as the nightmarish scene of her rape now returns to take her back to the place she never left. Particularly in a context in which pants "packed hard" with sand are compared to a "piece of torso," to "a broken statue, the human groin detached, only the loins left for kicking by strangers," the persistent *p-p-p* seems to conjure disjointed images of a hounded woman gasping for breath, of Rosa being mounted like a dog, pummeled on the inside, and smothered by the hot breath of a pack of strangers: " . . . hot, hot all night. No air. There was no air."[28]

In addition to being haunted by the visual and acoustic images associated with Rosa's being "forced . . . and more than once" (43), the scene set "at the edge of the waves" also in effect returns her to the "margin of the arena" where she was left at the end of "The Shawl," forced in this instance to look on in silence as her daughter was murdered. The sense of immobilization associated with both of these earlier moments now returns in the scene on the beach as a feeling of entrapment. "When she came back to the gate, the latch would not budge. A cunning design, it trapped the trespasser. She gazed up, and thought of climbing; but there was barbed wire on top" (48). As though standing still again at the "margin of the arena," Rosa sees in the gate looming before her the electrified fence into which Magda was thrown and hears in the noise resounding in her ears its electric voices. Only now, instead of the cries of "maamaa, maaamaaa" (9) that those voices had once "all hummed together," she seems to hear the "paapaa, paaapaaa" of Magda's anonymous fathers all panting together. More generally, it might be said that to be suspended in this way on the shore's sandy margin is to find oneself exposed once again to the violence of more than one traumatic experience, to the *repeated violation* of experiences belatedly breaking into and resonating through one another, to the violent shattering of an undelimitable traumatic scene which from the very first will have been *more and less than one.*

Just as in "The Shawl" the cry of "Maaa—" spilling from Magda's mouth like "a long viscous rope of clamor" served to mark a threefold connection—the tenuous attachment of mother and daughter in the process of separating; the conjunction of the lips above and those below at the moment of parting; and the sounding together of an infant's first cry with its last—in "Rosa" the verbal bridge of the perseverating *p* sound associated with Persky's dental work and the hotel roofs' "merciless teeth" joins the panting above to the underpants below in order to reinforce the link between Rosa's estranged lower parts and that which goes on, as it were, *sub rosa,* under the seal of silence, drowned out by another mouth, the deafening refrain of "Rosamunde." What thus returns as one panting refrain echoing through another, as the reverberation of pants within pants, are the remains of a traumatic violation heard through the deafening sound of its violent muting.

The stammering repetition of *p-p-p* in "The Shawl" thus opens another space, a different kind of pocket in the pants. Making toward "something standing open . . . ," it nevertheless remains—like the protagonist closed in on the water's edge—doubly marginalized, caught at the limit between speech and silence as though condemned to hover between two equally impossible alternatives. It is as though the moments of indecision repeatedly marked in the first part of the text by the rhythms of "if she . . . if she . . . ," rhythms, we recall, which themselves seemed to rise like waves of nausea toward the opening of the mouth, were made to return in the second part compacted into the *p* sound perseverating at the lips' edge. This stuttering thus has the effect of refocusing attention not just on the opening of the mouth, but, more specifically, on the very gesture of lips perpetually caught in the act of parting, on what remains to be said beyond the capacity of any mother tongue to speak or to silence it. It also suggests a model for the way in which the disjointed fragments of survivor testimony are condemned to remain, as it were, at the mouth of the ear—barely within earshot, incessantly in search of a hearing, incapable of being heard as such. Like the panting packed into and repeatedly impacting upon the closed pocket of the mouth, these infernal fragments ascending to the portals of the ear appear to beat away at the tympanum like shades at "black Dis's" door in Virgil's *Aeneid*, discussed below, like Celanian messages in a bottle nearing the shoreline of the heart caught in the wash and backwash of the surf. Ozick makes one hear in the panting at the edge of the waves, in the very noise of the pounding surf, the return of what Rosa cannot bear to hear interfused with her own desperate yearning to be heard.[29] "Do I still have ears? Am I all ear," she might ask with Nietzsche, "and nothing else?"

Here I stand in the midst of the surging breakers, whose white flames fork up to my feet;—from all sides there is howling, threatening, crying and screaming at me, while in the lowest depths the old earth shaker sings his aria hollow like a roaring bull; he beats such an earth shaker's measure thereto, that even the hearts of these weathered rock-monsters tremble at the sound.[30]

"Her Pants in His Pants"

Having traced the circular path by which Rosa is led back to the margin of the death camp, the place she will never have left, it is now necessary to follow the way this same path takes her back to something standing open, back to a pocket of difference at the heart of the same, to Persky, the man with "pants in his pockets," the thief whom she had in a sense been panting after all along in the guise of searching for a pair of missing underwear. Like the panties which, as it turns out, had been there the whole time, Rosa finds Persky waiting to greet her in the lobby of her hotel when she returns exhausted from her ordeal on the beach.

> "Lublin, Rosa! Where you been the whole night? I'm sitting hours."
> "I didn't tell you where I stay," Rosa accused.
> "I looked in the telephone book."
> "My phone's disconnected . . ."
> "All right. You want the truth? This morning I followed you, that's all. A simple walk from my place. I sneaked in the streets behind you. I found out where you stay, here I am." (53–54)

The circularity of the situation is obvious. Not only is the pursuer now the pursued, but Rosa is courted by the very man alleged to have "put her underpants in his pocket," a suitor initially considered to be "a criminal capable of every base act" (45). Coming full circle, Rosa thus returns to find what had in effect "been there" all along—not just the sought-after-suitor, the man with pants in his pockets and pockets in his pants, but Persky as the very figure of the vicious circle's own uncanny opening toward another, more elliptical heading. It is no doubt telling that upon seeing Persky, Rosa is reminded of the little circles he once sold for a living. "She considered Persky's life: how trivial it must always have been: buttons, himself no more significant than a button. It was plain he took her to be another button like himself, battered now and out of fashion, rolled into Florida" (55). Holding a mirror up to Rosa's own circular destiny, the pesky Persky appears not only as a threatening reflection, but already as the returning double of another, the anglicized doppelgänger of "Shimon Peres, the Israeli politician" who, Persky claims, is actually his "third cousin" (22). In view of this all-too-literal "family resemblance" (Peres, like Persky, emigrated from Poland where his name was originally Paretsky), and particularly in a context in which a certain panting is so patently associated with the initial sound of Persky's name, it should be noted that *peh* in the Israeli politician's adopted Hebrew tongue means *mouth*. Like the protagonist who now imagines "her pants in his pants" (54), this Hebrew mouth itself seems to pant through another, to signal through its own participation in this stammering colloquy without origin or end a different opening of the mouth and of the mother tongue, an opening of the static movement of circular return toward an unnameable Other returning to the same place as "you," an *impersonal* Other who can only be addressed indirectly or "in care of" a more easily identifiable "you." It is this Other (whose temporal structure and redemptive possibilities are explored with great subtlety in *The Messiah of Stockholm*) whom Rosa inadvertently prepares to address. It is this stranger whom she unexpectedly receives, in readying herself for the perpetually deferred arrival of Magda. "Her room was miraculously ready: tidy, clarified. It was sorted out: you could see where the bed ended and the table commenced. Sometimes it was all one jumble, a highway of confusion. Destiny had clarified her room just in time for a visitor" (55).

The preparations Rosa makes in anticipation of her daughter's deferred arrival as the shawl no doubt enable her to receive Persky in her or its place. Yet the play of substitutions in which this unexpected visitor is himself enmeshed suggest that his arrival is in its turn the deferral of another's. As though in preparation for the coming of this Other, Persky is now made to occupy the room initially cleared for the long-awaited daughter as a stand-in for the expectant mother as well, as a go-between acting on *her* behalf to do what she herself, after endless preparations, is finally unprepared to carry out. "What her own hands longed to do she was yielding to a stranger, a man with pockets" (59). In having Persky open the box which had been sitting there the whole time, and which, as it turns out, does not contain the shawl but the book on "repressed animation" sent by Dr. Tree, Rosa leaves it up to "a stranger" to discover for her what she herself on some level already knew.

This act of delegation also marks the beginning of a process of initiation, a ritual designed to test whether Persky, "himself no more significant than a button," is capable of bearing witness to the traumatized survivor, of entering Rosa's pantingly phantasmatic underworld in which something as insignificant as the unpacking of a small box can be experienced as a scene of labor and delivery. While Persky fails this initial test ("I can see I'm involved in a mistake . . . " [61]) and the attempt to "deliver" Magda once again miscarries, the scene nevertheless succeeds in clarifying his new role as a second-degree witness.[31] Henceforth he will be asked to serve not only as a kind of midwife but, moreover, as one whose task it is to assist a survivor condemned to circle incessantly around the central fatality of the "during" (58) in bringing *something unexpected* to life. Himself an unannounced visitor in the night, whose coming will still somehow have been "miraculously" anticipated in the guise of preparing for another's arrival, Persky seems to stand in here for an uncertain opening, for an unconscious (which is not to say wholly "unprepared") opening toward the Other.[32]

The very tentativeness of this opening is suggested by its mercurial appearance in the text, by the way it appears only to disappear, as though its first panting gasp were already its last. Indeed, no sooner does Rosa perceive that the anticipated "delivery" of Magda's shawl has been postponed yet again by the appearance of another in its place than she tears the new arrival out of Persky's hands and "hurl[s] it at the ceiling" (61). Her treatment of the unwanted "book" is no doubt meant to echo the camp guard's handling of her own lost child, a suggestion reinforced by the return of Magda's fall "from flight" after being "splashed against the fence" at the end of "The Shawl" in the description of the book's descent from the ceiling. "It slammed down into Persky's half-filled teacup. Shards and droplets flew" (61).

Although the night's false labors produce no new opening as such, they do signal a tentative movement in that direction. Thus, Rosa awakens the following morning to restart the failed initiative begun in a dreamlike state the night before. After washing her face and finding her missing underwear "curled inside a towel" (61), she goes downstairs to the desk to discuss the possibility of having her phone reconnected. As might be expected, this potential opening toward the Other takes her once again in two directions at once: back toward Magda and the closed circles of infernal repetition in which she had heretofore been condemned to orbit, and "toward something standing open, toward an addressable you." (It should be recalled that it is in a telephone book that Persky claims to have found Rosa's address.)

While making arrangements to have her phone service restored, Rosa is handed a package. "She lifted the lid of the box and looked down at the shawl; she was indifferent. . . . The colorless cloth lay like an old bandage; a discarded sling. For some reason it did not instantly restore Magda, as usually happened, a vivid thwack of restoration like an electric jolt. She was willing to wait for the sensation to surge up whenever it would" (62). The climactic arrival toward which "Rosa" will have been building from the first thus turns out to be an anticlimax. Yet, once again, this failure signals a different kind of opening. It is therefore no accident that the very nonsimultaneity of the two expected "deliveries" opens a space for the supplement of a telephone, which will also in its own way have "been there" the whole time lying dormant "under the bed" (62). Following an estab-lished pattern of doubling and deferral, the reconnected phone is now in its turn made to perform two functions at once. Serving, on the one hand, as a surrogate means of bringing Magda (back) to life, it also, on the other hand, provides a way of opening through Magda's own surrogacy the dif-ference of another place.

At the Mouth of the Ear

As though in accordance with the circularly repetitive logic of pant-ing we have been tracing, in which each gasp is at once a first *and* a last, Rosa's initial outgoing call turns out in retrospect to have been the only one she ever makes in the story. It is a call placed to Stella, whom she asks whether she should, as she puts it, "come back" (63) to New York. As is so often the case in *The Shawl*, this question ostensibly addressed to Rosa's niece is also one posed *through* her to an unaddressable other. For Stella is also in a sense a stand-in for Rosa's unapproachable tormentors. She is the one who not only allows the forbidden word *Aryan* to pass her lips, but the person through whose mouth the "Aryan" continues to speak. It is thus through Stella that Rosa obliquely asks those who had driven her away whether she can now finally "come back"—not just to New York but, via that way station, to her beloved Warsaw.

Surprised by the question, all Stella can think about is the cost of communicating in this new way. She therefore asks in return, "Is it an emergency? We could discuss this by mail. . . . I'm not a millionaire. What's the point of this call?" While Rosa goes right on speaking, "right over Stella's admonitions" (64), seemingly oblivious to everything her niece has to say, the point soon becomes clear. Indeed, what begins as a simple conversation with a single interlocutor gradually turns into a kind of séance with the dead, as another kind of connection is made through a dif-ferent kind of "medium" when Stella unwittingly puts the phone network itself on the line. "Rosa," she cries in exasperation, "this is long *dis*tance." "On that very phrase, 'long *dis*tance,' Magda sprang to life. Rosa took the shawl and put it over the knob of the receiver: it was like a little doll's head then. She kissed it, right over Stella's admonitions. 'Good-bye,' she told Stella, and didn't care what it had cost" (64).

Elaine Kauvar astutely connects the italicized portion of the phrase "long *dis*tance" to the "god of the lower world, Dis," an association supported by the explicit mention of Virgil in a letter Rosa writes to Magda shortly after hanging up the phone.[33] "My father," she notes, "knew the whole first half of the *Aeneid* by heart" (69). This reference to the father's knowledge functions in turn as a knowing allusion to the famous episode at the end of the *Aeneid*'s first half in which the hero is allowed to pass through the "door of gloomy Dis" in order to take counsel with the shade of his own dead father, Anchises. While Kauvar is right to recognize the resemblances Ozick establishes between Rosa and Aeneas, it is also necessary to remark a significant difference which emerges in her own reworking of the locus classicus of the hero's descent.[34] Whereas Aeneas, armed with the golden bough, is able "to pass beneath earth's hidden places" (6.140),[35] Rosa, holding just a phone in her hand, proceeds only as far as Dis's door. It is for this reason that Magda springs to life on the "very phrase, 'long *dis*tance'" (64). In clutching the receiver to her mouth and ear, Rosa summons her daughter back to this threshold of the underworld neither of them will ever have left, back to the "margin" that *is* their hell rather than its antiquated perimeter. Within the context of this scene, the margin is thus defined precisely as the place where the mouth *of* the ear meets the earphone and where a certain failure to hear what had "been there" all along now becomes painfully apparent. In other words, it is at this juncture that the call for a hearing is itself made strangely audible through the supplement of a telephonic hearing aid, through the introduction of a prosthetic device which in a sense adds nothing new to the deadlocked situation but a margin of *self-distance*.

It is this distension of a marginal space that now emerges in the text as a pocket of difference, a circuitous opening within the structure of the ear. Tellingly, the same letter in which Rosa recalls her father's knowledge of the *Aeneid* makes a point of mentioning a trip he took to Crete as an adolescent. The juxtaposition of these two classical references in the letter and, more generally, in a story in which Rosa fantasizes that her daughter will have become "a professor of Greek philosophy at Columbia University" (39), suggests not only a connection between Dis's door and the circuitous byways of the Cretan labyrinth, but, more dynamically, an unfolding of this single threshold in and as the manifold passageways of the Cretan maze. These supplementary folds at the labyrinthine margin of the

ear are the very space in which the unlistened-to survivor is herself condemned to wander as a kind of Minotaur. It is particularly telling in this
regard that the story of Pasiphaë's illegitimate offspring appears in the
Aeneid in an ekphrasis of the double doors of a temple built by Daedalas,
designer of the Minoan labyrinth. Within the architecture of the text itself
this temple stands at the very threshold of the sixth book (6.14–33)—that
is, as a doorway to the doorway through which Aeneus will soon descend
into the underworld (6.331–901).

Unlike the classical Minotaur described by Virgil as Pasiphaë's "child
of double form" concealed in "the puzzle of the house of Minos/The maze
none could untangle" (6.25–27; trans. modified), Ozick's much more monstrously mongrel protagonist—part Aeneus, part Pasiphaë, part Minotaur,
part Cecrops's children—*is hidden out in the open, doomed to grope her way,
blind and unseen, along invisible walls of silence.* While the labyrinthine passageways in which Rosa is enfolded in *The Shawl* may thus be said to form
an acoustic counterpart to the visually disorienting enclosure designed by
Daedalus, they also seem to recreate the architecture of the store she had
in New York, which she smashed up because, as she tells Persky, "whoever
came, they were like deaf people. Whatever you explained to them, they
didn't understand" (27). Rosa returns to this other version of the labyrinth
at the beginning of the aforementioned letter. "When I had my store I
used to 'meet the public,' and I wanted to tell everybody—not only our
story, but other stories as well. Nobody knew anything" (66).[36]

It is through these various reworkings of the classical locus of the
labyrinth, through the convoluted pathways of this mediating figure, that
the call initially made from Florida to New York and beyond is transferred
to the mouth of the ear. Relocated here, the telephone's "long *dis*tance" now
serves as a measure of the ear's own dis-stance from itself, an indication of
the distant vicinity in which stored-up stories in search of a hearing are, like
the storyteller herself, condemned to *stand apart*. The ear's status as a liminal
space of internal exile is further underscored by Magda's own return to it at
this point as the Minotaur she herself will have been. Whereas Kauvar in-
terprets the "two barrettes in the shape of cornets" (65) she wears in her hair
as emblems of Persephone's attribute, the cornucopia,[37] I would argue they
should be viewed instead as the horns of a bull, reminders of her fathers'
rather than her mother's "unspeakable lust [*Veneris monumenta nefandae*]"
(6.26). They should also be viewed, less literally, as the *horns of a dilemma*,

the sign of Rosa's own unacknowledged ambivalence toward her daughter. "She was always a little suspicious of Magda, because of the other strain, whatever it was, that ran through her. Rosa herself was not truly suspicious, but Stella was, and that induced perplexity in Rosa. The other strain was ghostly, even dangerous. It was as if the peril hummed out from the filaments of Magda's hair, those narrow bright wires" (65–66).

Rosa's maternal ambivalence is, as it turns out, but one side of the dilemma. The other surfaces through the mention of another set of horns in the letter and suggests the protagonist's equally ambivalent attitude toward her own Jewishness. Describing her confinement in the Warsaw Ghetto, itself another labyrinthine space of internal exile, Rosa writes, "We had to be billeted . . . with these old Jew peasants . . . *phylacteries on their foreheads sticking up so stupidly, like unicorn horns*" (67; emphasis added). Like the "other strain" running through Magda, these "ghetto Jews," who are linked to her through the mediating figure of the horn and who are described here as being "worn out from their rituals and superstitions" (67), embody for Rosa the "other strain" of Jewishness running through her.

The coupling of the two cornet-shaped barrettes with the "unicorn horns" of the phylacteries thus provides a figure for a dilemma which is itself ambivalently divided on each of its two sides. Beyond the immediate psychological implications of this pairing, the figure suggests a way of understanding the movement of the narrative itself, which, structured like a labyrinth, proceeds only by doubling and dividing itself, by moving along twin forking paths.[38] If figures such as the "if she" and the "margin of the arena" of the first part and the circular motifs of the second underscore the double binds and cycles of repetition in which Rosa had heretofore been caught, the double and divided sense of ambivalence which emerges here suggests a slight but decisive shift in the play of forces. Indeed, what begins to emerge under the sign of ambivalence is a different kind of opening toward the Other, an opening that does not occur punctually at any particular place or time, but is effected instead through a more general movement of dislocation.[39]

Emblematic of this movement is Magda's return as a different kind of Minotaur. Unlike the "twiformed offspring [*prolesque biformis*]" (6.25) described in the *Aeneid*, she comes back in *The Shawl* as an echo of that unspeakable and unsilenceable "strain" produced through the *poetic coupling* of two addresses: "dein goldenes Haar Margarete/dein aschenes Haar

Sulamith [your golden hair Margarete/your ashen hair Shulamith],” a strain of *dissonance* which is made to sound and resound from threshold to threshold, from the end of “Todesfuge” to the opening of *The Shawl* and beyond to the labyrinthine mouth of the ear. It is significant in this regard that Magda’s return at this point interrupts a call for a return to the same address. “Should I come back?” Rosa asks her niece shortly before Magda springs to life. “Rosa,” Stella replies, “if you want to come back, come back” (64).

While the pointed repetition of the verb *to come back* clearly prefigures Magda’s own disruptive return as a revenant, it also reminds us that what appears to come back under the proper name “Magda” is also and perhaps above all *a very different way* of returning as the spectral interruption of a more traditional, restricted economy of circular restitution.[40] What “comes back” “as Magda” is thus neither the Christ child Rosa had expected (“My purity, my snowqueen” [42], as she calls her in the letter cited earlier in which she herself is clearly identified with the Virgin Mother), nor a mode of return which could be described as a version of the Second Coming. What comes back in place of Rosa’s lost child, what returns in the guise of her return, is a revenant haunted by the ghost of other literary and historical monstrosities, the specter of “other stories” (66) told through “our story” (66) that is retold through them. What “comes back” here as strains of the other is also to be read as the haunting *revenance* of “our story’s” own dis-stance from and repeated interruption of itself, as a return from within a story Rosa does not herself fully possess of other scenes of repetition, of things already heard, almost heard, heard as if they were nothing, at the “edge of the waves” and the “margin of the arena.” In short, what “comes back” “as Magda” is an incessant call for an impossible hearing, the long-*dis*tance call of a *Shema* which nevertheless appears to ring differently each time it circles back to the “place” from which its solicitations will have sounded and resounded from the very first, each time it comes back to the distant proximity, the unfathomable intimacy of the labyrinth of the ear.

“How I Became Like the
Woman with the Lettuce”

This opening through Magda’s own surrogacy toward another place, toward a self-altering dislocation of the same place, seems in the end to take “Lublin, Rosa” back to the place from which she started, to Warsaw as the locus of a seemingly unbridgeable difference. "My Warsaw is not your Warsaw," she repeatedly reminds Persky. Yet, the Warsaw to which she now returns (after her call to "Stella") in her last letter to Magda is itself a pocket of otherness which will have opened within the city, a place of internal exile where disassimilated Jews like herself were thrown in together with that "other strain" of Jews who had heretofore resisted assimilation. "Can you imagine a family like us . . . who had lived in a tall house with four floors and a glorious attic . . . —imagine confining *us* with teeming Mockowiczes and Rabinowiczes and Perskys and Finkelsteins, with all their bad-smelling grandfathers and their hordes of feeble children!" (66).

Here Rosa's earlier contention that her Warsaw is not Persky's is given a bitterly ironic twist. For even after being confined with "teeming Mockowiczes and Rabinowiczes and Perskys," her Warsaw is still not his. Indeed, rather than fostering feelings of solidarity with this "other strain" of Jews, her confinement with them serves only to heighten her own sense of abasement. These feelings are no doubt exacerbated by the present situation in which she finds herself once again thrown in together with a different class of Jews, those retirees from the Northeast she encounters in the senior citizens ghetto of Miami Beach.[41] Here, however, the loss of social standing which had been such an obvious source of humiliation for her in the Warsaw Ghetto becomes a screen through which she experiences the related degradation of being a Holocaust survivor whose testimony goes essentially unheard. Persky serves as a stand-in both for the "other strain" of Jews in the Warsaw Ghetto toward whom Rosa's anger is still misdirected ("we were furious in every direction, but most immediately we were furious because we had to be billeted with such a class" [67]) and for those whose failure to hear her eyewitness testimony of the Holocaust effectively condemns her to remain confined in a ghetto of silence.

Rosa's memory of the Ghetto may thus be said to offer a particularly concrete image of the silenced survivor's current sense of alterity. Yet, her further description of that pocket of difference within Warsaw as a space on the inside traversed by the outside—a space, that is, in which tramcars that couldn't be rerouted around it "came right through the middle of the Ghetto" (67–68)—complicates the view one has of her place in and tenuous hold on the present. "The point is they couldn't reroute the whole tram system; so you know, they didn't. . . . What they did was build a sort of overhanging pedestrian bridge for the Jews, so they couldn't get near the tramcar to escape on it into the other part of Warsaw. The other side of the wall" (68). As Rosa recalls standing on this bridge looking down on the trams passing through, she seems once again to be straddling the horns of a dilemma, standing not just with one foot on either side but somewhere in the middle—precariously cut off both from the Jews within and the Poles without. It is from this point of double suspension that she sees the "most astounding thing" (68):

that the most ordinary streetcar, bumping along on the most ordinary trolley tracks, and carrying the most ordinary citizens going from one section of Warsaw to another, ran straight into the place of our misery. Every day, and several times a day, we had witnesses. Every day they saw us—women with shopping sacks; and once I noticed a head of lettuce sticking up out of the top of a sack—green lettuce! I thought my salivary glands would split with aching for that leafy greenness. (68)

Perhaps even more astounding than the scene recounted here are the last lines of the letter in which this account is found. There Rosa suddenly shifts back to the present (to a moment which itself hovers ambiguously between New York and Miami) in order to note how "in this place now I am like the woman who held the lettuce in the tramcar. I said all this in my store, talking to the deaf. How I became like the woman with the lettuce" (69). The space of identification opened in this passage in which the letter itself breaks off suggests that Rosa is still even now "in this place" on the Ghetto bridge standing outside herself; that this crossing from inside to inside, from outside to the outside, and in a certain sense between the inside and the outside, will have been a space of self-distance; that "the woman with the lettuce" will ultimately have been less a person than a place, a bridge suspended between the various segregated "sections" of "Lublin, Rosa's" disaggregated self.

That this woman with the head of lettuce is singled out not just as an eyewitness ("Every day . . . we had witnesses. Every day they saw us") but as one in possession of "leafy green" nourishment suggests that the act of witnessing she had been in a position to perform was—and still is—as vital to Rosa and as desired by her as actual food. It is therefore significant that she—and women like her—not only failed to bear witness to Rosa's ordeal but did so every day. Indeed, it is this quotidian violence, this daily humiliation of seeing oneself not being seen, of gradually being made *to view oneself* as invisible, as transparent as a ghost, that returns to haunt Rosa in her store in New York and again in Miami.

Like the woman with the lettuce, Rosa is herself potentially in a position to bear witness. Yet, having internalized the anonymous others' disregard for her ("no one regarded us as Poles anymore" [68]), she cannot testify alone. The point of these overdetermined identifications is thus to suggest that there will have been no witness without a witness to the witness, without the vital accompaniment of another, without someone prepared to listen with leafy fresh ears to what in a sense had "been there" the whole time, to hear in what will have been said time and again an unheard-of difference. "With salivary glands [that] would split with aching," it is ultimately Rosa's own words that she longs to taste through the ear of the other, through an act of listening which might belatedly bring something unexpected in her speech to life. In "On the Interlocutor," a text cited in Chapter 1 as an important point of reference for Celan, and as the source from which he derives the figure of the poem as a message in a bottle, Osip Mandelstam writes:

> when I speak to somebody, I do not know with whom I speak, and I do not wish to know him. There is no lyric without dialogue. Yet the only thing that pushes us into the arms of the interlocutor is the desire to be surprised by our own words, to be captivated by their novelty and unexpectedness. The logic is ineluctable. If I know to whom I speak, I know ahead of time how he will regard what I say, whatever I might say, and consequently I shall manage not to be astonished by his astonishment, to be overjoyed by his joy, or to love through his love.[42]

Rosa's return in her final letter to a Warsaw which will never have been either exactly hers or Persky's seems in the end to open another portal in the present through which the witness-to-the-witness may enter once again as if for the first time. "He's used to crazy women," Rosa tells the Cuban receptionist, "so let him come up" (70).

The Narrow Gate of the Second

It is all too easy to read *The Shawl* as a traditionally gendered narrative in which the violence directed against a woman takes the form of a rape, in which that violence is perpetuated in the form of an unwanted child the victim is made to conceive and bear, and in which a man appears in the end in the person of Simon Persky as the woman's rescuer and redeemer.[43] Yet, the narrative displaces these traditional gender roles in the place it makes for an *impersonal* Other. This Other is associated with a discourse that is never fully the speaker's own, that speaks otherwise in the self-estrangement of the speaking subject, speaking, as it were, out of the very space of dislocation and errancy which will have opened between Rosa's native Polish and her immigrant English. Indeed, in saying more and less than what the subject had "meant to say," such a discourse testifies to the unconscious binds which continue to hold Rosa in place and keep her hovering in a state of suspended animation and traumatic fixation. Yet, such a discourse which the subject does not herself mean to speak is also one that she alone cannot hear. It is therefore necessary to make a place in the act of testifying for an instance I have referred to as "a witness to the witness." It is in listening through the ear of such a second-degree witness that the speaker may begin to hear the very foreignness of "her own words." Indeed, it is precisely *in not knowing with whom* she speaks that the witness may be surprised and altered by the novelty and unexpectedness of these words.

"There is no lyric without dialogue," Mandelstam asserts. Yet, as was noted earlier, it is no longer dialogue in the sense of a reciprocal exchange of words and of illocutionary positions, of taking turns speaking and listening, but rather, as in Wolf, in the sense of discordant voices speaking with and through one another, at the same time. It is dialogue in which interruption is no longer the exception but the rule—and indeed the chance—dialogue in which one speaks in the hope not merely of being recognized finally as a subject but rather of being interrupted, provoked, and overtaken "by one's own words."

It is important to stress in this respect that the figure of Simon Persky be viewed ultimately less as a man than as a placeholder. Explicitly introduced as a kind of doppelgänger, he functions primarily as a stand-in for yet another Other which can only be addressed indirectly, if at all. Arriving in place of Magda and acting in Rosa's stead to carry out tasks she herself is unable to perform, he comes in lieu of a revenant that never "comes back" as itself. There is no doubt something messianic about Persky's comings in the text. Yet, it is not just because he is "used to crazy women" that Rosa tells the receptionist in the end to "let him come up." His coming stands instead for a certain opening of the unconscious, for a new mode of receptivity, a way of making a place for that which comes in the meantime in the very cracks and between-spaces of Rosa's broken English. The messianism of Persky's coming is therefore to be understood not in terms of a return of what was once present or of the Christian redeemer's Second Coming, but rather in terms suggested by Walter Benjamin in the last of his "Theses on the Philosophy of History." "The soothsayers," he writes,

who found out from time what it had in store certainly did not experience time as either homogeneous or empty. Anyone who keeps this in mind will perhaps get an idea of how past times were experienced in remembrance—namely, in just the same way. We know that the Jews were prohibited from investigating the future. The Torah and the prayers instruct them in remembrance, however. This stripped the future of its magic, to which all those succumb who turn to the soothsayers for enlightenment. This does not imply, however, that for the Jews the future turned into homogeneous, empty time. *For every second* [Sekunde] *of time was the narrow gate through which the Messiah might enter.*[44]

Here Benjamin is playing no doubt on the etymology of the word, *Sekunde*, or "second," derived from the Latin *secare*: to cut. It is thus a question for him of what may come in the very cutting or splitting of a second, of what may come between, come in the meanwhile, as an interruption or suspension of "homogeneous, empty time." Ozick's Persky is in this sense not just the all-too-familiar figure of a man who has come once again to rescue a woman in distress who has suffered terribly at the hands of other men. He figures instead the very wandering of the witness's words, the errancy of speech sent out, like Celan's message in a bottle, "in the—not always greatly hopeful—belief that it may somewhere and sometime wash up on land, on heartland perhaps." He stands as well for the place the survivor is herself unwittingly making toward, not necessarily located outside herself, the place, namely, "of something standing open," of a wound the "you" itself may have gathered around, the place of an Other which can only be addressed in speaking through the narrow gate of the *second person* toward something or someone other than "you."

If the Other whose place Persky holds and indeed *holds open* may be said to stand for a new psychic opening in Rosa, it also in the end perhaps stands for a repositioning of her desire with respect to him, with respect, that is, to the structural place he had occupied in her pantingly phantasmatic libidinal economy. In the course of the text Persky is cast in two related roles: either he is belittled as an uncultivated déclassé, insignificant button salesman, sexually frustrated husband of a crazy woman, and embodiment of all the "teeming Mockowiczes and Rabinowiczes and . . .

Filkelsteins" (66) with whom Rosa had been lumped together in the Warsaw Ghetto, or he is feared as a lascivious predator "with pants in his pockets," as a revenant of the thieves who had raped her and stolen her life. By
the end of the text, however, Rosa begins to see *through him* someone she
had never seen before. In the mirror of this perpetually displaced stand-in,
what may be glimpsed is a remobilization of her own traumatically fixated
desires, the fragile opening of a more libidinally available and erotically
vulnerable version of herself.

    In *The Shawl* Ozick uses the uncanniness of the mirror to help us see
repetition in an entirely new light—namely, as was suggested in Chapter 1,
as a double and divided *com*pulsion, an unconscious movement impelled
to move in two very different ways at once: primarily back toward the
sameness of the past, but also "secondarily" *and along the same paths* toward
the possible opening of a different future. It is in attuning ourselves to the
stammerings, perseverations, and pantings of *The Shawl* that we may begin to view repetition no longer simply as a compulsive acting out of the
past but also as an equally unconscious way of working through it, in
Celan's words, toward "something standing open, occupiable, . . . toward
an addressable reality." To move beyond traumatic fixation in the reading
of Holocaust literature, it is thus necessary, Ozick suggests, for us to go
even further in the direction of the unconscious toward a more complex
and conflictual understanding of repetition and the vital, if heretofore un-
foreseen, possibilities pulsing within it.

6

Silent Wine

The English term *belatedness* is often employed as a translation of the German *Nachträglichkeit*, which appears in various forms and often at critical junctures in Freud's work. It is glossed in Laplanche and Pontalis's *Language of Psychoanalysis*, under the heading of "deferred action," as follows: "Term frequently used by Freud in connection with his view of psychical temporality and causality: experiences, impressions and memory traces may be revised at a later date to fit in with fresh experiences or with the attainment of a new stage of development. They may in that event be endowed not only with a new meaning but also with psychical effectiveness."[1] Attention was first drawn to the peculiar temporal structure Freud struggled to articulate in his repeated use of the German term and its related adjectival and adverbial forms by Lacan in his self-described "return to Freud." That return, Laplanche elsewhere observes, was itself curiously marked by the structure of *après coup* or belatedness Lacan was to discover there—which is to say that it was a return to something which was not exactly *there* in the first place, something which was not to be encountered in the established theoretical core of Freud's thought but rather in the unassimilated margins of his texts, not in the central concepts explicitly elaborated by him but in the unthematized "paraconceptual" apparatus implicitly at work in his writing.

While the French reading of Freud has informed my own understanding of the structure of *Nachträglichkeit* in the preceding chapters, I use "belatedness" here also as a translation of the term *Spätmündigkeit*, a translation which is no doubt problematic since the word does not exactly exist in German. The term may be extrapolated, however, from processes silently at work in the writing of Paul Celan. In his poem "Die Winzer" (The Vintagers), written in September 1953 and published in the 1955 collection *Von Schwelle zu Schwelle* (From Threshold to Threshold), Celan brings together three related processes: the work of mourning, the making of wine, and the writing of poetry. In doing so, he locates "Die Winzer" as the site of a gathering of three interrelated processes and as the locus of a poetic reflection about the place and function of poetry after Auschwitz. As the site of such a reflection, the poem repeatedly turns back on itself, turning from the gathering of specific objects—be they the fruit of the vine or "the wine of the eyes"—to the activity of gathering itself. Reflexively turning this activity back on itself, the poem gathers the three processes mentioned above into and through one another, pressing them together in such a way as to open each to the difference of the others, *compressing* them so as to redefine each through its relation to the others. It is this *verdichtende* movement of poetic gathering that brings the poem's own body together, that draws it to a close by gathering it in the end toward the opening of a certain mouth, toward what is called a "latemouth" or *Spätmund*. Celan coins this term on the model of the more familiar vinicultural term *Spätlese*, traditionally used to describe wine made from grapes gleaned later than the general harvest. In what follows I argue that the neologism *Spätmund* should be read not only as a singular poetic orifice around which the body of the poem is organized and toward which it collects itself but—following a second possible derivation of the term from the German *Spätreife*—as the abbreviated or viniculturally compressed name of a belated maturation process, of what in German might be called a process of *Spätmündigkeit*.

Such a process, I argue, is not only implicitly at work in "Die Winzer" but, as a process of belated *overripening*, is one that will have carried the text beyond its own apparent end, leaving it to ripen after the fact in Celan's "Grabschrift für François" (Epitaph for François), written in commemoration of the tragic loss of his first-born son who died shortly after birth in October 1953. At stake in this reading is not only the nonlinear temporal structure of belatedness, which has played in such a crucial role in the texts discussed in the preceding chapters and which links the poems under discussion here in uncanny ways, but also the status of a translation that involves more than the mere transmission of what was already there in the original, "more than the mere transmission of subject manner." Such translations, Walter Benjamin remarks in "The Task of the Translator," "issue not from the life but from the 'Überleben' of the original."[2] They issue, in other words, not from its life but from a certain excess or surplus, from that which will have been *über-*, from that in the original which will have been not only more life or more than *its* life but from that which exceeds the very opposition of life and death. What is at stake again in this chapter is thus the question of a certain translational *sur*-vival.[3]

I begin then with Celan's poem, "Die Winzer," cited first in German and then in John Felstiner's English translation.

DIE WINZER
   Für Nani und Klaus Demus

Sie herbsten den Wein ihrer Augen,
sie keltern alles Geweinte, auch dieses:
so will es die Nacht,
die Nacht, an die sie gelehnt sind, die Mauer,
so forderts der Stein,
der Stein, über den ihr Krückstock dahinspricht
ins Schweigen der Antwort—
ihr Krückstock, der einmal,
einmal im Herbst,
wenn das Jahr zum Tod schwillt, als Traube,
der einmal durchs Stumme hindurchspricht, hinab
in den Schacht des Erdachten.

Sie herbsten, sie keltern den Wein,
sie pressen die Zeit wie ihr Auge,
sie kellern das Sickernde ein, das Geweinte,
im Sonnengrab, das sie rüsten
mit nachtstarker Hand:
auf daß ein Mund danach dürste, später—
ein Spätmund, ähnlich dem ihren:
Blindem entgegengekrümmt und gelähmt—
ein Mund, zu dem der Trunk aus der Tiefe emporschäumt, indes
der Himmel hinabsteigt ins wächserne Meer,
um fernher als Lichtstumpf zu leuchten,
wenn endlich die Lippe sich feuchtet.

THE VINTAGERS
   For Nani and Klaus Demus

They harvest the wine of their eyes,
they crush out all of the weeping, this also:

thus willed by the night,
the night, which they're leaning against, the wall,
thus forced by the stone,
the stone, over which their crook-stick speaks into
the silence of answers—
their crook-stick, which just once,
just once in fall,
when the year swells to death, swollen grapes,
which just once will speak right through muteness, down
into the mineshaft of musings.

They harvest, they crush out the wine,
they press down on time like their eye,
they cellar the seepings, the weepings,
in a sun grave they make ready
with night-toughened hands:
so that a mouth might thirst for this, later—
a latemouth, like to their own:
bent toward blindness and lamed—
a mouth to which the draught from the depths foams upward, meantime
heaven descends into waxen seas,
and far off, as a candle-end, glistens,
at last when the lip comes to moisten.[4]

"The Vintagers" opens with a potent ambiguity compressed in the phrase "wine of their eyes," an ambiguity which is maintained to the end. Poised between the verb *weinen* (to weep) and the noun *Wein* (wine), between the substantive *das Geweinte* (the weeping) and the past participle of the verb from which it is formed, it is uncertain whether the poem manages to give voice to inarticulate suffering or the poetic voice itself is engulfed in silence, whether tears of mourning are turned into the wine of elegy or a certain tradition of poetry intoxicated by its own transfigurative powers is turned in a more sober direction.[5] It is equally unclear at the conclusion of the poem whether the lip which "at last . . . comes to moisten" is wetted by a poetic "draught foaming up from the depths" or by tears prosaically trickling down the lines of a face from the eyes above. Maintaining this uncertainty from beginning to end, "The Vintagers" not only ends as uncertainly as it begins, but extends this uncertainty in the course of its own stammering movement to the very notions of beginning and ending.

As has often been noted, the poem appears to reach an impasse at the end of its first stanza and to begin again at the start of the second. Echoing the opening lines of the first: "They harvest the wine of their eyes,/they crush out all of the weeping," at the beginning of the second: "They harvest, they crush out the wine,/they press down on time like their eye," this return to the same simultaneously marks an opening of it, an opening of the "at the same time" to a pressing temporal difference. Opening between the wine and the eye, the phrase, "they press down on time" marks the difference in the repetition, the temporal difference that repetition makes as it rearticulates the traditional order of beginning and ending, first and second, original and translation suggesting, in short, that repetition will have taken place from and before the very first. The *Spätmund* or "latemouth," toward which the poem moves, should thus be read not merely as its telos but also and above all as the viniculturally compressed name of this repetitive movement. Decompressed as the term *Spätmündigkeit*, it names the belated structure of the poem's own deferred maturation process.

Repeatedly turning back on itself, the poem returns to the "same" both to mark the point at which it is stuck and in a belated attempt to open this "area of the given" to a pressing temporal difference, to delineate the "space of the possible." Circling back to the same, it endeavors to "pre-cise"—to invoke a central term of Celan's poetics—or to etch out the "contours" of a "reality" still "be searched for and won."[6] Moving forward and backward at once, the poem's faltering, *stockende* movement is itself that of the *Krückstock* named in the sixth line. No longer simply the *Weinstock* or staff of Dionysus, god of the vine and fecundity, this *Krückstock*, which "speaks through silence [*durchs Stumme hindurchspricht*]," is but a prosthetic, crutchlike limb with which this blind and crippled lyric seeks to orient itself in "the night, which they're leaning against, the wall," tapping its way like a probing question spoken into the "silence of answers." Such stonewalling responses not only leave unanswered the crook-stick's hesitantly posed questions, but, preemptively intervening in the very act of asking, they stifle its questions just as or even before they are asked. The poem's stammering movement bears witness to this tense stand-off, this intense interplay of opposing forces. Indeed, if Dionysus's thyrsus evoked by the figure of the *Krückstock* is still somehow present in the poem, it is there only in and as this intertwining of competing pressures being pressed through and compressed into one another.[7]

One might recall in this regard the distinction Freud draws in "Drives and Their Vicissitudes" between the "momentary impact" of an external stimulus and the "incessant urgency" or "constant pressure [*konstant drängende*]" of the drive. "The stimuli of the drives," he says, "oblige the nervous system to renounce its ideal intention of warding off stimuli, for they maintain an incessant and unavoidable afflux of stimulation."[8] The constant pressure exerted by the drives suggests not only an equally vigilant mode of defense, but a more intensely compromised relationship between these driving forces and the forces of repression.[9] The Freudian term *Verdrängung*, usually translated as "repression," captures precisely this compression of conflicting forces, suggesting as well the necessity of forging unstable compromise formations to accommodate their competing demands. Something like this sense of compression is evoked by Celan at the end of his Bremen address when he speaks of the "efforts of those who . . . carry their existence into language, racked by reality and in search of it [*wirklichkeitswund und Wirklichkeit suchend*]."[10]

Within "Die Winzer" these competing pressures are felt most strongly in the faltering cadences of the verse itself, in the beat crushed out by the vintagers' own heels, their *Fersen*. While this word does not appear as such in the poem, a connection between its feet of verse and the grape-stomping heels of the winemakers is implicit in the verb *keltern* (to crush), appearing in the second line, derived from the Latin *calcitrare*: to crush with the heels (*calx*).[11] Inhabited by these pressures, the poem presses toward the opening of a "latemouth," which critics often seek to locate in the moment of metrical decompression found in the only complete hexameter in the text:

ein Mund, zu dem der Trunk aus der Tiefe emporschäumt, indes

a mouth to which the draught from the depths foams upward, meantime

This argument, first advanced by Howard Stern, is compelling up to a point. For Stern it is not simply a question of long and short lines, but of complete and incomplete ones. In the early Celan, he contends, "the complete line is a dactylic hexameter . . . and very few poems in the first two volumes are free of its echoes."[12] Celan's decision "to compress the sonorous hexameters of his early maturity" into a radically reduced verse form would thus suggest greater "difficulty of expression, stammering, and hesitation." Yet, what the poem might lose in melodiousness through this increased metrical compression is compensated in Stern's view by what it will have gained in "evocative or incantatory power" (28). "The reformulations of the stammer" would thus imply that "whatever power is being invoked has multiple aspects or spheres of influence, and that the names corresponding to each aspect must be pronounced if the invocation is to be successful" (28). The measure of success, for Stern, is the reconstitution of a lost fullness. He therefore argues that such a reconstitution is not only predicted in the line cited above but, as the only complete hexameter in the poem, also accomplished by it.

John Felstiner also sees something magical happening in and around this line. "A ferment of syntax, punctuation, grammar, and prosody," he claims, "induces a kind of spell." An essential aspect of this incantation, he suggests, is the triple repetition of the noun *Mund*, which recalls the three-fold *einmal* of the first stanza as it summons up from the depths the very mouth of which it speaks:

so that a *mouth* might thirst for this, later—
a *latemouth*, like to their own:
bent toward blindness and lamed—
a *mouth* to which the draught from the depths foams upward

As was noted earlier, the neologism *Spätmund* plays on the vinicultural term *Spätlese* meaning a late gleaning of grapes. Describing the wine made from such grapes as "the richest," Felstiner sees in the corresponding appearance of the "latemouth" a belated fulfillment of the desire or "thirst . . . for utmost speech."[13]

This "latemouth," which Felstiner hears as "the poet's own," may also, however, be that of another still to come. On September 16, 1953, when "Die Winzer" was composed, Celan's wife was soon to give birth to their first child.[14] In describing the year as swelling to death "as grapes," the poem seems to allude not only to Gisèle Celan-Lestrange's richly swollen belly but also to certain fears the poet may have been harboring about this impending birth. Before examining more fully the circumstances surrounding the birth below, I want first to dwell a bit more both on the *Spätmund* toward which and around which the compressed energies of "The Vintagers" seem to be gathered and on the belated maturation process or *Spätmündigkeit* associated with it. While Stern locates the appearance of this mouth in a moment of reconstituted metrical fullness, Felstiner views its successful summoning from the depths in and around this same line as the belated realization of a wish for "utmost speech." In both cases one is made to witness the incantatory power of the poetic act, the still intoxicating potency of the Dionysian poet's transfiguring word. Yet, if it is indeed still a question of magic in this context, it must be asked not only how these spells successfully conjure the spirits they invoke but also how, in doing so, they manage to keep other, somewhat ghastlier and more deadly ones at bay. I am suggesting that both Stern's description of the "climax" of the poem as a "moment of sacramental communion" and Felstiner's accentuation of the richness of the wine known as a *Spätlese*—which, he tellingly adds, is made from grapes picked "*before* they rot"—tend to conjure away the haunting silences of a text that is not only pregnant with life but also very much swollen with death.

Beginning, then, with the spirits banned by these critics, which in their very banishment continue to hover at the periphery of their readings, one should note first that the wine known as a *Spätlese* may be made not just from grapes gleaned "before they rot" but from ones which have already begun to do so. The sweet, dark-gold dessert wine made in the environs of Tokaj, Hungary, is but one example. Like the year said to "swell to death, as grapes [*als Traube*]," in the tenth line of the poem, "The Vintagers" is itself swollen by a certain fatality ripening within it. This fatality, as well as the process by which it is belatedly brought to maturation (or rather to *over-ripening*) in the poem, may be specified by reference to Celan's Bremen speech, an address which is itself linked to "The Vintagers" by the strangely out-of-place vinicultural (and mineralogical) term *angereichert* Celan uses in quotation marks at a crucial moment in it. Before turning to that moment, it should be noted that a wine is said to be *angereichert* when it is "fortified" and "enriched" by the addition of sugar to sugar-deficient musts to make certain that the wine will have an alcoholic content commensurate with its other qualities. Used discretely, *Anreicherung* may bring alcohol into better balance with other constituents of the wine, but abused, it results in "wine" being made from grape skins, sugar, and acids.[15]

While Celan may not use the term exactly or exclusively in this sense in the passage from his Bremen speech, the quotation marks with which it is set off in his text nevertheless suggest both that it is used in a guarded and bitterly sarcastic way and that it is meant to resonate in more than one context.

Only this one thing remained reachable, close and un-lost amid all losses: language.

Yes, it, language, remained un-lost, in spite of everything. But it had to go through its own lack of answers, through terrifying silence, through the thousand darknesses of death-bringing speech. It went through and gave no words for what was happening; but went through it. Went through and could surface again, "en-riched" [*"angereichert"*] by it all.[16]

In both the vinicultural and mining contexts in which the term is used, the process of *Anreicherung* involves the addition of other materials to form new chemical concentrations which raise or potentiate the yield. Yet, as is suggested by the concatenation of the signifier *reich* in a chain extending from the *Bedeutungsbe*reich (semantic field) of the words *Denken und Danken* (thinking and thanking) with which this very brief speech begins, to the *Klang des Uner*reich*baren* (the sound of the unreachable), and via the substantives *Das Er*reich*bare*, *das zu Er*reich*ende*, and *Er*reich*barkeit* (the reachable, the place to be reached, and reachability) to the verb *ange*reich*ert*, what appears to have been "added to" this language in passing through everything it "went through" so that it now surfaces again "en-riched" is precisely the *Reich* through which it will have passed, the short-lived "thousand-year *Reich*," which, in living on beyond its own "premature" end, continues to hold this language in its spectral grasp. This is the double movement of "passing through" associated with the insistent repetition of the separable prefix *hindurch* at this point in the Bremen address. It is this thoroughgoing passage of speech through silence that is also performed in "Die Winzer" by the "Krückstock, . . . der . . . durchs Stumme hindurchspricht."

To be "angereichert," then, implies coming to the light of day again swollen with life-in-death-in-life, "mindful" in both the active and passive senses which the term *eingedenk bleiben* has for Celan of the "thousand darknesses of death-bringing speech."[17] Surrounded by quotation marks which do not so much delimit the term as suspend it in the midst of a number of signifying chains and semantic fields, *"angereichert"* may thus be read as a "citation" that is itself pregnant and saturated with these other contexts and especially with a *Reich* which, though never named as such in the speech, hauntingly resonates throughout it. It is this belated and necessarily excessive *over*ripening of life suffused with death, of death confused and transfused with life, that "The Vintagers" struggles to articulate as it presses toward the place of the *Spätmund*.

As a poem about gathering which itself gathers toward the "late-mouth" of which it speaks, "the lip" which finally "comes to moisten" in its last line, "The Vintagers" might also be described as a text *der im Munde mündet*, drawn on and drawn together by the latemouth it draws toward. In this way the various flows of the text—the draught which foams up from the depths, the tears which run down the face, the compressed time which flows backward and forward at once—may be said to open onto the mouth. Not only does this mouth mark a point of desired confluence but, as the nodal point at which the signifiers *Mund*, *münden*, and *Mündigkeit* meet—and with them the associated realms of the corporeal, fluvial, and temporal—it figures a moment of intense compression and condensation in the text. One might say that it is the fluidly diffuse, temporally dis-jointed body of the text itself that is gathered and drawn together around the potential opening of this mouth. In other words, it is only in being drawn toward this privileged orifice that the poetic corpus integrates, orga-nizes, and organicizes itself, that it draws itself literally to a close.

Yet this poem which closes just as a lip is beginning to moisten, as another seems about to speak, also takes the reader to the threshold of a certain silence. In order to approach this silence it is necessary to bear in mind Celan's derivation of *Spätmund* from *Spätlese*. Not only does a *mund* literally take the place of a *lese* here, but, in doing so, suggests more gener-ally that the mouth never exactly speaks for itself, that it speaks rather as a kind of cover or stand-in, not just in place of another voice but in lieu of engaging in other activities—instead, that is, of gleaning and reading, in short, of *Lesen*. One might recall in this context the way Heidegger, whom Celan had been reading since the early 1950s, seeks to move in a similar manner in his lecture on Heraclitus's fragment B50, from *logos* in the sense of *legein*, or saying aloud, to a process of gathering. In that lecture, pub-lished in 1951, Heidegger asks: "Who would want to deny that in the lan-guage of the Greeks from early on *legein* means to talk, say, or tell? How-ever, just as early and even more originally . . . it means what our similarly sounding *legen* means: to lay down and lay before. In *legen* a 'bringing to-gether' prevails, the Latin *legere* understood as *lesen*, in the sense of collect-ing and bringing together."[18]

There are no doubt important distinctions that need to be drawn between Heidegger's and Celan's work. While not wishing to minimize those differences, in the present context I want only to point to how speaking and gathering come together in the two texts, how a certain speaking *gathers in the place of* another way of thinking *legein*, another way of reading what the gathering of *logos* qua speech effectively mutes.

In "Die Winzer" that which resists being gathered into poetically potent speech or transfigured into the wine of elegy, and which marks the turning of poetry intoxicated with its own transfigurative powers in another direction, is silently inscribed there as *stummer* or *stumpfer Wein*, silent wine, or what in French is called *vin muet*. The Grimms' *Deutsches Wörterbuch* defines *stummer Wein* as wine that has ceased or has not yet begun to ferment; it is "motionless, flat." "One refers to wine as silent when it has been so sulfurized that it has lost its spirit [*den Geist verloren hat*]"; and "if the wine lacks spirit," the entry continues, "it cannot loosen the tongue [*es ist stumm . . . wenn . . . der Wein . . . ohne Geist ist, und daher nicht redselig macht*]."[19]

Stummer Wein is thus a term used to designate a suspension of the fermentation process, the silent insistence of that which remains to be *angereichert*, but also of that which remains undrinkable for having been excessively "enriched," "so sulfurized that it has lost its spirit."[20] As such, and particularly in a text engaged in harvesting the wine of the eyes, it figures a suspension of the work of mourning. It is the trace of that which remains to be mourned, of that which remains silently insistent in its unmournability.

While the term itself never appears in Celan's text, this "silent wine" nevertheless insists there as a traumatic subtext, as a silence around which and against which the text gathers itself together. This other wine silently surfaces in the poem like the floating fragment of another muted text, like the trace of the text's own irreducible otherness to itself, at two points—one in the second-to-last line of the first stanza, the other in the same place in the second—a parallel structure that invites one to read the second as a belated repetition of the first. The first is the word *Stumme* (silence) paratactically set off in the phrase *durchs Stumme hindurchspricht* by the signifier *durch*, which, appearing twice in this line and nowhere else in the poem, seems to frame it in quotation marks. Such invisible quotes, Celan stresses in "The Meridian," should be viewed less as *Gänsefüsschen* or goose feet than as "rabbit's ears which listen . . . for something else, something beyond words."[21] The second is the word *Lichtstumpf* (candle end or stump of light), which also gets the fifth and sixth beats of the line and is itself paratactically set off by an *um . . . zu* construction. The parallel placement of these terms silently marks the phantom presence in "Die Winzer" of an unincorporable, unspiritualizable subtext.

This lingering "presence" is also remarked by the floating seal of the *Lichtstumpf* formed from the heavens' descent into "waxen seas" at sunset. Its seal of silence remains afloat not only in the positive, spatial sense of a stump of sunlight hovering at the horizon where sea and sky appear to meet, but also in the more equivocal sense of being suspended between two ways of reading a twilit moment at the horizon of the text. Indeed, at the moment this candle stump appears in the poem it is unclear whether its molten seal is just being impressed upon the lip positioned directly below it or just beginning to melt away. As it seals and unseals the lip below it *in* the text, the floating *Lichtstumpf* also sheds its twilight on the haunting "presence" of a text below the text, the muted subtext of silent wine, which is itself said to be *stumpf* to the extent that it has ceased or not yet begun to "mature."

While the poem appears to draw to a close around the deferred opening of the *Spätmund* whose lips seem to part slightly in the fractured endrhyme of *leuchten* and *feuchtet*, the *Spätmündigkeit* at work in the text from the very beginning will have moved it in the end beyond this carefully circumscribed opening at the close. Closing only to open again, the ending of "Die Winzer" is itself but a repetition of the ending/beginning performed at its meridianal midsection in the transition from the first twelve-line stanza to the second one of equal length. As though playing out this logic of repetition and deferred maturation at work within it, the poem continues to "ripen" beyond its own apparent end, belatedly opening again in the midst of another, Celan's "Grabschrift für François" (Epitaph for François). Written in October 1953, it is the only poem Celan ever printed with its date.

> Die beiden Türen der Welt
> stehen offen:
> geöffnet von dir
> in der Zwienacht.
> Wir hören sie schlagen und schlagen

und tragen das ungewisse,
und tragen das Grün in dein Immer.
Oktober 1953[22]

Both doors of the world
stand open:
opened by you
in the twilight.
We hear them beating and beating
and bear the uncertain,
and bear the green into your Ever.
October 1953[23]

Haunted by a fatality ripening within it, "The Vintagers" writes a certain future into its own belated structure, its *Spatmündigkeit*. I would suggest, in other words, that the loss of the Celans' first child is already uncannily inscribed in "Die Winzer," in which the year is said to swell like an overripe grape to death, in which time itself is swollen with death, in which *Winter* (itself a paronomasia of *Winzer*) comes early in the fall.

In a undated letter to Isac Chiva, Celan describes the circumstances surrounding the birth of his son on October 8, 1953, and his death shortly thereafter: "L'enfant est mort. Il a survécu l'accouchement—très difficile, trois fois forceps, puis finalement, pour le sauver, césarienne—il a survécu cet accouchement de 30 heures./Mon fils, notre fils, notre fils François. /Gisèle est bien, la pauvre, son état évolue normalement [The child is dead. He survived the delivery—very difficult, three times forceps, then finally to save him a cesarean—he survived the 30-hour long delivery. /My son, our son, our son François. /Gisèle is OK, the poor thing, and her condition is progressing normally]."[24] While one might assume, as I had at the time the present chapter was first drafted, that Celan's commemorative poem could only have been written some time *after* the traumatic birth and death of his first-born son, it has recently been reported that the poem was actually composed a few days *before* the fact. Identifying the poet's close friend Yves Bonnefoy as his source, the editor of the recently published correspondence of Paul Celan and Gisèle Celan-Lestrange, Bertrand Badiou, notes that "*Celan donne au poème* écrit quelques jours avant la naissance et la mort de son fils, *y voyant* une prémonition des événements, le titre de 'Grabschrift für François' [Writing the poem a few days *before* the birth and death of his son and seeing in it *a premonition of what was to come*, Celan gave it the name 'Epitaph for François']" (emphasis added).[25]

As was noted earlier, both "The Vintagers" and "Epitaph for François" are contained in the volume *Von Schwelle zu Schwelle*. Not only does the latter poem relate this movement "from threshold to threshold" to "both doors of the world," to the thresholds of birth and death, but in leaving them open so that "we hear them beating and beating," it also makes us hear the one beating through, beating at the heart of the other. Each of these *Schwellen* is in this sense already swollen with the other, pregnant with a death inside a life inside a death, "bearing . . . and bearing." If "Die Winzer" may be said to ripen belatedly, carrying on beyond its own twilit ending, overripening in the medial "twinight" of "Grabschift," it is, I would suggest, because the latter poem will itself have already been inscribed in the former as the latemouth toward which it speaks. Such a circularly repetitive temporality of belatedness is suggested in the lines which figure poetic desire as a movement not of "thirst[ing] *for*," as Felstiner translates it, but of thirsting *after*.

> auf daß ein Mund danach dürste, später—
> ein Spätmund, ähnlich dem ihren:
> Blindem entgegengekrümmt und gelähmt—
>
> so that a mouth might thirst after this, later—
> a latemouth, like to their own:
> bent toward blindness and lamed—

Preparing for "a latemouth . . . bent toward blindness and lamed," "Die Winzer" will not only have made a place for the latter poem's *Grabschrift* over the "sun grave" which it itself makes ready, but it already seems to have envisioned the poet in a blind and unconscious manner as a sightless and crippled Oedipus stranded in the meridianal "twinight" of the present, in exile from the past and from the future, twice orphaned as a survivor both of his parents and of his own offspring. Celan's poetry, I would suggest, is shadowed by this traumatic moment—by the death of his infant son, whose French name echoes that of the poet's newly adopted *patrie*, and by his own haunting sense of being exiled at the threshold of life/death, a threshold to which he repeatedly returns in "The Meridian," asking at each turn how it is possible to live on beyond one's own life-in-death.[26]

Celan's discussion of Georg Büchner's *Lenz* in "The Meridian" is exemplary in this regard. Beginning with the last lines of the text, "His existence was a necessary burden for him.—Thus he lived on . . . ," and adding, "Here the narrative breaks off," Celan draws attention to the way the text founders on the point of an existential impasse, remaining stuck at a moment associated with the protagonist's separation from the pastor Oberlin and his reluctant return to his widowed father and forsaken *Vaterstadt*. Indeed, it is no exaggeration to say that Büchner's mention of Lenz's living death in the phrase "So lebte er hin . . . " stops the narrative dead in its tracks. In order to move the fragment beyond this existential and narrative impasse, Celan suggests that it is necessary not just to return to the beginning of the text but to begin again at the very place where an impossible desire for another kind of gait, a way of moving which might itself incisively carve out new paths, is expressed for the first and only time in the text: " . . . only it sometimes bothered him that he could not walk on his head." For Celan this return to a path not taken, which might be (re)opened only by the trenchant gait of a character walking on his head, has the structure of a "step" (*Schritt*).[27] Such a step which Lenz might have taken on January 20, on a date which now returns as the anniversary of the 1942 Wannsee Conference, is associated in the immediate context of the Büchner fragment with the possibility of beginning again, of beginning to move in a necessarily circular and belated manner beyond the living death at the text's end. It is also associated more generally with a way of opening a stagnating movement in place to "something" that, in Celan's words, "dazwischen kommt." What "comes between," "comes in the meantime," in the time-space of an interval, comes in the context of "The Meridian" as an intervention of the Other. It comes as an interruption that may reorient a fatally closed circle of repetition, silently respacing and rearticulating a closed, exclusive, and isolating ring of circular return so as to transform it into an alliance with the Other, into the kind of alliance forged in a poem such as "In Eins" (In One). It is in view of such interventions that Celan asks the following questions at this point in his discussion of Lenz: "Can we now, perhaps, find the place where strangeness was present, the place where a person succeeded in setting himself free, as an—estranged— I? Can we find such a place, such a step? Is perhaps at this point, along with the I—with the estranged I, set free . . . —is perhaps at this point an Other set free?" Returning to Celan's "Grabschrift für François," it should be noted that the poem opens the central cycle, "Mit wechselndem Schlüssel" (With a Changing Key) of *Von Schwelle zu Schwelle*. While the first poem of this cycle is dedicated to the memory of Celan's son, the last Hölderlinian poem, "Andenken" (Remembrance), has been read as a memorial to his father.[28] In this movement from threshold to threshold at the center of Celan's 1955 collection, the poet himself appears suspended in the doubly abyssal "twinight" of the present as an orphaned son and a sonless father. "Grabschrift für François" is the open crypt of this empty present.

The "beating and beating" "we hear" in this poem is not only that of "both doors of the world" standing open but of the clock striking yet another meridianal moment. Like the phonograph needle scratching at a record's inner lip in Mann's *The Magic Mountain*, a scratching sound that makes audible the sand coursing through the narrow neck of an hourglass, the "beating and beating" of "Grabschrift" resonates with the sound of time at a standstill. Indeed, what is sounded out in the ticking of its "schlagen und schlagen," a beat which is itself audibly carried over by the anaphora "und tragen . . . und tragen" in the last two lines of the poem, is time's (and the text's) own movement in place. Making us hear the sound of "dead time" as the sounding of time's own death knell, the poem also evokes the *Totenuhr*, or deathwatch, of Büchner's mortally bored prince Leonce, whose fatally ticking heart is now relocated in the dead center of the poem's own open doorways,[29] in the open grave which the threshold of the moment will have become for the radically uprooted survivor.[30]

What is written and dated as a poetic epitaph must also be read therefore as a temporal cenotaph.[31] Erected over the open grave of a voided present, the title "Grabschrift für François" stands over a text that itself stands as open as the doors which open it—as open, that is, as the doors of a crypt "opened by you/in the twinight." This movement of opening is repeated throughout the poem: in its incipit; in its third line; in the entry of a new subject "We" at the beginning of the fifth line, which also begins a new sentence; and even in the stuttering overlap of "the uncertain" end of the sixth line and the "green" middle of the seventh. Because the adjective *ungewisse* (uncertain) remains uncapitalized in the nominal contruction *das ungewisse*, it may be read not only *in tandem* with *das Grün* (the green) occupying the same place in the line directly below but as a modification of it. In other words, rather than bearing *both* "the uncertain" *and* "the green" "into your Ever," what the "we" of the poem bears there is *das ungewisse Grün* (the uncertain green). This additional stutter would hardly be worth mentioning were it not for the fact that the "Ever" toward which the poem appears teleologically to gather, toward which its "we" bears its dead as though delivering it in the end into the eternal rest of a timeless present, were not itself but the fragmentary beginning of a word whose ending has itself been broken off and buried elsewhere. That word is *Immergrün*. Capitalized as a noun, the term may refer to a flower known in English as a periwinkle. Left uncapitalized like the word *ungewisse*, discussed above, it may be translated more literally by the adjective "evergreen." Broken in two and divided between its nominal and adjectival senses, this wounded flower of speech stands as uncertainly open as the doors at the other thresholds of the poem. Like them, it marks yet another opening of the crypt over which the gravestone of the title, "Epitaph for François," is placed.

Standing open like the broken doors of a vacant crypt, this word fragment must also be read in the end as a symbolon imparted in silence at the threshold, in the very movement from threshold to threshold, of the text. This symbolon which is broken and shared in the open doorways of the text is the "uncertain green" that the poem gives in promise, as though giving its own hand as it reaches uncertainly toward another, pledging thereby to leave itself open to the untimely interventions of another that never speaks for itself or in its own behalf.[32] It is in this way that one may begin to understand Celan's contention that there is "no fundamental difference between a handshake and a poem."

REFERENCE MATTER

Notes

CHAPTER 1: INTRODUCTION

1. Cited in Shoshana Felman and Dori Laub, M.D., *Testimony: Crises of Witnessing in Literature, Psychoanalysis, and History* (New York: Routledge, 1992), 78.

2. This relationship between narration and survival is discussed at length by Laub in his essay "An Event Without a Witness: Truth, Testimony, and Survival," in Felman and Laub, *Testimony*. See in particular the section "The Imperative to Tell," 78–79.

3. Jean-François Lyotard, *The Differend: Phrases in Dispute*, trans. Georges Van Den Abbeele (Minneapolis: University of Minnesota Press, 1988), 57. Lyotard defines the differend as

> the unstable state and instant of language wherein something which must be able to be put into phrases cannot yet be. This state includes silence, which is a negative phrase, but it also calls upon phrases which are in principle possible. This state is signaled by what one ordinarily calls a feeling: "One cannot find the words," etc. A lot of searching must be done to find new rules for forming and linking phrases that are able to express the differend disclosed by the feeling, unless one wants this differend to be smothered right away in a litigation and for the alarm sounded by the feeling to have been useless. What is at stake in a literature, in a philosophy, in a politics, perhaps, is to bear witness to differends by finding idioms for them. (13)

These are very much the stakes of the readings proposed in the present study.

4. The reorientation proposed here has strong affinities with a line of thought developed by Thomas Trezise in his essay "Unspeakable," *Yale Journal of Criticism* 14, no. 1 (2001): 39–66.

5. The bodies in question here are not only those of Holocaust survivors and their descendants but of certain children of the Third Reich, as well. Thus, Chapter 4 examines the autobiographical researches of the (East) German writer Christa Wolf, into a childhood played out in a petit bourgeois milieu during the Nazi period. In a highly illuminating reading of Wolf's novel *Patterns of Childhood*, Eric

Santner examines the "substantial archive" of bodily symptoms in the text, noting that such symptoms "may be the traces of conflicts that have been repressed, that is, forgotten by consciousness but remembered by the body. The body, then, functions in this novel as a sort of writing tablet and mnemonic device of the unconscious." Eric Santner, *Stranded Objects* (Ithaca, N.Y.: Cornell University Press, 1990), 157.

6. Paul Celan, *Collected Prose*, trans. Rosemarie Waldrop, (New York: Sheep Meadow Press, 1986), 34; trans. modified.

7. Ibid.; trans. modified.

8. Celan, *Collected Prose*, 16.

9. Ibid.

10. While the term *encounter* is often employed as a translation of the French *rencontre*, the English term fails to capture many crucial resonances which the French term has in the writings of Lacan and Derrida, to which my own understanding of the notion is indebted. In teasing out the logic implicit in what Celan himself refers to as the "Geheimnis der Begegnung" (secrecy of encounter), Derrida writes, "'*Rencontre*'—in the French word two values come together [*dans le mot français se rencontrent deux valeurs*] without which there would be no date: '*la rencontre*' as it suggests the random occurrence, the chance meeting, the coincidence or conjuncture that comes to seal one or more than one event *once*, at a given hour, on a given day, in a given month, in a given region; and then '*rencontre de l'autre*,' an encounter with the other, the ineluctable singularity out of which and destined for which the poem speaks." Jacques Derrida, "Shibboleth for Paul Celan," trans. Joshua Wilner, *Word Traces*, ed. in Aris Fioretos (Baltimore: Johns Hopkins University Press, 1994), 11; trans. modified.

11. Wiesel, "The Loneliness of God," cited in Felman's translation as it appears in her essay "The Return of the Voice: Claude Lanzmann's *Shoah*," in *Testimony: Crises of Witnessing in Literature, Psychoanalysis, and History* (New York: Routledge, 1992), 204.

12. In a related context Henry Greenspan and Sidney Bolkovsky, interviewers from the University of Michigan who have worked extensively with Holocaust survivors, stress that an

> interview is . . . not an interrogation. In those sorts of encounters the so-called interviewer certainly labors, often very hard to "get" certain things— some specific data or information—while the interviewee does his or her best to surrender the goods or fend off the eager collector. . . . Like speech delivered to a single listener, the interrogation of a particular survivor entails an encounter between two different people, but not a meeting, a shared engagement, between two minds. There is . . . this view and that view, but there is not an interview.

Henry Greenspan and Sidney Bolkovsky, "When Is an Interview an Interview? Notes on Listening to Holocaust Survivors," paper presented at the Fortunoff

Video Archive Conference, The Contribution of Oral Testimony to Holocaust and Genocide Studies, Yale University, October 6, 2002.

13. Laub, "Bearing Witness," in Felman and Laub, *Testimony*, 57–58; references to this essay will henceforth appear in parentheses in the body of the text.

14. On the notion of belatedness, see Laplanche's essential study *Life and Death in Psychoanalysis*, trans. Jeffrey Mehlman (Baltimore: Johns Hopkins University Press, 1976), particularly chapter 2, "Sexuality and the Vital Order." There Laplanche lays stress on the role of sexuality in the structure of belatedness, noting that "sexuality alone is available for that action in two phases which is also an action 'after the event' [*après coup*]." While I do not share this limited view, which Laplanche himself would revise in his later work, and while I attempt in what follows to view belatedness more in terms of a Derridian structure of supplementarity, the German term *nachträglich* meaning both belated and supplementary, I find it useful to think of belatedness in Laplanche's terms as a "complex and endlessly repeated interplay—midst a temporal succession of missed occasions—of 'too early' and 'too late'" (ibid., 43).

In its standard psychoanalytic sense, *Nachträglichkeit* designates the transformation and rewriting of experiences, impressions, and memory traces on the basis of later experiences and in the context of a new phase of development. Yet, as Rainer Nägele stresses in *Reading After Freud* (New York: Columbia University Press, 1987), the object of such transformations, rewritings, and reorderings is not the totality of the past, but *fragments that, at the time of the event, could not be integrated into a context of significance.*

All phenomena of belatedness—including its discovery—are marked by a period of latency. Indeed, as Laplanche and Pontalis have noted, Freud employed the noun *Nachträglichkeit* and the adjectival and adverbial forms from which it is derived on numerous occasions and often at crucial moments in his writings about individual and collective trauma. While no doubt recognizing its essential and constitutive function in the formation of traumatic histories, Freud did not discover the phenomenon of belatedness per se. Such a discovery, as they note, was itself curiously belated, and credit for its elaboration is usually attributed to Jacques Lacan.

In his famous "return to Freud," Lacan, like Spiegelman, went back to a certain bleeding of the paternal corpus; that is, he returned to aspects of the founding father's work that had remained relatively undeveloped and insufficiently theorized, thereby making contact in this "return" not with established concepts but with energies and processes *silently at work* in Freud. Lacan will have made contact, in other words, with something unacknowledged and unassimilated in the body of Freud's work, with fragments that, at the time of their initial inscription, could not be integrated into a context of significance. What Lacan discovered, in a sense, was a certain belatedness of Freudian thought, something—at once meaning and force—that exceeded Freud's own grasp and that, in its very excessiveness, continued to drive that thought, making it possible for later generations to inherit from Freud a certain way of thinking with and beyond him. For Derrida's own "return to Freud," in which the concept of *Nachträglichkeit* plays a similarly decisive and unsettling role, see his seminal essay "Freud and the Scene of Writing," in *Writing and Difference*, trans. Alan Bass (Chicago: University of Chicago Press, 1978), 196–231. For close readings of the workings of *Nachträglichkeit* in the text of Freud see Rainer Nägele, *Reading After Freud*, and Cathy Caruth, *Unclaimed Experience* (Baltimore: Johns Hopkins University Press, 1996). For Laplanche's later thinking about what he now proposes to translate as "afterwardsness," see Cathy Caruth, "An Interview with Jean Laplanche," in the e-journal, *Postmodern Culture* 11, no. 2 (January 2001), http://muse.jhu.edu/journals/postmodern_culture/toc/pmc11.2.html; as well as Jean Laplanche, *Essays in Otherness*, ed. John Fletcher (New York: Routledge, 1998).

15. Primo Levi, *Survival in Auschwitz*, trans. Stuart Woolf (New York: Macmillan/Collier, 1961), 52.

16. This notion of co-responsibility is indebted to Laub's discussion of it in "An Event Without a Witness," in Felman and Laub, *Testimony*. See the section "Witnessing and Restoration," 85–86.

17. Bessel A. van der Kolk and Onno van der Hart, "The Intrusive Past: The Flexibility of Memory and the Engraving of Trauma," in *Trauma: Explorations in Memory*, ed. Cathy Caruth (Baltimore: Johns Hopkins University Press, 1995), 163.

18. Laub, "The Event Without a Witness," in Laub and Felman, *Testimony*, 81–82.

19. Celan's strange injunction is discussed at length in the context of a reading of Ozick's *The Shawl*, in Chapter 5.

20. Osip Mandelstam, *Selected Essays*, ed. and trans. Sidney Monas (Austin: University of Texas Press, 1977), 62–63.

21. Celan, *Collected Prose*, 49; trans. modified.

22. Ibid., 50; emphasis added.

23. At the conclusion of his discussion of the trope of the "unspeakable" in Holocaust literature, referred to above, Trezise notes,

> the survivor who says "I" does not speak with one voice, but with several. This plurality is not only an effect of the Holocaust, it is also a way of resisting what Kenneth Burke once called the "sinister unifying" of Hitler's rhetoric. And in order for these voices to be heard—which is not the same as to be understood—one must listen to the silences or read between the lines, attentive to what impels and exceeds understanding and hence, in Semprun's words, to "that possibility of going on forever." Listening or reading is in this case a resistance to the somnolence of sense, or as Adorno suggests, a sleeplessness nurtured by the static of the unspeakable. (Trezise, "Unspeakable," 62)

24. "In literature as in psychoanalysis," Laub's coauthor, Shoshana Felman, notes,

> and conceivably in history as well, the witness might be—as the term suggests and as Freud knew only too well (as is evidenced by his insistence on "der Zeuge")—the one who (in fact) *witnesses*, but also, the one who *begets*, the truth, through the speech process of the testimony. This begetting of the truth is also what Freud does, precisely, through his witness and his testimony to the Irma dream, out of which he will *give birth* to the entire theory of dreams, and to its undreamt of implications.

Felman and Laub, 16; emphasis in original. Later in the same essay, this time in the context of a reading of Mallarmé's "La Musique et les lettres," Felman pursues this double sense of *zeugen*, figuring the act of bearing witness no longer simply as an act of begetting but instead as a *premature or precocious birth*. "In a way," she writes,

> Mallarmé suggests that he speaks too soon, before he is quite ready, before he quite knows what his subject is about. And yet, since he has been a witness to "an accident known," since he does know that an accident has taken place, and since the accident "pursues him," he has got to speak "already," almost compulsively, even though he has not had as yet the time to catch his breath. He thus speaks in advance of the control of consciousness; his *testimony is delivered "in breathless gasps"*: in essence, it is a precocious testimony. Such precocious testimony in effect becomes, with Mallarmé, the very principle of poetic insight and the very core event of poetry, which makes precisely language—*through its breathless gasps—speak ahead of knowledge and awareness and break through the limits of its own conscious understanding*. . . . [P]oetry will henceforth speak beyond its means, to testify—precociously—to ill-understood effects and to the impact of an accident whose origin cannot precisely be located but whose repercussions, in their very uncontrollable and unanticipated nature, still continue to evolve even in the very process of the testimony.

Laub and Felman, *Testimony*, 21–22; emphasis added. In shifting the focus from the traveler's message, from the content of Mallarmé's testimony, to the *manner of its delivery* "in breathless gasps," Felman suggests that testimony henceforth be viewed less as a *discrete* birth, a creative *product*, and more as an interminable *process*—a labor that never exactly culminates in a delivery or, to be more precise, that delivers its testimony in an altogether different way, in another manner of speaking. She invites us to attune ourselves to testimony that never, as it were, comes out whole, but is instead only stammeringly delivered in panting gasps. Such testimony, as the example of Mallarméan free verse suggests, is borne not only—or even primarily—as an intact meaning conveyed by the words of the text but instead as an opening of that text to the accident of which it speaks, to an accident whose impact is registered in its own fragmentation. Yet, this unprecedented "accidenting" of verse in particular (and of the stable syntax and predictable rhythms of the language of consciousness in general) is precisely what now leaves the testimonial text open to chance, open to the possibility of *happening upon* what cannot be encountered in any more direct, immediate, or predictable way, upon an event that, in Laub's words, "*has not yet come into existence*" (emphasis added), and whose very advent cannot be anticipated, calculated, or prepared for in advance. I pursue the interrelated motifs of panting, birthing, and bearing witness in my reading of Ozick's *The Shawl* in Chapter 5.

Felman and Laub are not the only ones to figure the act of bearing witness as a kind of birth. In their article on the testimonial interview cited above, Greenspan and Bolkovsky use similar language to describe their work with survivors, stressing that there has to be the shared sense that there is a

> working relationship—a collaboration in the sense of laboring together. The essence of that labor is a shared commitment to bring forth, as fully as they may be retrievable, the survivor's tellable memories of the destruction. Expressions like "labor" and "bringing forth" are deliberately used because there is a kind of birthing and midwifery that goes on here—a creation that required more than one person at the start and needs more than one person all along the way. Conversely, a testimony that is simply given by one side, and gathered up by the other, need not entail any collaboration at all. It is more like a speech delivered to an audience of one. . . . That sort of "delivery" (showing the limits of metaphor) is not what we have in mind.

Henry Greenspan and Sidney Bolkovsky, "When Is an Interview an Interview? Notes on Listening to Holocaust Survivors," paper presented at the Fortunoff Video Archive Conference, The Contribution of Oral Testimony to Holocaust and Genocide Studies, Yale University, October 6, 2002. Other examples of this figurative pattern in which the act of bearing witness is linked to scenes of labor and delivery and the interviewer-listener is troped as a kind of midwife are adduced and analyzed in Chapter 2.

25. The title of Celan's 1955 collection of poems is *Von Schwelle zu Schwelle* (From Threshold to Threshold), discussed in Chapter 6 and mentioned at the end of this chapter.

26. The term *cervix* refers at once to the neck and to the neck-shaped, narrow outer end of the uterus; cf. the French *col de l'utérus* and German *Hals*.

27. The Celanian figure of an *Engführung* is discussed in the context of a reading of Wolf's autobiographical novel, *Patterns of Childhood*, in Chapter 4.

28. LaCapra, *Writing History, Writing Trauma*, 66.

29. "In acting out," LaCapra writes,

> tenses implode, and it is as if one were back there in the past reliving the traumatic scene. Any duality (or double inscription) of time (past and present or future) is experientially collapsed or productive only of aporias and double binds. In this sense, the aporia and the double bind might be seen as marking a trauma that has not been worked through. Working through is an articulatory practice: to the extent one works through trauma (as well as transferential relations in general), one is able to distinguish between past and present and to recall in memory that something happened to one (or one's people) back then while realizing that one is living here and now with openings to the future. This does not imply either that there is a pure opposition between past and present or that acting out—whether for the traumatized or for those empathetically relating to them—can be fully transcended toward a state of closure or full identity. But it does mean that processes of working through may counteract the force of acting out and the repetition compulsion. These processes of working through, including mourning and modes of critical thought and practice, involve the possibility of making distinctions or developing articulations that are recognized as problematic but still function as limits and as possibly desirable resistances to undecidability. (ibid., 21–22)

30. Celan, *Collected Prose*, 44–46 (trans. modified).

31. The phrase "to bestir herself . . . ," is from Christa Wolf, *Patterns of Childhood*, trans. Ursule Molinaro and Hedwig Rappolt (New York: Farrar, Straus and Giroux, 1980), 24; *Kindheitsmuster* (Darmstadt: Luchterhand, 1979), 28. The phrase "limits of the expressible" is from the same texts, pages 407, 378. "Sentences that stick in our throats" is from Wolf, *The Author's Dimension* (New York: Farrar, Straus and Giroux, 1993), 62.

CHAPTER 2: NECESSARY STAINS

1. Here I follow the distinction Spiegelman draws between "comics" and "comix." "Rather than comics," he writes, "I prefer the word comix, to mix together, because to talk about comics is to talk about mixing together words and pictures to tell a story." Art Spiegelman, "Commix: An Idiosyncratic Historical and Aesthetic Overview," *Print* 42 (November–December 1988): 61. I also follow Spiegelman's practice of writing the title MAUS in capital letters.

2. For a further discussion of this turning point see Geoffrey H. Hartmann, "Learning from Survivors: The Yale Testimony Project," in *The Longest Shadow: In the Aftermath of the Holocaust* (Bloomington: Indiana University Press, 1996), 133–50.

3. Marianne Hirsch, "Mourning and Postmemory," in *Family Frames: Photography, Narrative, and Postmemory* (Cambridge, Mass.: Harvard University Press, 1997), 17–40.

4. Ibid., 27.

5. Ibid., 21.

6. An excerpt from *Buch der Könige* appears in English translation in Klaus Theweleit, "The Politics of Orpheus Between Women, Hades, Political Power and the Media: Some Thoughts on the Configuration of the European Artist, Starting with the Figure of Gottfried Benn or: What Happens to Eurydice?" *New German Critique: An Interdisciplinary Journal of German Studies* 36 (Fall 1985): 133–56.

7. Hirsch, "Mourning and Postmemory," 21.

8. James E. Young, "The Holocaust as Vicarious Past: Art Spiegelman's *Maus* and the Afterimages of History," in *Critical Inquiry*, no. 24 (Spring 1998): 686.

9. Ibid., 678.

10. Ibid., 678–79. Later in the essay Young makes a related point about Art's interest in knowing more about his origins and his mother (about the mother as origin). Referring to a scene in which Vladek guilts a supermarket clerk into giving him a refund on groceries he had bought, a scene in which he "trades even his story of survival for food," Young notes, "While this kind of self-interested storytelling might drive the son a little crazy, Art must face the way he too has come to the story as much to learn about his origins, his dead mother, his own *mishugas*, as he does to learn Holocaust history" (ibid., 692).

11. Ibid. 669–70.

12. Being "out of joint" implies not only that past and present stand in a different relation to each other, but also that the temporal and logical priority of an original over a translation, speech over writing, immediate over mediated experience, is being rearticulated at such moments. In contrast to Hirsch, who asserts that "*once in a while*, something breaks out of the rows of frames, or out of the frames themselves, upsetting and disturbing the structure of the entire work," I view these moments of rupture not as sporadically occurring exceptions but as the general structural rule in MAUS. Hirsch, "Mourning and Postmemory," 26–27 (emphasis added).

13. See Alan Rosen's insightful study "The Language of Survival: English as Metaphor in Spiegelman's *Maus*" (*Prooftexts*, no. 15 [1995]: 257), in which he makes the crucial observation that "Vladek's 'tortured visualized prose' (the phrase is Nancy Miller's) is not only meant to represent an English-speaking 'foreigner' but is also meant to torture English into being a foreign language."

14. As Marianne Hirsch observes, "*Maus* sounds like mouse but its German spelling echoes visually the recurring Nazi command 'Juden raus' ('Jews out'— come out or get out) as well as the first three letters of 'Auschwitz,' a word that in itself has become an icon of the Holocaust. Spiegelman reinforces this association

when, in the second volume, he refers to the camp as 'Mauschwitz.'" Hirsch, "Mourning and Postmemory," 11.

15. Franz Kafka, *Letters to Friends, Family, and Editors*, trans. Richard Winston and Clara Winston (New York: Schocken, 1977), 288; trans. modified.

16. Jonathan Rosen, "Spiegelman: The Man Behind *Maus*," interview, *Forward*, January 17, 1992, 11.

17. Mark Anderson, *Kafka's Clothes: Ornament and Aestheticism in the Habsburg Fin de Siècle* (Oxford: Clarendon, 1992), 205. Elsewhere in his chapter entitled "'Jewish' Music? Otto Weininger and 'Josephine the Singer,'" Anderson discusses Wagner's notorious claim that "works of Jewish music often produce in us the kind of effect we would derive from hearing a poem by Goethe, for example, translated into that jargon we know as Yiddish." As Anderson comments, this "claim . . . fed on the street-level perception of recently 'emancipated' Jews as being incapable of speaking High German without a peculiar 'Yiddish' intonation, a 'hissing', abrasive sound accompanied by aggressive gesticulation" (197).

18. As James Young notes, "Subjugated groups have long appropriated the racial epithets and stereotypes used against them in order to ironize and thereby neutralize their charge, taking them out of the oppressors' vocabulary" ("The Holocaust as Vicarious Past," 690). While I agree with Young up to a point, I would still question whether the ultimate intent of Spiegelman's displacement of certain German stereotypes is merely to "neutralize their charge." I would also strongly take issue with Alan Rosen's claim that "by deploying the German word for the title, Spiegelman is asking the reader to view Jews/mice through the Germans'/cats' eyes." Rosen, "The Language of Survival," 261.

19. "The aspiring cartoonist," Spiegelman notes, "must master the conventions of picture-writing. . . . I remember looking at old cartooning books when I was a kid and learning that a Jew had a hooked line for a nose and large animated hands. . . . MAUS, my comic book about my parents' life in Hitler's Europe that uses cats to represent Germans and mice to represent Jews, was made in collaboration with Hitler. . . . My anthropomorphized mice carry trace elements of Fips' antisemitic Jew-as-rat cartoons for *Der Stürmer*." "Little Orphan Annie's Eyeballs," in Spiegelman, *Comix, Essays, Graphics, and Scraps: From MAUS to Now to MAUS to Now* (New York: Raw, 1998), 17. In the same letter to Max Brod cited above, Kafka also describes the pleasure of rummaging "with excessively lively Jewish hands."

20. Cited in Shoshana Felman and Dori Laub, M.D., *Testimony: Crises of Witnessing in Literature, Psychoanalysis, and History* (New York: Routledge, 1992), 241–42.

21. Rosen, "Spiegelman: The Man Behind *Maus*," 9.

22. In a related context, Michael Herr, writing about his work as a journalist during the Vietnam war, notes, "it took the war to teach it, that you were as responsible for everything you saw as you were for everything you did. The problem

was that you didn't always know what you were seeing until later, maybe years later, that a lot of it never made it in at all, it just stayed there in your eyes." Michael Herr, *Dispatches* (New York: Vintage, 1991), 20.

23. Art Spiegelman, MAUS: *A Survivor's Tale. My Father Bleeds History* (New York: Pantheon Books, 1986), 30. All references to MAUS will henceforth appear in the body of the text, by volume and page number. Volume 2 (MAUS II: *A Survivor's Tale. And Here My Troubles Began*) was also published by Pantheon (New York, 1991).

24. Excerpts from this anthology appear in *Comix, Essays, Graphics, and Scraps*, 28.

25. Lawrence Weschler, "Art's Father, Vladek's Son," in *Shapinsky's Karma, Bogg's Bills, and Other True-Life Tales* (San Francisco: North Point, 1988), 56.

26. *Raw* is of course also the name of the comix journal edited by Spiegelman and his wife, Françoise Mouly.

27. Spiegelman, "Dirty Little Comics," in *Comix, Essays, Graphics and Scraps*, 100.

28. There are marked similarities between Spiegelman's art of the slow-motion picture and Jorge Semprun's evocation of the difference between documentary realism and lived reality in *Literature or Life* (trans. Linda Coverdale [New York: Viking, 1997], 201; trans. modified). "The film," he writes,

> should have been worked through, in its filmic substance, by arresting the march of images, by fixing an image to enlarge certain details; sometimes the projection should have been slowed, and, at other times, speeded up. Above all, the scenes should have been provided with commentary, to make them less cryptic, to place them not only in historical context but in a continuum of thoughts and emotions. . . . In short, documentary reality should have been handled like fictional material.

29. In "Little Orphan Annie's Eyeballs" Spiegelman describes the masks themselves as projection surfaces: "In MAUS, the mouse heads are masks, virtually blank, like Little Orphan Annie's eyeballs, a white screen the reader can project on." Spiegelman, *Comix, Essays, Graphics and Scraps*, 17.

30. Spiegelman, "Looney Tunes, Zionism, and the Jewish Question," in *Comix, Essays, Graphics and Scraps*, 15.

31. The repetition of *about* in three successive panels not only draws attention to this seemingly innocuous preposition, but, in doing so, helps to sound out various related senses of the term. The first definition given in *Webster's* is, in fact, "in a circle around: around: on every side."

32. Laub suggest that we can try to understand what is happening in the "testimonial interview" by viewing it as a kind of "brief treatment contract," a contract, he describes as one

> between two people, one of whom is going to engage in a narration of her trauma, through the unfolding of her life account. Implicitly, the listener says to the testifier: "For this limited time, throughout the duration of the

testimony, I'll be with you all the way, as much as I can. I want to go wherever you go, and I'll hold and protect you along this journey. Then, at the end of the journey, I shall leave you." Bearing witness to a trauma is, in fact, a process that includes the listener. For the testimonial process to take place, there needs to be a bonding, the intimate and total presence of an *other*—in the position of one who hears. Testimonies are not monologues; they cannot take place in solitude. The witnesses are talking *to somebody*: to somebody they have been waiting for for a long time. (*Testimony*, 70–71)

33. Art Spiegelman, *The Complete* Maus *CD-ROM* (New York: Voyager, 1994).

34. Another notable exception is Marianne Hirsch's "Family Pictures," referred to earlier.

35. Nancy K. Miller, "Cartoons of the Self: Portrait of the Artist as a Young Murderer. Art Spiegelman's *Maus*," in *Considering Maus: Approaches to Art Spiegelman's "Survivor's Tale" of the Holocaust*, ed. Deborah R. Geis, 44–59 (Tuscaloosa: University of Alabama Press, 2003), 49.

36. Andreas Huyssen, "Von Mauschwitz in die Catskills und zurück: Art Spiegelmans Holocaust-Comic *Maus*," in *Bilder des Holocaust: Literatur—film—bildende Kunst*, ed. Manuel Köppen and Klaus Scherpe (Cologne: Böhlau, 1997), 184.

37. The centrality of this panel is underscored by its location at the degree zero of the page's horizontal-vertical axis.

38. Louise Kaplan, "Images of Absence, Voices of Silence," in *No Voice Is Ever Wholly Lost* (New York: Simon and Schuster, 1995), 224.

39. Ibid., 222–23.

40. The repeated killing of the mother may also be read as the figure of the way her own death stands in for others—as though the temporally inflected notion of repetition were also a spatial movement of substitution.

41. As was suggested earlier, the language of turning plays an integral part in the penultimate scene leading up to the mother's death. The figure of the cord is introduced by Art's words "I turned away" and is accompanied by a visual depiction of him doing just that. As though to underscore the importance of this gestural language, Spiegelman uses it once again in the penultimate panel of volume 2, a scene to which we will return below.

42. Saul Friedlander, *Memory, History, and the Extermination of the Jews of Europe* (Bloomington: Indiana University Press, 1993), 132.

43. In changing the topic so abruptly, Vladek may also be attempting to avoid any potentially embarrassing questions concerning the timing of Richieu's conception.

44. Speaking about the photograph of Richieu displayed in the dedication of the second volume of MAUS and referred to by Art in a conversation with Françoise, Hirsch writes, "The parents keep it in their bedroom to refer to, Art competes with it, and we take it as the ultimately unassimilable fact that it is of a

child who died unnaturally, before he had a chance to live" ("Mourning and Post-memory," 23).

45. This initial scene of pill spilling should also be read in relation to another moment of rupture in the text. As Young has pointed out, "as the father recounts the days in August 1939 when he was drafted, just as he gets to the outbreak of war itself: 'and on September 1, 1939, the war came. I was on the front, one of the first to . . . Ach!' His elbow knocks two bottles of pills onto the floor. 'So. Twice I spilled my drugstore.'" Young, "The Holocaust as Vicarious Past," 684.

46. Spiegelman, "Mad Youth," first published in *Life* magazine in August 1992, reprinted in *Comix, Essays, Graphics, and Scraps*, 21.

47. "Things Are More Like They Are Now . . . " in Spiegelman, *Comix, Essays, Graphics, and Scraps*, 23. As Spiegelman notes in "Prisoner on the Hell Planet," his nervous breakdown in winter 1967–68 preceded his mother's suicide by a little more than three months.

48. CD-ROM version, audio appendix to 89.

49. Lawrence Weschler, "Art's Father, Vladek's Son," originally published in *Shapinsky's Karma, Bogg's Bills, and Other True-Life Tales*, is reproduced in full in the appendix to the CD-ROM version of MAUS. The passages quoted above appear on pp. 5–7 of the article in the appendix.

50. Throughout his work Spiegelman plays on the language of publishing and graphic art. The title of his 1977 anthology, *Breakdowns*, is a case in point. See also his "dog-eared" children's book, *Open Me . . . I'm a Dog* (New York: Joanna Cotler, 1997).

51. It should further be noted that Spiegelman figures the publication of the second volume as a kind of birth when he thanks Paul Pavel, Deborah Karl, and Mala Spiegelman "for helping this volume into the world." In the German trans-lation of MAUS this connection is made even more explicit as the phrase "helping this volume into the world" is rendered as "zur Geburt verholfen haben [assisted in the birth]." MAUS: *Geschichete eines Überlebenden*, trans. Christine Brinck and Josef Joffe (Reinbek bei Hamburg: Rowolt, 1999). One might also note that the publi-cation of each of the two volumes of MAUS coincided roughly with the birth of Spiegelman's two children. Volume 1 appeared in 1986; Nadja was born in 1987. Both the second volume, subtitled "And Here My Troubles Began," and his sec-ond child, Dashiell, came out in 1991. In an interview which appeared in the *Forward* shortly after the completion of MAUS Spiegelman responds to a question con-cerning the recent birth of his son and the potential danger of becoming in his turn what his own father had been for him—namely a parent who *was* Auschwitz as much as its victim. "I was terrified of having a boy child," he says. "It involved having to move carefully around and not recapitulate that particular set of prob-lems but create new ones . . . for years my fears of having a child would be that I just didn't want anybody to think about me with the same complexity I had to

think about my father with . . . ." Rosen goes on then to ask Spiegelman about Nadja. "Did having a daughter in the course of writing a book that takes on such a dark subject make you more hopeful?" "No," Spiegelman responds, "it probably got me more scared because now I have even a greater vested interest in seeing this thing not all go to pieces. And that's always been a fear about having a child." It is unclear whether "this thing" refers to his work, his family, or both. Rosen, *Forward*, 9, 11.

52. Ibid., 1.

53. Elsewhere Spiegelman uses similarly hyperbolic language to describe the medium of the comic strip itself as a monstrous offspring, as "the hunchback, half-witted bastard dwarf step-child of the graphic arts." "Comix: An Idiosyncratic Historical and Aesthetic Overview," in Spiegelman, *Comix, Essays, Graphics, and Scraps*, 74.

54. See in this connection the passage from Shakespeare's *Richard II* and Slavoj Žižek's superb reading of it in *Looking Awry: An Introduction to Jacques Lacan Through Popular Culture* (Cambridge, Mass: MIT Press, 1991), 8–12. One portion of Bushy's speech is particularly relevant here:

> Each substance of a grief hath twenty shadows,
> Which show like grief itself, but are not so.
> For sorrow's eye, glazed with blinding tears,
> Divides one thing entire to many objects;
> Like perspectives, which rightly gaz'd upon
> Show nothing but confusion; ey'd awry
> Distinguish form; so your sweet majesty,
> Looking awry upon your lord's departure,
> Finds shapes of grief more than himself to wail;
> Which look'd on as it is, is nought but shadows
> Of what is not.
>
> —William Shakespeare, *Richard II*, 2.2, in
> *The Pelican Shakespeare*, ed. Frances E. Dolan
> (New York: Penguin, 2000), 41–42.

We will return to the question of "perspective" addressed here in a discussion of the structural and thematic significance of vanishing points in MAUS II.

55. It might be added that the glowing tip of the cigarette occupies the same structural position in the scene as the glass panes of the window insofar as both mark the point at which inside and outside meet.

56. In addition to the various senses of the word *drawing* Spiegelman plays on here and elsewhere, one might recall that the word *contract* itself derives from the Latin *contractus*, past participle of *contrahere*: to draw together.

57. I would like to acknowledge my debt to Richard Klein's analysis of smoking in *Cigarettes Are Sublime* (Durham, N.C.: Duke University Press, 1993), 105.

58. In a draft attached to the CD-ROM version of this page Spiegelman makes clear that the chimney itself is to be viewed as a smoking cigarette. "Cremo = cigarette," he adds in a note to himself.

59. See, for example, Miles Orvell's "Writing Posthistorically: *Krazy Kat, Maus,* and the Contemporary Fiction Cartoon" (*American Literary History* 4, no. 1 [Spring 1992]: 118), in which he describes *Maus* as a

> frame story with an external narrative enfolding an inner one: in the surrounding story, Art Spiegelman, a cartoonist, is writing a cartoon-fiction about his father Vladek, a refugee from Nazi Europe now living in Rego Park, Queens. The inner story is Vladek's. . . . What adds a crucial dimension to the novel is the frame surrounding that [story]—the relationship between father and son and the process of transmitting the story from one to the other, so that the book as a whole asks, what does it cost to survive?

60. It is no doubt telling in this regard that when Vladek actually burns the diaries he describes himself as having been "so DEPRESSED" that "I didn't know if I'm coming or going" (1:159).

61. It should be noted that it is on this trip to the bank that Vladek also relates the heartbreaking story of Richieu's tragic death (1:109).

62. Spiegelman, *Comix, Essays, Graphics, and Scraps,* 52.

63. Spiegelman, "Looney Toons, Zionism, and the Jewish Question," in *Comix, Essays, Graphics, and Scraps,* 16.

64. As Helen Epstein writes, "Our family tree had been burnt to a stump. Whole branches, great networks of leaves had disappeared into the sky and ground. *There was no stone that marked their passage.*" Epstein, *Children of the Holocaust: Conversations with Sons and Daughters of Survivors* (New York: Penguin, 1979), 11; emphasis added.

CHAPTER 3: THE VANISHING POINT

1. Interestingly, in the interview transcript from which this scene is taken there is no mention of the phrase "here my troubles began." The transcript reads, "Finally we came to Dachau. Then it started my misery. I went through this much that I cannot even tell anybody what I went through in Dachau." Audio appendix to 227 in CD-ROM.

2. "Translation," Benjamin asserts, "is a form. To comprehend it as form one must go back to the original. For in it resides the law of that form as the original's translatability." Walter Benjamin, "The Task of the Translator," in *Illuminations,* trans. Harry Zohn (New York: Schocken, 1978), 70. The translation is modified in order to draw attention to Zohn's curious rendering of the German word *Form* by "mode." In his illuminating commentary on this passage Samuel Weber observes that

such a refusal [by Zohn] of the literal is highly symptomatic. The translator was obviously unsatisfied or highly uncomfortable with the word "form" in this context. . . . The reason why "mode" is substituted for "form" is because the translator senses a tension between the autonomy and integrity associated with form, on the one hand— . . . Kant's definition of it as "the unification of a manifold"—and the subordination or dependence generally associated with translation and endorsed here by Benjamin: a translation is precisely not autonomous, self-contained, integral: it consists in a relationship to something outside of it, to something it is not and yet to which it owes its existence; the "original" work. "Mode" suggests a way of being rather than any sort of independent structure. And yet it is just such independence that Benjamin endorses, provocatively, in extending the term "form" to cover not only the original work but that of "translation" as well. And it is this extension which is unusual, which shocks, and which is reflected in the American translation of "form" by "mode." What is unfortunate in this translation, however, is that precisely the provocative tension between the relative independence of translation and its dependency upon something other than itself—an "original," a work—that drives Benjamin's effort to articulate "The Task of the Translator."

Weber, "Benjamin's 'The Task of the Translator,'" unpublished manuscript, 7. I am grateful to Professor Weber for sharing this essay with me.

3. See Chapter 2, note 30.

4. In earlier drafts of this panel Spiegelman uses the German word RAUS which, as Marianne Hirsch has noted, rhymes with the text's title, MAUS, a name which itself appears to be an abbreviation of the title of this particular chapter, "Mauschwitz."

5. As has already been noted, this circular movement is set in motion at the very beginning of MAUS, volume 1, in the scene in which Art circles tentatively about Vladek and the question of the book he wishes to "draw about" him as the latter pedaling his stationary bike visually surrounds his son with his own cycling frame. If Vladek contests the frame of the book and seeks implicitly to redraw it about its would-be framer, Art, he does so not only because, as he says, "it would take MANY books, my life, and no one wants anyway to hear such stories" (1:12), but also, as Art's therapist Pavel later suggests, because Vladek in fact sees Art rather than himself as the real survivor of the tale. "Maybe your father needed to show that he was always right—that he could always SURVIVE—because he felt GUILTY about surviving. And he took his guilt out on YOU, where it was safe . . . on the REAL survivor" (2:44).

6. Witek's discussion of the expressionist style employed in "Prisoner on the Hell Planet," a style Spiegelman had at one point considered using for the book-length version of MAUS, is of particular relevance here. "The rejected woodcut style

contained so much information as to trap the reader's gaze within individual panels. But the more open and spare panels of *Maus* allow one's eye to flow smoothly from scene to scene, and we fail to sense that we are constantly being manipulated into reading at a predetermined pace." Joseph Witek, *Comic Books as History: The Narrative Art of Jack Jackson, Art Spiegelman, and Harvey Pekar* (Jackson: University of Mississippi, 1989), 106. Witek adds in a note that Spiegelman discusses the flow of the text at greater length in an interview with Joey Cavalieri, published under the title "Jewish Mice, Bubblegum Cards, Comics Art, and Raw Possibilities," in *Comics Journal*, no. 65 (August 1981): 116–17.

7. Needless to say, the insect repellent is linked to the pesticide Zyklon B used in the gas chamber evoked here as the ultimate vanishing point and center of death.

8. Bingo is defined in *Webster's Third New International Dictionary* as a game in which the playing card is "a grid on which five numbers that are covered in a row in any direction constitute a win, the center square being counted as an already drawn number."

9. Charlotte Delbo, *Auschwitz and After*, trans. Rosette C. Lamont (New Haven, Conn.: Yale University Press, 1995), 267. The passage appears in a section called "The Measure of Our Days," under the heading, "Mado."

10. Cf. the famous checkerboard tile pattern in the ground plane of Lorenzetti's *Annunciation*, which, according to Panofsky, "becomes an index for spatial values and indeed as much for those of the individual bodies as for those of the intervals," enabling us to "express both bodies and intervals . . . numerically, as a number of floor squares." Erwin Panofsky, *Perspective as Symbolic Form*, trans. Christopher S. Wood (New York: Zone, 1991), 57–58.

11. Ibid., 31.

12. Shoshana Felman and Dori Laub, M.D., *Testimony: Crises of Witnessing in Literature, Psychoanalysis, and History* (New York: Routledge, 1992), 209–10.

13. Panofsky, *Perspective as Symbolic Form*, 27. In adopting this definition initially proposed by Dürer, Panofsky adds: "We shall speak of a fully 'perspectival' view of space not when mere isolated objects, such as houses or furniture, are represented in 'foreshortening,' but rather only when the entire picture has been transformed—to cite another Renaissance theoretician—into a 'window,' and when we are meant to believe we are looking through this window into a space" (ibid.).

14. There is a similar strategy at work in Anselm Kiefer's series of photographs entitled *Besetzungen* (Occupations), from 1969. The work consists of photographs taken at various locations all over Europe—historical spaces, landscapes—all of which feature the artist himself performing, citing, embodying the Sieg Heil gesture. I agree with Andreas Huyssen that this gesture

> be read as a conceptual gesture reminding us that indeed Nazi culture had
> most effectively occupied, exploited, and abused the power of the visual,

especially the power of massive monumentalization *and of a confining, even disciplining, central-point perspective.* Fascism had furthermore perverted, abused, and sucked up whole territories of a German image-world, turning national iconic and literary traditions into mere ornaments of power and thereby leaving post-1945 culture with a tabula rasa that was bound to cause a smoldering crisis of identity.

Andreas Huyssen, *Twilight Memories: Marking Time in a Culture of Amnesia* (New York: Routledge, 1995), 216–17; emphasis added.

15. See Derrida, "La Séance continue," a section of "To Speculate—on 'Freud,'" 320–37.

16. Cf. the "sun umbrella" in the shadow of which mother and son sit in a 1960 snapshot taken by Vladek which Spiegelman reproduces in his *Life* magazine article "Mad Love." Spiegelman, *Comix, Essays, Graphics and Scraps: From* MAUS *to Now to* MAUS *to Now* (New York: Raw, 1998), 21–22.

17. Cf. Benjamin's "On Some Motifs in Baudelaire," Poe's "Man of the Crowd," and Freud's "Drives and Their Vicissitudes." See also Nadine Fresco's eloquent discussion of the "empires" of silence, in "Remembering the Unknown," *International Review of Psycho-Analysis* 11, no. 4 (1984): 417–27. This text is a translation (by Alan Sheridan) of her essay "La Diaspora des cendres."

18. Cf. Wiesel's statement, "If someone else could have told these stories, I would not have done so." Cited in Felman and Laub, *Testimony*, 204. Spiegelman's strategic use of upper- and lower-case letters is referred to explicitly in an audio appendix to the beginning of the "Time Flies" section of volume 2:

> Before there was a present with Vladek and me talking and then there was a past with his story. All of a sudden we now have a kind of supra-present and the supra-present is done with certain devices; for one thing the upper- and lower-case writing which is used only a few times earlier in the book. It's used when you very first enter into the story and in a couple of captions like "I went back to visit my father" or something like that and that implies that all of that upper and lower case comes from a different present.

Appendix to 178 of CD-ROM.

19. The voice-over superimposed on the preceding panel located in the bottom right-hand corner of the page before reads: "For over two months I stayed here safe and taught him English" (2:35).

20. See Richard Klein's superb chapter "What Is a Cigarette?" in *Cigarettes Are Sublime* (Durham, N.C.: Duke University Press, 1993), where he observes that the cigarette "is at most a vanishing being. . . . The cigarette not only has little being of its own, it is hardly ever singular, rather always myriad, multiple, proliferating. Every single cigarette numerically implies all the other cigarettes, exactly alike, that the smoker consumes in a series; each cigarette immediately calls forth its inevitable

successor and rejoins the preceding one in a chain of smoking more fervently forged than that of any other form of tobacco" (26). Speaking later of the cigarette's "eminent countability," Klein adds,

> The distinctive character of cigarettes compared to other forms of tobacco is their indistinctness; one cannot distinguish one smoke from another. Each cigarette is exactly, mechanically, indifferently like every previous cigarette one has smoked, perhaps hundreds of thousands of them. Each individual cigarette has its identity insofar as it is like every other one, mere interchangeable tokens. . . . Deprived of any irreducible specificity or distinguishing characteristics, the cigarette has only a collective identity not an individual one. The one is the many; number seems to belong to its identity. (30–31)

21. These juxtaposed passages should themselves be read in relation to the scene in which Vladek obsessively re-adds the figures on his "bank papers" until they "come out so as on the statement" even though, as Art insists, "it's off by less than a buck" (2:23). If Vladek here attacks this problem of addition as though it were a matter of life and death, it is perhaps because in a related series of panels set in Auschwitz it was indeed just that. In this scene a priest is shown studying the number 175113 tattooed on Vladek's arm and exclaiming, "LOOK! added together it totals 18. That's 'Chai,' the Hebrew number of life. I can't tell if I'll survive this hell, but I'm certain YOU'LL come through all this alive!" As the scene shifts back into the present Vladek shows Art his arm, adding, "and whenever it was very bad I looked and said: 'Yes, the priest was right! It totals eighteen'" (2:28).

22. See chapter 2, note 47.

23. "In some ways he DIDN'T survive" (2:90), Art tells Françoise as they wait for Vladek parked outside a supermarket where, as Young observes, the father has gone to trade his story of survival for food.

24. See draft of p. 237 in CD-ROM, "At the Tail-End Of MAUS."

25. Speaking of the collaboration of witness and listener and of testimony as "the narrative's address to hearing," Laub notes that "in the center of this massive dedicated effort remains a danger, a nightmare, a fragility, a woundedness that defies all healing." Felman and Laub, *Testimony*, 73. Needless to say, it is also this center that is very much at the core of MAUS.

26. This is obviously a very traditional privilege particularly in the legal profession. As John Kaplan notes, "Lawyers have innumerable rules involving hearsay, the character of the defendant or of the witness, opinions given by the witness, and the like, which are in one way or another meant to improve the fact-finding process. But more crucial than any one of these—possibly more crucial than all put together—is the evidence of eyewitness testimony." John Kaplan, foreword to Elizabeth F. Loftus, *Eyewitness Testimony* (Cambridge, Mass.: Harvard University Press, 1979), vii.

27. For a detailed discussion of these two frames see Chapter 1, pp. 51–53.

28. See in particular the chapter on deictics, "The Unraveled Calligram," in Michel Foucault, *This Is Not a Pipe*, trans. James Harkness (Berkeley: University of California Press, 1983), 19–31.

29. Apropos of writing, erasure, and saving, Françoise elsewhere tells Art, "I'll bet you that Anja's notebooks were written on both sides of the page. . . . If there were any BLANK PAGES Vladek would never have BURNED them" (2:89).

30. Actually, if one really scrutinizes the drawings, it is possible to detect the shadowy presence of a few scattered figures in the first panel presumably representing the tinmen assigned to remove the pipes and ventilation fans from the underground gas room. Similarly, if one looks carefully at the second panel, there appears to be a pile of mouse corpses located in the far right-hand corner.

31. Indeed, as Vladek observes in a rare moment of metatestimonial reflection, "If I saw a couple of months before how it was all arranged here, only ONE time I could see it!" (2:70).

32. Laub discusses a related "explosion of vitality" in the course of another "survivor's tale" in his chapter "Bearing Witness." The relevance of this discussion is such that it is worth citing at length:

> A woman in her late sixties was narrating her Auschwitz experience to interviewers from the Video Archive for Holocaust Testimonies at Yale. She was slight, self-effacing, almost talking in whispers, mostly to herself. Her presence was indeed barely noteworthy in spite of the overwhelming magnitude of the catastrophe she was addressing. She tread lightly, leaving hardly a trace.
>
> She was relating her memories as an eyewitness of the Auschwitz uprising: a sudden intensity, passion and color were infused into the narrative. She was fully there. "All of sudden," she said, "we saw four chimneys going up in flames, exploding. The flames shot into the sky, people were running. It was unbelievable." There was a silence in the room, a fixed silence against which the woman's words reverberated loudly, as though carrying along an echo of the jubilant sounds exploding from behind barbed wires, a stampede of people breaking loose, screams, shots, battle cries, explosions. It was no longer the deadly timelessness of Auschwitz. A dazzling, brilliant moment from the past swept through the frozen stillness of the muted, grave-like landscape with dashing meteoric speed, exploding it into a shower of sights and sounds. Yet the meteor from the past kept moving on. The woman fell silent and the tumults of the moment faded. She became subdued again and her voice resumed the uneventful, almost monotonous and lamenting tone. The gates of Auschwitz closed and the veil of obliteration and of silence, at once oppressive and repressive, descended once again. The comet of intensity and of aliveness, the explosion of vitality and of resistance faded and receded into the distance.

Felman and Laub, *Testimony*, 59.

33. It is therefore telling that Vladek's next sentence immediately shifts back into the past tense, while in the next panel the narrative itself returns directly to a scene staged as a present moment in the past.

34. In attempting to analyze MAUS as a story of narrative ruptures, a tale of tales prematurely broken off and belatedly begun again, I have sought not only to re-define the "margins" of the text but, in doing so, to bring the question of spec-trality more consistently to the fore.

35. In his reading of *Hamlet* Derrida situates "hauntology" in the following way: as a "logic" which "would not be merely larger and more powerful than an ontology or a thinking of Being (of the 'to be,' assuming that it is a matter of Be-ing in the 'to be or not to be,' but nothing is less certain). It would harbor within itself, but like circumscribed places or particular effects, eschatology and teleology themselves. It would *comprehend* them, but incomprehensibly. How to *compre-hend* in fact the discourse of the end or the discourse about the end? Can the ex-tremity of the extreme ever be comprehended?" Jacques Derrida, *Specters of Marx*, trans. Peggy Kamuf (New York: Routledge, 1994), 10.

36. This essay, originally published in *The Village Voice*, June 6, 1989, accom-panied by a prepublication excerpt of MAUS II, is reprinted in *Comix, Essays, Graphics, and Scraps*, 14–16.

37. For a further discussion of the last scene of MAUS II, see Gertrud Koch, "'Against All Odds'; or, The Will to Survive: Moral Conclusions from Narrative Closure," in *History and Memory: Studies in Representations of the Past* 9, nos. 1–2 (Fall 1997): 393–408.

38. Art Spiegelman, interview on *Fresh Air*, National Public Radio, December 1986, cited in "History and Talking Animals: Art Spiegelman's *Maus*," in *Comic Books as History: The Narrative Art of Jack Jackson, Art Spiegelman, and Harvey Pekar*, (Jackson: University of Mississippi Press, 1989) 101. See Theodor W. Adorno, "What Does Coming to Terms with the Past Mean?" trans. Timothy Bahti and Geoffrey Hartman, in *Bitburg in Moral and Political Perspective*, ed. Ge-offrey H. Hartman (Bloomington: Indiana University Press, 1986), 114–29; origi-nally published in German as "Was heisst Aufarbeitung der Vergangenheit?" in *Eingriffe* (Interventions). Translation based on Adorno's *Gesammelte Schriften*, vol. 10, pt. 2 (Frankfurt am Main: Suhrkamp Verlag, 1977), 555–72.

CHAPTER 4: WRITING ANXIETY

1. Trans. Margaret Sayers Peden, in Christa Wolf, *Patterns of Childhood*, trans. Ursule Molinaro and Hedwig Rappolt (New York: Farrar, Straus and Giroux, 1980). The Neruda quote serves as the epigraph to the novel and appears on an un-numbered page.

2. Wolf, *Patterns of Childhood*, 67; *Kindheitsmuster* (Darmstadt:Luchterhand, 1979), 67. The novel was initially published in the GDR by Aufbau Verlag in 1976.

All references to the English and German editions will henceforth appear in parentheses in the body of the text, the English page number first, the German one second.

3. I am grateful to Jenny Kassanoff for her help in locating the Faulkner citation, which is to be found in act 1, scene 3 of *Requiem*.

4. I have attempted elsewhere to elaborate the split temporality of such encounters in the context of a reading of Freud and the censorship of dreams, in *Writing Through Repression: Literature, Censorship, Psychoanalysis* (Baltimore: Johns Hopkins University Press, 1994). See especially pp. 31–32 and 78.

5. The language of "coming to oneself [*zu sich kommen*]" appears early on in chapter 5, when a call to reason is sounded only to be echoed and parodically displaced: "She is finally listening to reason. Understanding and listening to reason. Thus: to come to one's senses. (Come to your senses!) [*Jetzt hat sie endlich Vernunft angenommen. Einsicht haben und Vernunft annehmen. Auch: Zu sich kommen. (Komm zu dir!)*]" (92, 89). The chapter opens with a reflection on the vicissitudes of reason and on "reason as grounds for approval [*Vernunft als Übereinstimmung*]" (91, 88). I will return to this notion of *Übereinstimmung* below.

6. These are the two most common ways of interpreting the narrator 's substitution of the third person for the first when referring to herself as a child. Many critics take as their point of departure a statement found at the beginning of the novel, "to remain speechless, or else to live in the third person. The first is impossible, the second strange [*unheimlich*]" (3, 9). Among the numerous studies of "persons" and pronouns in *Patterns of Childhood*, see Bella Brodzki, "Mothers, Displacement, and Language in the Autobiographies of Nathalie Sarraute and Christa Wolf," in *Life/Lines*, ed. Bella Brodzki and Celeste Schenk (Ithaca, N.Y.: Cornell University Press, 1988, 243–59); Kathleen L. Komar, "The Difficulty of Saying 'I': Reassembling a Self in Christa Wolf's Autobiographical Fiction," in *Redefining Autobiography in Twentieth-Century Women's Fiction*, ed. Janice Morgan and Colette T. Hall (New York: Garland, 1991), 261–79; Judith Ryan, "The Discontinuous Self: Christa Wolf's *A Model Childhood*," in *The Uncompleted Past: Postwar German Novels and the Third Reich* (Detroit: Wayne State University Press, 1983); Anna Kuhn, "*Patterns of Childhood:* The Confrontation with the Self," in *Christa Wolf's Utopian Vision: From Marxism to Feminism* (Cambridge: Cambridge University Press, 1988); Ruth Ginsburg, "In Pursuit of Self: Theme, Narration, and Focalization in Christa Wolf's *Patterns of Childhood*" *Style* 26, no. 3 (Fall 1992): 437–46; Catherine Viollet, "Nachdenken über Pronomina: Zur Entstehung von Christa Wolfs Kindheitsmuster," *Zeitschrift für Literaturwissenschaft und Linguistik* 17, no. 68 (1987): 52–62; see also Wolf's own discussion of *Kindheitsmuster* in "A Model of Experience," in *The Fourth Dimension*, trans. Hilary Pilkington (London: Verso, 1988), 39–63.

7. This passage, curiously omitted from the English translation, is to be found on page 9 of the German edition. Previously unpublished translations are by the author of the present volume.

8. Wolf's ongoing concern with this question in the new context of a reunified German state and in the aftermath of the heated debates surrounding her controversial involvement with the Stasi, the East German secret police, is reflected in the title of her collection of essays *Auf dem Weg nach Tabou* (On the Way to Tabu). This collection has appeared in English translation under the title *Parting from Phantoms*, trans. Jan van Heurck (Chicago: University of Chicago Press, 1997).

9. Compare in this regard the following passage: "Such then is the cascade of voices. As if someone had opened the sluice gates behind which these voices had been dammed up [*Solche Stimmen nun, haufenweise. Als hätte jemand eine Schleuse hochgezogen, hinter der die Stimmen eingesperrt waren*]" (32, 35; trans. modified).

10. For a sensitive discussion of "the *unheimlich*" and its relation to questions of anxiety in the novel, see the epilogue to Eric Santner's *Stranded Objects* (Ithaca, N.Y.: Cornell University Press, 1990), 156–62.

11. One is reminded here of a situation Jabès has described as "the bitter stubbornness of a wandering question [*l'amère obstination d'une question errante*]." Edmond Jabès, *The Book of Questions*, trans. Rosmarie Waldrop (Hanover, N.H.: Wesleyan University Press, 1991), 26.

12. Early on in the novel the narrator sounds out various resonances of the term *Kindheitsmuster*:

> Tentative titles. . . . Zeroing in on the unknown word, seemingly hidden under a parchment-thin layer, but eluding the brain's antennae. Basics Patterns, Behavior Patterns, Childhood Patterns. A Model Childhood. . . . A model [*Muster*] is used for demonstration. To demonstrate is derived from the Latin "monstrum," which originally meant "showpiece," or "model," which suits you perfectly. But "monstrum" can also become "monster" in today's sense of the word. Right now, as a matter of fact: Standartführer Rudi Arndt (an animal, believe me, nothing but an animal. A statement by Charlotte Jordan). Except that this particular animal doesn't rouse your interest half as much as the hordes of half-men, half-beasts with whom, generally speaking, you're more familiar from within yourself. (36, 39)

The English edition inexplicably omits the entire next sentence, which continues this meditation, focusing, in turn, on "the anxiety which gushes forth from the obscure abyss between man and beast [*die Angst, die aus dem dunklen Abgrund zwischen Mensch und Vieh hoch aufschießt*]." On the interrelationship between the *Muster* as model, example, and monster and a certain mustering [*Musterung*] of examples, see Samuel Weber's reading of Freud's "The Uncanny," an essay in which questions of anxiety also play a crucial role. Weber, "The Sideshow; or, Remarks on a Canny Moment," *MLN* 88 (1973): 1102–33.

13. Commenting in a related context on the question of "indifference," Adorno writes, "A very large number of people claim not to have known what was hap-

pening then, although Jews were disappearing everywhere, and although it can hardly be assumed that those who experienced events in the East would always have kept silent about what must have been an unbearable burden for them. One may certainly suggest that a proportional relation exists between the gesture of 'I didn't know anything about all that' and an indifference that is obtuse and frightened, at the very least." Theodor Adorno, "What Does Coming to Terms with the Past Mean?" in *Bitburg in Moral and Political Perspective*, ed. Geoffrey H. Hartman (Bloomington: Indiana University Press, 1986), 116.

14. One might note in passing the unsuspected formal similarity between the second-person narration, in which the narrator always implicitly addresses her reader, "you," while apparently speaking only to herself and the use of the third person, Nelly, as an "innocent" address to whom or rather in care of whom questions destined for other unnamed "persons" may be sent.

15. The cinematic notion of an "afterimage" [*Nachbild*] is used here in the particular sense given to it by Benjamin in his essay "On Some Motifs in Baudelaire," in which he writes of the way Bergson "manages . . . to stay clear of that experience from which his own philosophy evolved or, rather in reaction to which it arose. It is the inhospitable, *blinding* age of big-scale industrialism. In *shutting out* this experience the eye perceives an experience of a complementary nature in the form of its spontaneous *afterimage*, as it were." Walter Benjamin, *Illuminations*, trans. Harry Zohn, ed. Hannah Arendt (New York: Schocken, 1969), 157. For further discussion of this passage see the chapter "*En Garde!* Benjamin's Baudelaire and the Training of Shock Defense," in my book *Writing Through Repression*, 91–113. See also Henry Sussman, *Afterimages of Modernity* (Baltimore: Johns Hopkins University Press, 1990).

16. Shoshana Felman and Dori Laub, M.D., *Testimony: Crises of Witnessing in Literature, Psychoanalysis, and History* (New York: Routledge, 1992), 223–24.

17. While Felman never uses the term *fugue* in her essay "The Return of the Voice: Claude Lanzmann's *Shoah*," she does describe the film at one point "as a chorus of performances and testimonies, [which creates] within the framework of its structure, a communality of singing, an odd community of testimonial incommensurates which held together [i.e., differently and differentially con-tained], have an overwhelming testimonial impact" (ibid., 279). One might also cite in this context Lanzmann's assertion, "*Shoah* had to be built like a musical piece, where a theme appears at a lower level, disappears, comes back again at a higher level or in full force, disappears, and so on. It was the only way *to keep several parameters together* (cited in ibid., 277; emphasis added).

18. Christa Wolf, *The Author's Dimension* (New York: Farrar, Straus and Giroux, 1993), 58.

19. Peter Szondi, "Reading '*Engführung*': An Essay on the Poetry of Paul Celan," trans. David Caldwell and S. Esh, in *boundary 2* 11, no. 3 (1983): 232.

20. One might recall in this connection a passage cited earlier in which the signifiers *eng* and *Angst* are metonymically "coupled." "Seit wann," the narrator asks, "*ist Elternliebe so* eng mit Angst *verkoppelt*" (119).

21. Obviously, the phrase "Ich weiß es nicht" is an expression of uncertainty difficult to confuse with the blissful ignorance of a saying like "Was ich nicht weiß, macht mich nicht heiß" (141). I would suggest only that by the time the first-person singular actually appears in the novel we are prepared both by the preceding narrative and by the all too obvious signs of uncertainty marking its appearance to look for other, less obvious and less certain ones.

22. As if to suggest that *Kindheitsmuster* itself be read as a book of (open) questions, the first two questions asked by the narrator in this passage repeat almost verbatim the opening lines of the text's epigraph, taken from Neruda's *Book of Questions*.

23. The text continues, "One day I will even talk about it in that other language which, as of yet, is in my ear but not on my tongue. Today I knew would still be too soon. But would I know when the time was right? Would I ever find my language?" Christa Wolf, *What Remains and Other Stories*, trans. Heike Schwarzbauer and Rick Takvorian (New York: Farrar, Straus Giroux, 1993), 231; *Was bleibt* (Frankfurt am Main: Luchterhand, 1990), 7. For a sensitive discussion of *What Remains* and the debates following its West German publication in early June 1990, see Andreas Huyssen, *Twilight Memories: Marking Time in a Culture of Amnesia* (New York: Routledge, 1995), 49–66; see also Thomas Anz, ed., "*Es geht nicht um Christa Wolf": Der Literaturstreit im vereinten Deutschland* (Munich: Spangenberg, 1991).

24. Wolf, *The Author's Dimension*, 62–63.

CHAPTER 5: TOWARD AN ADDRESSABLE YOU

1. The poem "Die Posaunenstelle" was first published in the posthumous collection *Zeitgehöft* (Homestead of Time) in 1976 and appears in *Selected Poems and Prose of Paul Celan*, trans. John Felstiner (New York: Norton, 2001), under the title "The Shofar Place" (360–61). Whereas Felstiner renders these lines as "hear deep in/with your mouth," I would translate them more simply as "listen in/with your mouth." For a very eloquent reading of the poem, see Stéphane Moses, "Patterns of Negativity in Paul Celan's 'The Trumpet Place,'" trans. Ken Frieden, in *Languages of the Unsayable: The Play of Negativity in Literature and Literary Theory*, ed. Sanford Budick and Wolfgang Iser (Stanford, Calif.: Stanford University Press, 1987), 209–24.

2. Émile Benveniste, *Indo-European Language and Society*, trans. Elizabeth Palmer (Coral Gables, Fla.: University of Miami Press, 1973), 393; emphasis added.

3. "The Question of Our Speech: The Return to Aural Culture," reprinted in Cynthia Ozick, *Metaphor and Memory* (New York: Knopf, 1989), 146. All references to this essay will henceforth appear in parentheses in the body of the text.

4. Cynthia Ozick, *The Puttermesser Papers* (New York: Vintage, 1998), 7. All references to this novel will henceforth appear in parentheses in the text.

5. Cynthia Ozick, *The Cannibal Galaxy* (New York: Syracuse University Press, 1983), 12. All references will henceforth appear in parentheses.

6. Cynthia Ozick, *The Shawl* (New York: Vintage, 1990), 19. All references will henceforth appear in parentheses.

7. Cynthia Ozick, *The Messiah of Stockholm* (New York: Vintage, 1988), 101. All references will henceforth appear in parentheses.

8. Since it is a question here of vomiting, it should be noted that the upside-down mouth stands not only as a locus of inverted doubling but also as the place where the body threatens to turn itself inside out. We will return to this question below.

9. These dead letters are often filled not only with a mother's longing for her lost child, but for her home in Warsaw and her own mother, for the Madonna-like purity of Motherhood, and the unbroken flow of the mother tongue. "A pleasure, the deepest pleasure," Rosa writes from Miami to Magda in their native Polish, "home bliss, to speak in our own language" (40). In another letter all these longings are brought together in a highly sanitized vision of motherhood. "Motherhood," she writes, "is a profound distraction from philosophy, and all philosophy is rooted in suffering over the passage of time. I mean the *fact* of motherhood, the physiological fact. To have the power to create another human being, to be the instrument of such a mystery. To pass on a whole genetic system. I don't believe in God, but I believe, like the Catholics, in mystery. My mother wanted so much to convert; my father laughed at her. But she was attracted. She let the maid keep a statue of the Virgin and Child in the corner of the kitchen. Sometimes she used to go in and look at it. I can even remember the words of a poem she wrote about the heat coming up from the stove, from the Sunday pancakes—

> Mother of God, how you shiver
> in these heat-ribbons!
> Our cakes rise to you
> and in the trance of His birthing
> you hide. (41–42)

However idealized the figure of the Mother, however illusory the dream of restoring a certain "before" may be, such illusions are the stuff, the very warp and woof, of a dream the protagonist clearly cannot bear to live without. Living within that dream, wrapping herself in it as though she were now the daughter swaddled in her beloved shawl, she seeks to protect herself from the overwhelming reality of the "during." If, according to Rosa, it is only this during that stays, it does so, the text suggests, not so much as a memory she conjures at will, but rather as an ongoing nightmare from which she rarely, if ever, awakens. It is this struggle *within* dreams, on the part of one kind of dream to stave off another, to dream, as it were, both on this side of the pleasure principle and beyond it, that gives *The Shawl* its peculiar texture.

10. There are numerous similarities between Rosa and the protagonist of *The Cannibal Galaxy*, Joseph Brill. Like Rosa, Brill is said to be "dying of lack of death—his reason deprived, he was like a barbarian who cannot fathom the link between copulation and procreation" (86).

11. That Magda's mouth is a locus of death-in-life is suggested by a description of her teeth just starting to break through the gums: "One mite of a tooth tip sticking up in the bottom gum, how shining, an elfin tombstone of white marble gleaming there" (4).

12. It should be noted that the distinction between third- and first-person narration also seems to dissolve here.

13. For a discussion of the shawl in Winnicottian terms, see Andrew Gordon, "Cynthia Ozick's 'The Shawl' and the Transitional Object," in *Literature and Psychology* 30, nos. 1 and 2 (1994): 1–9.

14. Julia Kristeva, *Tales of Love*, trans. Leon S. Roudiez (New York: Columbia University Press, 1987), 24.

15. My reading of this passage runs counter to the more redemptive interpretations proposed by other Ozick critics. Margot Martin, for example, draws the dubious conclusion that "the soldier has freed [Magda] from her bondage to enjoy immortality, to join with the humming voices, and possibly to cross into that beautiful world beyond the fence." I also take issue with Amy Gottfried's suggestion that "Magda's metaphoric transformation into a butterfly" be read as "a gift of redemption for those who suffered in the Holocaust," adding that her "graceful death signifies an instant of transcendence." Margot Martin, "The Theme of Survival in Cynthia Ozick's 'The Shawl,'" *RE: Artes Liberales* 14, no. 1 (Fall–Spring 1988): 31–36; Amy Gottfried, "Fragmented Art and the Liturgical Community of the Dead in Cynthia Ozick's *The Shawl*," *Studies in American Jewish Literature* 13 (1994): 39–51.

16. Hana Wirth-Nesher, "The Languages of Memory: Cynthia Ozick's *The Shawl*," in *Multilingual America: Transnationalism, Ethnicity, and the Languages of American Literature*, ed. Werner Sollers (New York: New York University Press, 1998), 316.

17. Konnilyn G. Feig, *Hitler's Death Camps: The Sanity of Madness* (Holmes and Meier, 1981), 321. The exact number seems to vary. Konstantin Simonov gives the figure of 18,000, the eyewitness Paul Trepman as 22,000, while Feig maintains that 18,400 Jews were killed on that day.

18. Paul Trepman, *Among Men and Beasts*, trans. Shoshana Perla and Gertrude Hirschler (South Brunswick, N.J.: Barnes, 1978), 138.

19. Ibid., 137–43. While Trepman recalls the date of these mass executions as being that of September 3, Feig maintains that they took place on November 3, 1943.

20. Shoshana Felman and Dori Laub, M.D., *Testimony: Crises of Witnessing in Literature, Psychoanalysis, and History* (New York: Routledge, 1992), 29–33. The following discussion of Celan's poem is greatly indebted to Felman's analysis.

21. See Primo Levi's mention of "Rosamunde" in *Survival in Auschwitz*, trans. Stuart Woolf (New York: Macmillan/Collier, 1961), 30.

22. John Felstiner, *Paul Celan: Poet, Survivor, Jew* (New Haven, Conn.: Yale University Press, 1995), 28.

23. Wirth-Nesher, "The Languages of Memory," 321–23.

24. *Selected Poems and Prose of Paul Celan*, trans. John Felstiner (New York: Norton, 2001), 30–33 (trans. mod.).

25. Felman and Laub, *Testimony*, 33.

26. Paul Celan, "Speech on the Occasion of Receiving the Literature Prize of the Free Hanseatic City of Bremen," in *Selected Poems and Prose*, 396; trans. modified.

27. Various senses of the verb *to pant* are sounded out in *The Cannibal Galaxy*, where it is a question at one point of "a Jew *panting* for Jerusalem" (22), at another of "a prayer of the lung [which] was merely *panting* and throat-pain" (24), at still another of "the wife, always out of breath, *panting* faintly in a way that ravished, [who] pleaded so passionately for the actuality of the Savior . . . " (59), and then finally, in words addressed by Hester Lilt to Joseph Brill, of "'anguish over the graveyards of the world! Anguish over school failure . . . ! What you can't swallow! It won't go down your gullet! Principal Brill can't be put in a position where he might have to flunk the fruit of his own loins! Tell me—am I right? Am I right? Say it!' She was *panting*; he heard it clearly" (112–13; emphasis added).

28. Whereas Kauvar links the mention of the "wolf's screech" to a pattern of associations leading back to Virgil's *Aeneid* (and the founding of Rome), I am more inclined to read it in terms of Hitler's so-called "Wolf's Lair" and, more generally, as an allusion to the strangeness of the familiar, the werewolf, the seemingly domestic and civilized creature as wild beast. See Elaine Kauvar, *Cynthia Ozick's Fiction: Tradition and Invention* (Bloomington: Indiana University Press, 1993), 197.

29. Vulcan's hammer introduced through the mention of Pompeii's "volcanic ash" is not far off. More generally it should be noted that to be stuck in the time frame of the "during" ("Before is a dream. After is a joke. Only during stays. And to call it a life is a lie," Rosa tells Persky [58]) is to be trapped in the enduring frozenness of life-in-death. This time frame is associated here and elsewhere in Ozick's work with the figure of "waves." For example, in *The Cannibal Galaxy*, "'the Principal' of the Edmond Fleg School (Fleg as in 'Phlegmatic' or 'Flegethon, the river of fire that runs through Hell')" (5) is described at one point as seeing "how he had not died in the middle of the time of dying. And then he saw how they would continue to pass before him, these children who were eternally children, who could never grow beyond the age of pubescence; they passed before him, always the same, always the same. . . . Wave after wave, and always the same wave. They were like stars that are still alive, or possibly dead" (45). Like Rosa, Principal

Brill is a Holocaust survivor. Yet, unlike her, he is hidden in the cellar of a convent and thereby avoids being sent to the camps. Still he finds himself later in the novel stranded like Rosa at the water's edge at the limit of life-death. "On the beach of the Phlegethon, seeing each new wave identically supplant the previous wave, it came to him one freezing dawn that he was dying of unchangingness: he was dying of lack of death" (86).

30. Nietzsche, *The Gay Science*, bk. 2, § 60, trans. Josefine Nauckhoff (New York: Cambridge University Press, 2001), 71; trans. modified.

31. Compare this scene and the logic of deferred parturition enacted throughout *The Shawl* to Ozick's description of Hester Lilt in *The Cannibal Galaxy*: "The more she delivered," it is said, "the more she withheld" (92).

32. The messianic overtones of this scene—the place it makes for the "unexpected" coming of an Other—echo an enigmatic remark made by Hester Lilt in *The Cannibal Galaxy*. "To expect, to welcome, exactly that which appears most unpredictable. To await the surprise which, when it comes, turns out to be not a surprise after all, but a natural path" (68).

33. Kauvar, *Cynthia Ozick's Fiction*, 199.

34. In her 1988 essay "Primo Levi's Suicide Note," Ozick describes Levi as "a Darwin of the death camps: not the Virgil of the German hell but its scientific investigator." The essay was later republished in Ozick, *Metaphor and Memory*, where the citation appears on 37.

35. Virgil, *Eclogues, Georgics, Aeneid I–VI*, trans. H. Rushton Fairclough, Loeb Classical Library (Cambridge, Mass.: Harvard University Press 1999), 543.

36. Unlike the rest of her one-sided correspondence with Magda, this particular "letter" is not written with a "regular pen" on paper, but is inscribed instead directly within the folds of the "brain": " . . . she was writing inside a blazing flying current, a terrible beak of light bleeding out a kind of cuneiform on the underside of the brain" (69).

37. Kauvar, *Cynthia Ozick's Fiction*, 199.

38. In *The Cannibal Galaxy* the figure of the labyrinth is again associated with the structure of an enigma in a phrase used to describe Hester Lilt. Brill "kept himself informed—he watched over whatever came from her lips or her pen. The heat, *the mazy network of enigma*, the conflagration of Hester Lilt's mind!" (74; emphasis added).

39. The messianic overtones of this unconscious opening toward the Other, toward that which never exactly comes as such, become clearer when one reads *The Shawl* in conjunction with a text dear to Ozick, Bruno Schulz's *Sanitorium Under the Sign of the Hourglass*, where the Messiah's coming is staged as a curiously—and I dare say *necessarily*—"missed encounter," as a scene played out under the sign of the unconscious in which all those involved seem like somnambulists to sleepwalk through their parts in a world which appears to stand as open as the "addressable you" toward which Celan's own errant "messages in a bottle" are said

to be drifting. "We could have divided it between us and renamed it, so open, un-protected, and unattached was the world. On such a day the Messiah advances to the edge of the horizon and looks down on the earth. And when He sees it, white, silent, surrounded by azure and contemplation, He may lose sight of the boundary of clouds that arrange themselves into a passage, and, *not knowing what He is doing*, He may descend upon earth. And in its reverie the earth won't even notice Him, who has descended onto its roads, and people will wake up from their afternoon nap remembering nothing. The whole event will be rubbed out, and everything will be as it has been for centuries, as it was before history began." Bruno Schulz, *Sanitorium Under the Sign of the Hourglass*, trans. Celina Wieniewska (New York: Walker, 1978), 21; emphasis added. Here the timelessness of paradise seems to intervene in the world as a scene in which "nothing happens." Compare in this regard the sublime thirteenth chapter of *The Messiah of Stockholm* in which the protagonist, Lars Andemening, is said to fall into the text of *The Messiah*

> with the force of a man who throws himself against a glass wall. He crashes through it to the other side, and what was there? Baroque arches and niches, intricately hedged byways of a language so incised, so *bleeding*—a touch could set off a hundred slicing blades—that it could catch a traveler anywhere along the way with this knife or that prong. Lars did not resist or hide; he let his flesh rip. . . . Always afterward Lars remembered the rising of his lamentation. It was as if he had been accumulating remorse even as he fled through passage after passage. He could not contain what he met; he could not keep it. Amnesia descended with the opacity of a dropped hood. What he took he lost. And instantly grieved, because he could not keep it. (105–6)

See also the description of Paradise (or PRDS) in the final pages of *The Puttermesser Papers*. "In Paradise, where sight and insight, inner and outer, sweet and salt, logic and illogic, are shuffled in the manner of a kaleidoscope, nothing is permanent. Nothing will stay. All is ephemeral. . . . the images within the soul shift, drift, wander. Paradise is a dream bearing the inscription on Solomon's seal: *this too will pass*" (234).

40. As the last line of the text punningly suggests, Magda is not just "away" in the end but, more silently and enigmatically, *a way* (70).

41. Of note here is the way Rosa views the other women she sees milling around the lobby of her Miami hotel. That view is itself not direct but instead clouded by the conflation of third- and first-person voices, through what the narratologist, Gérard Genette, has termed "free indirect style." The problem of identifying who or what Rosa sees in this scene—the object of vision—is thus compounded by and reflected in the related difficulty of specifying its viewing subject.

> The "guests"—some had been residents for a dozen years—were already milling around, groomed for lunch, the old women in sundresses showing

their thick collar-bones and the bluish wells above them. Instead of napes they had rolls of wide fat. They wore no stockings. Brazen blue-marbled sinews strangled their squarish calves; in their reveries they were again young women with immortal pillar legs, the white legs of strong goddesses; it was only that they had forgotten about impermanence. In their faces, too, you could see everything they were not noticing about themselves—the red gloss on their drawstring mouths was never meant to restore youth. It was meant only to continue it. Flirts of seventy. Everything had stayed the same for them: intentions, actions, even expectations—they had not advanced. They believed in the seamless continuity of the body. (28)

That this lobby is to be viewed as a space of reflection, a hall of mirrors in which depictions of the other become a privileged mode of self-description, in which the recognition of other women's apparent credulity becomes a way of identifying Rosa's own delusional blind spots, is suggested by the account of that space given in the next paragraph. "It was real and it was not real. Shadows on a wall, the shadows stirred, but you could not penetrate the wall. . . . Every wall of the lobby a mirror. Every mirror hanging thirty years. Every table surface a mirror. In these mirrors the guests appeared to themselves as they used to be" (29). The disorienting play of reflections in this scene makes Rosa appear to be gazing at herself in the mirror of the other—which is to say that the other women's lack of self-awareness ("you could see everything they were not noticing about themselves"), their belief in "the seamless continuity of the body" and their desire for bodily integrity are also in some sense her own. The scene suggests, in other words, that Rosa is able to assume such things about herself only in the mode of denegation. The space described here as being both "real" and "not real" might thus be viewed as the very space of desire, defined as that which places the protagonist in a kind of double bind, that which she finds impossible to assume as her own and yet impossible not to. More generally, it should be noted that the spatial problem of distinguishing "who stands before" from "what takes after" in this scene of reflection, this *mise-en-abîme* structure of mirroring desires, must in its turn be read in relation to the temporal issues raised in Rosa's claim that "before is a dream" and "after is a joke." At this point it becomes clear that if "only during stays," it does so not simply because it is a time set apart from the other two time frames, but rather because all three are subjected to a different temporal logic, a "timelessness" of the unconscious, in which before, during, and after may no longer be viewed as successive or mutually exclusive moments. It is a question here of a "certain 'timelessness,'" because, as Derrida has stressed, what is at stake is not merely "a negation of time, a cessation of time in a present or a simultaneity, but a different structure, a different stratification of time" (Jacques Derrida, *Writing and Difference*, trans. Alan Bass [Chicago: University of Chicago Press, 1978], 214–15).

It is this timelessness of the unconscious to which Rosa inadvertently alludes in her description of "before" as a dream and "after" as a joke. That her words at this moment betray her intentions, only to give voice to a more general textual strategy of privileging the very language of dreams and jokes, is significant. For it is in this language of the Other that Rosa's story is written. Scripted in a language she herself does not comprehend, it is the story first and foremost of her *dispossession*, the story not of her life but of its loss—"You ain't got a life?" Persky asks. "Thieves took it," the survivor laconically replies (28). It is a story that paradoxically is Rosa's own precisely to the extent that she herself does not have access to it.

That story, one particular version of which is the dream of a certain life "before," is not told by any one person in *The Shawl* but is instead inscribed there as a kind of *Traumschrift*, a text which remains by definition indecipherable to the dreaming subject enmeshed in it and which is nevertheless only hers to decipher as the very enigma of her survival. "A terrible beak of light bleeding out a kind of cuneiform on the underside of her brain" (69), this dream text is not only one in which Rosa is enmeshed, but moreover one which is itself inscribed as a palimpsest on the tissue of her body. Inhabited by this indecipherable text, the body itself becomes the generalized locus of an enigma, a dark continent Rosa explores as though groping her way toward the solution of a riddle. Mystified by the enigma it has become, Rosa also perceives this body as vaguely threatening, as though it itself were a foreign body, another body within her own, posing *as* her own, as though it were a body which seemed to her to be perpetually coming apart at the seams.

42. Osip Mandelstam, *Selected Essays*, ed. and trans. Sidney Monas (Austin: University of Texas Press, 1977), 62–63.

43. I am grateful to Janet Jakobsen, director of the Women's Center at Barnard College, for comments on an earlier draft of this chapter and particularly for her reflections on the traditional gendering of the narrative.

44. Walter Benjamin, *Illuminations*, trans. Harry Zohn (New York: Schocken Books, 1969), 264; emphasis added. "Theses on the Philosophy of History" is a translation of "Über den Begriff der Geschichte," now to be found in Benjamin, *Gesammelte Schriften*, vol. 1, pt. 2. The passage cited here appears in the German on 704.

CHAPTER 6: SILENT WINE

1. Jean Laplanche and J.-B. Pontalis, *The Language of Psychoanalysis*, trans. Donald Nicholson-Smith (New York: Norton, 1973), 111.

2. Walter Benjamin, *Illuminations*, trans. Harry Zohn (New York: Schocken, 1976), 71.

3. The belatedness of Lacan's return to the thresholds of Freud's text is itself marked by a peculiar movement of translation, by a way of translating from the German that which was never exactly there in the first place. This is most strikingly evident in his reading of the famous dream of the burning child, in *The Interpretation of Dreams*. Laying particular stress on the doorways explicitly mentioned in that dream, as well as the dream's own location at the threshold between

chapters 6 and 7 of Freud's text, Lacan describes the question, "Father, can't you see I'm burning?" as "itself a firebrand." "One cannot see," he continues, "what is burning, for the flames blind us to the fact that the fire bears on [*porte sur*] the *Un-terlegt*, on the *Untertragen*, on the real." Jacques Lacan, *The Four Fundamental Concepts of Psychoanalysis*, trans. Alan Sheridan (New York: Norton, 1978), 59. Curiously, Lacan uses the term *Untertragen*, which does not exist in German, as though it were already there in original and which his own notion of *souffrance* appears merely to translate. Here the place of the "porte" marks the opening of another kind of question concerning the very movement of bearing and of bearing across, the question, that is, of Lacan's own translation or *Übertragung* of *Untertragen* as *souffrance*. Earlier in this lecture Lacan writes, "To this requirement correspond those radical points that I call encounters, and which enable us to conceive reality as *unterlegt, untertragen*, which, with the superb ambiguity of the French language, appear to be translated by the same word—*souffrance*. Reality is in abeyance there, awaiting attention" (55–56). Needless to say, it is not merely a question here of the "superb ambiguity of the French" but of what happens in the course of Lacan's own ferrying movement back and forth "between" languages. On the "seesaw effect between the two events" associated with the Freudian notion of belatedness, see Laplanche, *Life and Death in Psychoanalysis*, trans. Jeffrey Mehlman (Baltimore: Johns Hopkins University Press, 1976), 41ff. For a discussion of questions of translation as they relate to the structure of belatedness in Lacan's reading of the dream of the burning child, see Cathy Caruth's chapter "Traumatic Awakenings," in her book *Unclaimed Experience* (Baltimore: Johns Hopkins University Press, 1996), 91–112.

   4. Paul Celan, *Gesammelte Werke* (Frankfurt am Main: Suhrkamp, 1986), 1:140; *Selected Poems and Prose of Paul Celan*, trans. John Felstiner (New York: Norton, 2001), 82–83.

   5. In her persuasive reading of Celan's "Todesfuge," Felman writes,

> The violence is all the more obscene by being thus *aestheticized* and by aestheticizing its own dehumanization, by transforming its own murderous perversity into the cultural sophistication and the cultivated trances of a hedonistic art performance. But the poem works specifically and contrapuntally to dislocate this masquerade of cruelty as art, and to exhibit the obscenity of this aestheticization, by opposing the melodious ecstasy of the aesthetic pleasure to the dissonance of the commandant's speech acts and to the violence of his verbal abuse, and by reintroducing into the amnesia of the "fugue"—into the obliviousness of the *artistic drunkenness*—the drinking of black milk as *the impossibility of forgetting* and of getting a reprieve from suffering and memory, and as the sinister, insistent, *unforgettable return of what the aesthetic pleasure has forgotten.*

Later in the same essay Felman adds, "To prevent the possibility of an aesthetic, drunken infatuation with its own verse, the later poetry rejects, within the language, not its music and singing—which continue to define the essence of poetic language for Celan—but a certain predetermined kind of recognizably *melodious* musicality." Shoshana Felman and Dori Laub, M.D., *Testimony: Crises of Witnessing in Literature, Psychoanalysis, and History* (New York: Routledge, 1992), 31, 35.

While I agree in general with the latter claim, I see such a strategy at work not only in Celan's later poetry but already in earlier poems like "Die Winzer." On the question of poetry's transfigurative powers see also Adorno's essay "Commitment," in which he writes, "The aesthetic principle of stylization . . . make[s] an unthinkable fate appear to have had some meaning; it is transfigured, something of its horror is removed. This alone does an injustice to the victims. . . . [Some] works . . . are even willingly absorbed as contributions to clearing up the past." Adorno, "Commitment" (1962), trans. Francis McDonagh, in *The Essential Frankfurt School Reader*, ed. Andrew Arato and Eike Gebhardt, intro. Paul Ricoeur (New York: Continuum, 1982), 313.

6. In his 1958 reply to a questionnaire from the Flinker Bookstore, Celan writes,

> German poetry is going in a very different direction from French poetry. No matter how alive its traditions, with most sinister events in its memory, most questionable developments around it, it can no longer speak the language which many willing ears seem to expect. Its language has become more sober, more factual. It distrusts "the beautiful," it tries to be truthful. If I may search for a visual analogy while keeping in mind the polychrome of apparent actuality: it is a "greyer" language, a language which wants to locate even its "musicality" in such a way that it has nothing in common with the "euphony" which more or less blithely continued to sound alongside the greatest horror. The concern of this language is in all the irreducible polyvalence of the term: precision [*geht es, bei aller unabdingbaren Vielstelligkeit des Ausdrucks um Präzision*]. It does not transfigure or render "poetical": it names, it posits, it tries to measure the area of the given and of the possible. True, this is never the working of language itself, language as such, but always of an "I" who speaks from the particular angle of inclination which is his existence and who is concerned with outlines [*Kontur*] and orientation. Reality is not simply there, it must be searched for and won.

Paul Celan, *Gesammelte Werke* (hereafter *GW*), 3:167–68; *Collected Prose*, trans. Rosmarie Waldrop (New York: Sheep Meadow Press, 1986), 15–16; trans. modified. Emphasizing the polyvalence of the term *precision*, Celan suggests it be understood not only in the more common sense of exactness but, more literally, as an act of precutting related to what is described in the same paragraph as the speaker's concern with outlines (*Kontur*) and orientation. Like its English cognate, the German *Kontur* suggests a particular kind of outline, one which turns around a curving or irregular figure. The "precision" Celan speaks of may thus also be read as an act of circumcision, which at once circles around and etches out a reality that "must searched for and won."

7. This intertwining evokes that of Baudelaire's prose poem, "Le Thyrse": "physiquement ce n'est qu'un bâton, un pur bâton, perche à houblon, tuteur de vigne, sec, dur et droit. Autour de ce bâton, dans des méandres capricieux, se jouent et folâtrent des tiges et des fleurs, celles-ci sinueuses et fuyardes, celles-là penchées comme des choches ou des coupes renversées. Et une gloire étonnante jaillit de cette complexité de lignes et de couleurs, tendres ou éclatantes." Baudelaire, *Le Spleen de Paris* (Paris: Gallimard, 1973), 467.

8. Sigmund Freud, *The Standard Edition of the Complete Psychological Works of Sigmund Freud*, vol. 14, trans. James Strachey (London: Hogarth, 1953), 120.

9. I discuss the altered temporality of this relationship in the context of Freud's writings on censorship and repression in chapters 2 and 4 of *Writing Through Repression: Literature, Censorship, Psychoanalysis* (Baltimore: Johns Hopkins University Press, 1994).

10. Celan, *GW*, 3:186; *Collected Prose*, 35.

11. Volker Kaiser, *Das Echo jeder Verschattung: Figur und Reflexion bei Rilke, Benn und Celan* (Vienna: Passagen, 1993), 111.

12. Howard Stern, "Verbal Mimesis," in *Studies in Twentieth Century Literature* 8, no. 1 (Fall 1983): 27. Hereafter cited in parentheses within the text.

13. John Felstiner, *Paul Celan: Poet, Survivor, Jew* (New Haven, Conn.: Yale University Press, 1995), 89.

14. Ibid., 86.

15. Alexis Lichine, *Alexis Lichine's New Encyclopedia of Wine and Spirits* (New York: Knopf, 1985), 44–45.

16. Celan, *GW*, 3:185; *Collected Prose*, 34; trans. modified.

17. Celan uses the phrase *eingedenk bleiben* in his "Meridian" address when speaking about the dates from which and toward which we write. *GW*, 3:196; *Collected Prose*, 47.

18. Martin Heidegger, *Early Greek Thinking*, trans. David Farrell Krell and Frank A. Capuzzi (New York: Harper and Row, 1984), 60.

19. Jacob Grimm and Wilhelm Grimm, *Deutsches Wörterbuch* (Leipzig: Hirzel, 1942), 20:390; trans. mine. Cf. the entry on the English term *stum* in *The Oxford English Dictionary*.

20. Ibid.

21. Celan, "Der Meridian," *GW* 3:202; *Collected Prose*, 54.

22. Celan, *GW*, 1:105.

23. This translation is a modified version of the one appearing in Celan, *Selected Poems*, trans. Felstiner, 72.

24. Cited in Paul Celan and Gisèle Celan-Lestrange, *Correspondance, Commentaires et illustrations*, vol. 2 of *Correspondance*, ed. and with a commentary by Bertrand Badiou, with Eric Celan (Paris: Seuil, 2001), 493; trans. mine.

25. Ibid.

26. While it is impossible to say how deeply the moment marked by "Die Winzer" and "Grabschrift für François" will have affected Celan, it should be noted that the last poem he wrote before committing suicide in April 1970 begins:

REBLEUTE graben	VINTAGERS dig up
die dunkelstündige Uhr um,	the dark-houred clock,
Tiefe um Tiefe,	deep upon deep

—Celan, *GW*, 2:123; *Selected Poems*, 376–77.

27. To appreciate the trenchancy of the gait of one who "walks on his head [*auf den Kopf geht*]" and how it is not merely a way of walking on one's hands, it is necessary to recall all the rolling heads in Büchner's texts. Such heads are not merely cut or guillotined (as in *Danton's Death*) but are themselves razor-sharp. One might recall in this regard the Hauptmann's description of Woyzeck as someone who rushes "through the world like an open razor," in a play which itself begins with the eponymous character's vision of a curiously "spiked" head rolling in the grass, a head which "someone" once mistook for the quill-covered body of a hedgehog. If he who walks on his head is said by Celan to have the sky as an abyss beneath him, it is because such a gait cuts open the sheltering tent of the heavens, opening in it an abyss out of whose depths a terrible voice begins to speak precisely at the moment of the meridian, at a moment when a solar cycle is about to come full circle. "Sometimes," Woyzeck tells the Doctor who has been performing medical experiments upon him, "when the sun's up high in the middle of the day and it seems like the world is bursting into flames, this terrible voice starts talking to me." Georg Büchner, *Complete Plays, Lenz, and Other Writings*, trans. John Reddick (London: Penguin, 1993), 122; *Werke und Briefe* (Munich: dtv Weltliteratur, 1980), 168.

28. Israel Chalfen, *Paul Celan: Eine Biographie seiner Jugend* (Frankfurt am Main: Insel, 1979), 127; Klaus Manger, "Die Königszäsur: Zu Hölderlins Gegenwart in Celans Gedicht," *Hölderlin-Jahrbuch* 23 (1982–83): 161–64.

29. "Leonce (träumend vor sich hin): O, jeder Weg ist lang! Das Picken der Totenuhr in unserer Brust ist langsam und jeder Tropfen Blut mißt seine Zeit und unser Leben ist ein schleichend Fieber. Für müde Füße ist jeder Weg zu lang [Leonce (dreaming to himself): Oh every way is long! The ticking deathwatch in our breast is slow, each drop of blood is measured in its pace, our entire life's a creeping fever. For tired feet, every way is long]." *Leonce und Lena*, act 2, scene 2, in Büchner, *Werke und Briefe*, 108; *Complete Plays*, 96–97.

30. It should be recalled that a year earlier the poet, still going by the name of Paul Antschel, had married Gisèle Lestrange over the violent objections of her family to her liason with "un Juif . . . apatride . . . de langue allemande," and that shortly before "Die Winzer" and "Grabschrift für François" were written he had submitted yet another "demande de naturalisation française et de 'francisation' du

nom d'Antschel en Celan." He was to wait more than two years for the first part of the request to be granted. Indeed, it was only on July 8, 1955, approximately a month after the premature birth of his second son, Claude François Eric, that the "décret de naturalisation de Paul Antschel" was published in the *Journal officiel*, his request for the "francisation" of his name having been turned down on April 6 by the Ministry of Public Health and Population, which considered his proposed translation of Antschel into Celan as constituting "un véritable changement de nom." *Correspondance*, 2:492, 500.

31. Cf. the poem "Kenotaph," included like "Die Winzer" in the final cycle, "Inselhin," of *Von Schwelle zu Schwelle* (*GW*, 1:134).

32. "True," Celan concedes in "The Meridian," the poem "speaks only on its own, its very own behalf," only to add: "But I think—and this will hardly surprise you—that the poem has always hoped, for this very reason, to speak also on behalf of the *strange*—no, I can no longer use this word here—*on behalf of the other*, who knows, perhaps of an *altogether other*." Celan *GW*, 3:196; *Collected Prose*, 48; emphasis in original.

Bibliography

Adorno, Theodor. "Commitment" (1962). Trans. Francis McDonagh. In *The Essential Frankfurt School Reader*, ed. Andrew Arato and Eike Gebhardt, intro. Paul Ricoeur, 300–318. New York: Continuum, 1982.

———. "What Does Coming to Terms with the Past Mean?" In *Bitburg in Moral and Political Perspective*, ed. Geoffrey H. Hartman, 114–29. Bloomington: Indiana University Press, 1986.

Anderson, Mark. *Kafka's Clothes: Ornament and Aestheticism in the Habsburg Fin de Siècle*. Oxford: Clarendon, 1992.

Anz, Thomas, ed. *"Es geht nicht um Christa Wolf": Der Literaturstreit im vereinten Deutschland*. Munich: Spangenberg, 1991.

Baer, Ulrich. *Remnants of Song: Trauma and the Experience of Modernity in Charles Baudelaire and Paul Celan*. Stanford, Calif.: Stanford University Press, 2000.

———, ed. *Niemand zeugt für den Zeugen*. Frankfurt am Main: Suhrkamp, 2000.

Baudelaire, Charles. *Le Spleen de Paris*. Paris: Gallimard, 1973.

Benjamin, Walter. *Gesammelte Schriften*. Ed. Rolf Tiedemann and Hermann Schweppenhäuser. 7 vols. Frankfurt am Main: Suhrkamp, 1972.

———. *Illuminations*. Trans. Harry Zohn. New York: Schocken, 1978.

Benveniste, Émile. *Indo-European Language and Society*. Trans. Elizabeth Palmer. Coral Gables, Fla.: University of Miami Press, 1973.

Bergmann, Martin S., and Milton E. Jucovy, eds. *Generations of the Holocaust*. New York: Columbia University Press, 1990.

Brodzki, Bella. "Mothers, Displacement, and Language in the Autobiographies of Nathalie Sarraute and Christa Wolf." In *Life/Lines*, ed. Bella Brodzki and Celeste Schenk, 243–59. Ithaca, N.Y.: Cornell University Press, 1988.

Büchner, Georg. *Complete Plays, Lenz, and Other Writings*. Trans. John Reddick. London: Penguin, 1993.

———. *Werke und Briefe*. Munich: dtv Weltliteratur, 1980.

Caruth, Cathy. "An Interview with Jean Laplanche." *Postmodern Culture* 11, no. 2 (January 2001). http://muse.jhu.edu/journals/postmodern_culture/toc/pmc11.2.html.

———, *Unclaimed Experience*. Baltimore: Johns Hopkins University Press, 1996.

Celan, Paul. *Collected Prose*. Trans. Rosemarie Waldrop. New York: Sheep Meadow Press, 1986.

———. *Gesammelte Werke*. 3 vols. Frankfurt am Main: Suhrkamp, 1986.

———. *Selected Poems and Prose of Paul Celan*. Trans. John Felstiner. New York: Norton, 2001.

Celan, Paul, and Gisèle Celan-Lestrange. *Commentaires et illustrations*. Vol. 2 of *Correspondance*, ed. and with a commentary by Bertrand Badiou, with Eric Celan. Paris: Seuil, 2001.

Chalfen, Israel. *Paul Celan: Eine Biographie seiner Jugend*. Frankfurt am Main: Insel, 1979.

de Man, Paul. *The Resistance to Theory*. Minneapolis: University of Minnesota Press, 1986.

Delbo, Charlotte. *Auschwitz and After*. Trans. Rosette C. Lamont. New Haven, Conn.: Yale University Press, 1995.

DeLillo, Don. *White Noise*. New York: Penguin, 1986.

Derrida, Jacques. *The Postcard*. Chicago: University of Chicago Press, 1987.

———. "Shibboleth for Paul Celan." Trans. Joshua Wilner. In *Word Traces*, ed. Aris Fioretos, 3–72. Baltimore: Johns Hopkins University Press, 1994.

———. *Specters of Marx*. Trans. Peggy Kamuf. New York: Routledge, 1994.

———. *Writing and Difference*. Trans. Alan Bass. Chicago: University of Chicago Press, 1978.

Emmerich, Wolfgang. *Paul Celan*. Reinbek bei Hamburg: Rowolt, 1999.

Epstein, Helen. *Children of the Holocaust: Conversations with Sons and Daughters of Survivors*. New York: Penguin, 1979.

Faulkner, William. *Requiem for a Nun*. New York: Vintage, 1975.

Feig, Konnilyn G. *Hitler's Death Camps: The Sanity of Madness*. Holmes and Meier, 1981.

Felman, Shoshana, and Dori Laub, M.D. *Testimony: Crises of Witnessing in Literature, Psychoanalysis, and History*. New York: Routledge, 1992.

Felstiner, John. *Paul Celan: Poet, Survivor, Jew*. New Haven, Conn.: Yale University Press, 1995.

Foucault, Michel. *This Is Not a Pipe*. Trans. James Harkness. Berkeley, Calif.: University of California Press, 1983.

Fresco, Nadine. "Remembering the Unknown." *International Review of Psycho-Analysis* 11, no. 4 (1984): 417–27.

Freud, Sigmund. *The Standard Edition of the Complete Psychological Works of Sigmund Freud*. Vol. 14. Trans. James Strachey. London: Hogarth, 1953.

Friedlander, Saul. *Memory, History, and the Extermination of the Jews of Europe*. Bloomington: Indiana University Press, 1993.

Ginsburg, Ruth. "In Pursuit of Self: Theme, Narration, and Focalization in Christa Wolf's *Patterns of Childhood*." *Style* 26, no. 3 (Fall 1992): 437–46.

Gordon, Andrew. "Cynthia Ozick's 'The Shawl' and the Transitional Object." *Literature and Psychology* 30, nos. 1 and 2 (1994): 1–9.

Gottfried, Amy. "Fragmented Art and the Liturgical Community of the Dead in Cynthia Ozick's *The Shawl.*" *Studies in American Jewish Literature* 13 (1994): 39–51.

Greenspan, Henry, and Sidney Bolkovsky. "When Is an Interview an Interview? Notes on Listening to Holocaust Survivors." Paper presented at Fortunoff Video Archive Conference, The Contribution of Oral Testimony to Holocaust and Genocide Studies, Yale University, October 6, 2002.

Grimm, Jacob, and Wilhelm Grimm. *Deutsches Wörterbuch.* Vol. 20. Leipzig: Hirzel, 1942.

Hartman, Geoffrey H. *The Longest Shadow: In the Aftermath of the Holocaust.* Bloomington: Indiana University Press, 1996.

Heidegger, Martin. *Early Greek Thinking.* Trans. David Farrell Krell and Frank A. Capuzzi. New York: Harper and Row, 1984.

Herr, Michael. *Dispatches.* New York: Vintage, 1991.

Hirsch, Marianne. "Mourning and Postmemory." In *Family Frames: Photography, Narrative, and Postmemory.* Cambridge, Mass.: Harvard University Press, 1997.

Huyssen, Andreas. *Twilight Memories: Marking Time in a Culture of Amnesia.* New York: Routledge, 1995.

Huyssen, Andreas. "Von Mauschwitz in die Catskills und zurück: Art Spiegelmans Holocaust-Comic *Maus.*" In *Bilder des Holocaust: Literatur—film—bildende Kunst*, ed. Manuel Köppen and Klaus Scherpe, 171–89. Cologne: Böhlau, 1997.

Jabès, Edmond. *The Book of Questions.* Trans. Rosmarie Waldrop. Hanover, N.H.: Wesleyan University Press, 1991.

Kafka, Franz. *Letters to Friends, Family, and Editors.* Trans. Richard Winston and Clara Winston. New York: Schocken, 1977.

Kaiser, Volker. *Das Echo jeder Verschattung: Figur und Reflexion bei Rilke, Benn und Celan.* Vienna: Passagen, 1993.

Kaplan, Louise. *No Voice Is Ever Wholly Lost.* New York: Simon and Schuster, 1995.

Kauvar, Elaine. *Cynthia Ozick's Fiction: Tradition and Invention.* Bloomington: Indiana University Press, 1993.

Klein, Richard. *Cigarettes Are Sublime.* Durham, N.C.: Duke University Press, 1993.

Koch, Gertrud. "'Against All Odds'; or, The Will to Survive: Moral Conclusions from Narrative Closure." *History and Memory: Studies in Representations of the Past* 9, nos. 1–2 (Fall 1997): 393–408.

Komar, Kathleen L. "The Difficulty of Saying 'I': Reassembling a Self in Christa Wolf's Autobiographical Fiction." In *Redefining Autobiography in Twentieth-Century Women's Fiction*, ed. Janice Morgan and Colette T. Hall, 261–79. New York: Garland, 1991.

Kristeva, Julia. *Tales of Love*. Trans. Leon S. Roudiez. New York: Columbia University Press, 1987.

Kuhn, Anna. *Christa Wolf's Utopian Vision: From Marxism to Feminism*. Cambridge: Cambridge University Press, 1988.

Lacan, Jacques. *The Four Fundamental Concepts of Psychoanalysis*. Trans. Alan Sheridan. New York: Norton, 1978.

———. "Seminar on the 'The Purloined Letter.'" In *The Purloined Poe*, ed. John Muller and William Richardson. Baltimore: Johns Hopkins University Press, 1988.

LaCapra, Dominick. *Writing History, Writing Trauma*. Baltimore: Johns Hopkins University Press, 2001.

Laplanche, Jean. *Essays in Otherness*. Ed. John Fletcher. New York: Routledge, 1998.

———. *Life and Death in Psychoanalysis*. Trans. Jeffrey Mehlman. Baltimore: Johns Hopkins University Press, 1976.

Laplanche, Jean, and J.-B. Pontalis. *The Language of Psychoanalysis*. Trans. Donald Nicholson-Smith. New York: Norton, 1973.

Levi, Primo. *The Drowned and the Saved*. Trans. Raymond Rosenthal. New York: Summit, 1988.

———. *Survival in Auschwitz*. Trans. Stuart Woolf. New York: Macmillan/Collier, 1961.

Levine, Michael G. *Writing Through Repression: Literature, Censorship, Psychoanalysis*. Baltimore: Johns Hopkins University Press, 1994.

Lichine, Alexis. *Alexis Lichine's New Encyclopedia of Wine and Spirits*. New York: Knopf, 1985.

Loftus, Elizabeth F. *Eyewitness Testimony*. Cambridge, Mass.: Harvard University Press, 1979.

Lyotard, Jean-François. *The Differend: Phrases in Dispute*. Trans. Georges Van Den Abbeele. Minneapolis: University of Minnesota Press, 1988.

Mallarmé, Stéphane. "La Musique et les lettres." In *Oeuvres completes*, ed. Henri Mondor and G. Jean-Aubry, 635–60. Paris: Gallimard, 1945.

Mandelstam, Osip. *Selected Essays*. Ed. and trans. Sidney Monas. Austin: University of Texas Press, 1977.

Manger, Klaus. "Die Königszäsur: Zu Hölderlins Gegenwart in Celans Gedicht." *Hölderlin-Jahrbuch* 23 (1982–83): 161–64.

Martin, Margot. "The Theme of Survival in Cynthia Ozick's 'The Shawl.'" In *RE: Artes Liberales* 14, no. 1 (Fall–Spring 1988): 31–36.

Miller, Nancy K. "Cartoons of the Self: Portrait of the Artist as a Young Murderer. Art Spiegelman's *Maus*." In *Considering Maus: Approaches to Art Spiegelman's "Survivor's Tale" of the Holocaust*, ed. Deborah R. Geis, 44–59. Tuscaloosa: University of Alabama Press, 2003.

Moses, Stéphane. "Patterns of Negativity in Paul Celan's 'The Trumpet Place.'" Trans. Ken Frieden. In *Languages of the Unsayable: The Play of Negativity in Literature and Literary Theory,* ed. Sanford Budick and Wolfgang Iser, 209–24. Stanford, Calif.: Stanford University Press, 1987.

Nägele, Rainer. *Reading After Freud.* New York: Columbia University Press, 1987.

Nietzsche, Friedrich. *The Gay Science.* Trans. Josefine Nauckhoff. New York: Cambridge University Press, 2001.

Orvell, Miles. "Writing Posthistorically: *Krazy Kat, Maus,* and the Contemporary Fiction Cartoon." *American Literary History* 4, no. 1 (Spring 1992): 110–28.

Ozick, Cynthia. *The Cannibal Galaxy.* New York: Syracuse University Press, 1983.

———. *The Messiah of Stockholm* (New York: Vintage, 1988).

———. "Primo Levi's Suicide Note." In *Metaphor and Memory,* by Cynthia Ozick, 34–48. New York: Knopf, 1989.

———. *The Puttermesser Papers.* New York: Vintage, 1998.

———. "The Question of Our Speech: The Return to Aural Culture." In *Metaphor and Memory,* by Cynthia Ozick, 146–72. New York: Knopf, 1989.

———. *The Shawl.* New York: Vintage, 1990.

Panofsky, Erwin. *Perspective as Symbolic Form.* Trans. Christopher S. Wood. New York: Zone, 1991.

Poe, Edgar Allan. *The Annotated Edgar Allan Poe.* Garden City, N.J.: Doubleday, 1981.

Rosen, Alan, "The Language of Survival: English as Metaphor in Spiegelman's *Maus.*" *Prooftexts,* no. 15 (1995): 249–62.

Rosen, Jonathan. "Spiegelman: The Man Behind *Maus.*" Interview. *Forward,* January 17, 1992.

Ryan, Judith. *The Uncompleted Past: Postwar German Novels and the Third Reich.* Detroit: Wayne State University Press, 1983.

Santner, Eric. *Stranded Objects.* Ithaca, N.Y.: Cornell Univesity Press, 1990.

Scarry, Elaine. *The Body in Pain: The Making and Unmaking of the World.* New York: Oxford University Press, 1985.

Schindel, Robert. *Gebürtig.* Frankfurt am Main: Suhrkamp, 1992. Trans. Michael Roloff as *Born-Where.* Riverside, Calif.: Ariadne, 1995.

Schulz, Bruno. *Sanitorium Under the Sign of the Hourglass.* Trans. Celina Wieniewska. New York: Walker, 1978.

Semprun, Jorge. *Literature or Life.* Trans. Linda Coverdale. New York: Viking, 1997.

Shakespeare, William. *The Pelican Shakespeare.* Ed. Frances E. Dolan. New York: Penguin, 2000.

Spiegelman, Art. *Comix, Essays, Graphics, and Scraps: From MAUS to Now to MAUS to Now.* New York: Raw, 1998.

———. "Comix: An Idiosyncratic Historical and Aesthetic Overview." *Print* 42 (November–December 1988).

———. *The Complete* Maus *CD-ROM*. New York: Voyager.

———. Interview on *Fresh Air*, National Public Radio, December 1986. Cited in "History and Talking Animals: Art Spiegelman's *Maus*." In *Comic Books as History: The Narrative Art of Jack Jackson, Art Spiegelman, and Harvey Pekar*, by Joseph Witek. Jackson: University of Mississippi Press, 1989.

———. "Jewish Mice, Bubblegum Cards, Comics Art, and Raw Possibilities." Interview by Joey Cavalieri. *Comics Journal*, no. 65 (August 1981).

———. MAUS: *A Survivor's Tale. My Father Bleeds History*. New York: Pantheon, 1986.

———. MAUS II: *A Survivor's Tale. And Here My Troubles Began*. New York: Pantheon, 1991.

———. MAUS: *Die Geschichte eines Überlebenden*. Trans. Christine Brinck and Josef Joffe. Reinbek bei Hamburg: Rowolt, 1999.

———. *Open Me . . . I'm a Dog*. New York: Joanna Cotler, 1997.

Stern, Howard. "Verbal Mimesis." *Studies in Twentieth Century Literature* 8, no. 1 (Fall 1983): 23–39.

Sussman, Henry. *Afterimages of Modernity*. Baltimore: Johns Hopkins University Press, 1990.

Szondi, Peter. "Reading '*Engführung*': An Essay on the Poetry of Paul Celan." Trans. David Caldwell and S. Esh. *boundary 2* 11, no. 3 (1983): 231–64.

Trepman, Paul. *Among Men and Beasts*. Trans. Shoshana Perla and Gertrude Hirschler. South Brunswick, N.J.: Barnes, 1978.

Trezise, Thomas. "Unspeakable." *Yale Journal of Criticism* 14, no. 1 (2001): 39–66.

van der Kolk, Bessel A., and Onno van der Hart. "The Intrusive Past: The Flexibility of Memory and the Engraving of Trauma." In *Trauma: Explorations in Memory*, ed. Cathy Caruth, 158–82. Baltimore: Johns Hopkins University Press, 1995.

Viollet, Catherine. "Nachdenken über Pronomina: Zur Entstehung von Christa Wolfs Kindheitsmuster." *Zeitschrift für Literaturwissenschaft und Linguistik* 17, no. 68 (1987): 52–62.

Virgil. *Ecologues, Georgics, Aeneid I–VI*. Trans. H. Rushton Fairclough. Loeb Classical Library. Cambridge, Mass.: Harvard University Press 1999.

Weber, Samuel. "The Sideshow; or, Remarks on a Canny Moment." *MLN* 88 (1973): 1102–33.

———. "Benjamin's 'The Task of the Translator.'" Unpublished ms.

Weschler, Lawrence. "Art's Father, Vladek's Son." In *Shapinsky's Karma, Bogg's Bills, and Other True-Life Tales*, by Lawrence Weschler, 53–68. San Francisco: North Point, 1988.

Wieviorka, Annette. *The Era of the Witness*. Trans. Jared Stark. Ithaca, N.Y.: Cornell University Press, 2006.

Wirth-Nesher, Hana. "The Languages of Memory: Cynthia Ozick's *The Shawl*." In *Multilingual America: Transnationalism, Ethnicity, and the Languages of*

American Literature, ed. Werner Sollers, 313–26. New York: New York University Press, 1998.

Witek, Joseph. *Comic Books as History: The Narrative Art of Jack Jackson, Art Spiegelman, and Harvey Pekar*. Jackson: University of Mississippi Press, 1989.

Wolf, Christa. *The Author's Dimension*. New York: Farrar, Straus and Giroux, 1993.

———. *The Fourth Dimension*. Trans. Hilary Pilkington. London: Verso, 1988.

———. *Kindheitsmuster*. Darmstadt: Luchterhand, 1979.

———. *Parting from Phantoms*. Trans. Jan van Heurck. Chicago: University of Chicago Press, 1997.

———. *Patterns of Childhood*. Trans. Ursule Molinaro and Hedwig Rappolt. New York: Farrar, Straus and Giroux, 1980.

———. *Was bleibt*. Frankfurt am Main: Luchterhand, 1990.

———. *What Remains and Other Stories*. Trans. Heike Schwarzbauer and Rick Takvorian. New York: Farrar, Straus and Giroux, 1993.

Young, James E. "The Holocaust as Vicarious Past: Art Spiegelman's *Maus* and the Afterimages of History." In *Critical Inquiry*, no. 24 (Spring 1998): 666–99.

Žižek, Slavoj. *Looking Awry: An Introduction to Jacques Lacan Through Popular Culture*. Cambridge, Mass.: MIT Press, 1991.

Index

Cultural Memory | *in the Present*

Stuart McLean, *The Event and its Terrors: Ireland, Famine, Modernity*

Beate Rössler, ed., *Privacies: Philosophical Evaluations*

Bernard Faure, *Double Exposure: Cutting Across Buddhist and Western Discourses*

Alessia Ricciardi, *The Ends Of Mourning: Psychoanalysis, Literature, Film*

Alain Badiou, *Saint Paul: The Foundation of Universalism*

Gil Anidjar, *The Jew, the Arab: A History of the Enemy*

Jonathan Culler and Kevin Lamb, eds., *Just Being Difficult? Academic Writing in the Public Arena*

Jean-Luc Nancy, *A Finite Thinking*, edited by Simon Sparks

Theodor W. Adorno, *Can One Live after Auschwitz? A Philosophical Reader*, edited by Rolf Tiedemann

Patricia Pisters, *The Matrix of Visual Culture: Working with Deleuze in Film Theory*

Andreas Huyssen, *Present Pasts: Urban Palimpsests and the Politics of Memory*

Talal Asad, *Formations of the Secular: Christianity, Islam, Modernity*

Dorothea von Mücke, *The Rise of the Fantastic Tale*

Marc Redfield, *The Politics of Aesthetics: Nationalism, Gender, Romanticism*

Emmanuel Levinas, *On Escape*

Dan Zahavi, *Husserl's Phenomenology*

Rodolphe Gasché, *The Idea of Form: Rethinking Kant's Aesthetics*

Michael Naas, *Taking on the Tradition: Jacques Derrida and the Legacies of Deconstruction*

Herlinde Pauer-Studer, ed., *Constructions of Practical Reason: Interviews on Moral and Political Philosophy*

Jean-Luc Marion, *Being Given That: Toward a Phenomenology of Givenness*

Didier Maleuvre, *Museum Memories: History, Technology, Art*

Jacques Derrida, *Monolingualism of the Other; or, The Prosthesis of Origin*

Andrew Baruch Wachtel, *Making a Nation, Breaking a Nation: Literature and Cultural Politics in Yugoslavia*

Niklas Luhmann, *Love as Passion: The Codification of Intimacy*

Mieke Bal, ed., *The Practice of Cultural Analysis: Exposing Interdisciplinary Interpretation*

Jacques Derrida and Gianni Vattimo, eds., *Religion*